M000248034

STERLING
Test Prep

AP Physics 1
Review

4th edition

4 3 2 1

ISBN-13: 978-0-9977782-9-8

Sterling Test Prep products are available at special quantity discounts for sales, promotions, academic counseling offices and other educational purposes.

Contact our sales department at: info@sterling–prep.com

Sterling Test Prep
6 Liberty Square #11
Boston, MA 02109

Published by Sterling Test Prep

Printed in the U.S.A.

Congratulations on joining thousands of students using our study aids to achieve high test scores!

Scoring well on the AP exams is essential to earn placement credits and admission into a competitive college, which will position you for a successful future. This book prepares you to achieve a high score on the AP Physics 1 exam by developing the ability to apply your knowledge and quickly choose the correct answer. Understanding key concepts, extracting and analyzing information from the question, and distinguishing between similar answer choices are more effective skills than merely memorizing terms.

This book provides a thorough review of all topics tested on the AP Physics 1 exam. The content covers the foundational principles and theories necessary to answer test questions. Physics instructors with years of teaching experience prepared this material by analyzing the AP Physics 1 exam content and developing preparation material that builds your knowledge and skills crucial for success on the test. Our editorial team reviewed and systematized the content to ensure adherence to the current College Board AP Physics 1 curriculum. Our editors are experts on preparing students for standardized tests and have coached thousands of undergraduate and graduate school applicants on test preparation and admission strategies.

The review content is clearly presented and systematically organized to provide you with a targeted preparation for AP Physics 1. You will learn the scientific foundations and details of essential physics topics needed to answer exam questions. By reading these review chapters thoroughly, you will learn important physics concepts and the relationships between them. This will prepare you for the exam and significantly improve your AP score.

We wish you great success in your academics and look forward to being an important part of your successful test preparation!

Visit www.sterling-prep.com for more test prep resources.

230525akp

Advanced Placement (AP) prep books

Biology Practice Questions	Psychology
Biology Review	U.S. History
Physics 1 Practice Questions	World History
Physics 1 Review	European History
Physics 2 Practice Questions	U.S. Government and Politics
Physics 2 Review	Comparative Government and Politics
Environmental Science	Human Geography

Visit our Amazon store

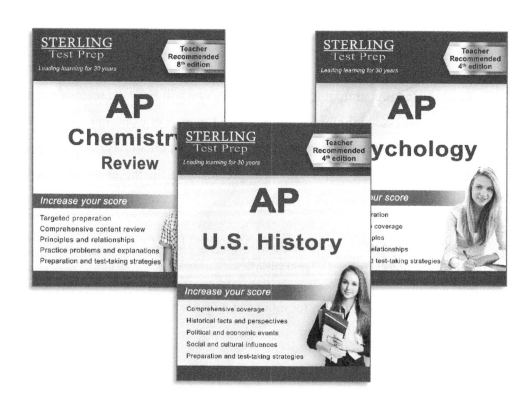

AP Chemistry, Biology and Physics online practice tests

Our advanced online testing platform allows you to take AP practice questions on your computer to generate a Diagnostic Report for each test.

By using our online AP tests and Diagnostic Reports, you will:

Assess your knowledge of subjects and topics to identify your areas of strength and weakness

Learn important scientific topics and concepts for comprehensive test preparation

Improve your test-taking skills

To access AP questions online
at special pricing for book owners, see page 314

**For best results, supplement this book with
"AP Physics 1 Practice Questions"**

AP Physics 1 Practice Questions provides high-yield practice questions with detailed explanations covering all topics tested on AP Physics 1.

· Kinematics & dynamics

· Force, motion, gravitation

· Equilibrium & momentum

· Work & energy

· Rotational motion

· Waves & periodic motion

· Sound

· DC circuits

· Electrostatics

Table of Contents

Table of Contents (*continued*)

Table of Contents (*continued*)

AP Physics Test-Taking Strategies

The best way to do well on AP Physics 1 is to be really good at physics. There is no way around that. Prepare for the test as much as you can, so you can answer with confidence as many questions as possible. With that being said, there are strategies you should employ when you approach a question on the exam.

The task of pacing yourself will become easier if you are aware of the number of questions you need to answer to reach the score you want to get. Always strive for the highest score, but be realistic about your level of preparation. It may be helpful if you research what counts as a good score for the colleges you are applying to. You can talk to admissions offices at colleges, research college guidebooks or specific college websites, or talk to your guidance counselor. You should find out which score would earn you a college placement credit and which score would be beneficial to your application without earning credit.

Below are some test-taking strategies to help you maximize your score. Many of these strategies you already know and they may seem like common sense. However, when a student is feeling the pressure of a timed test, these common-sense strategies might be forgotten.

Mental Attitude

If you psych yourself out, chances are you will do poorly on the test. To do well on the test, particularly physics, which calls for cool, systemic thinking, you must remain calm. If you start to panic, your mind won't be able to find the correct solutions to the questions.

Many steps can be taken before the test to increase your confidence level. Buying this book is a good start because you can begin to practice, learn the information you should know to master the topics and get used to answering physics questions. However, there are other things you should keep in mind:

Study in advance. The information will be more manageable, and you will feel more confident if you've studied at regular intervals during the weeks leading up to the test. Cramming the night before is not a successful tactic.

Be well rested. If you are up late the night before the test, chances are you will have a difficult time concentrating and focusing on the day of the test, as you will not feel fresh and alert.

Come up for air. The best way to take this three-hour-long test is not to keep your head down, concentrating intensely for the entire time. Even though you only have 1 minute and 48 seconds per question (on the multiple-choice section) and there is no time to waste, it is recommended to take a few seconds between the questions to take a deep breath and relax your muscles.

Time Management

Aside from good preparation, time management is the most important strategy that you should know how to use on any test. You have an average time of 1 minute 48 seconds for each question on the multiple choice section. Even though, you will breeze through some in less than a minute, with others you may be stuck on for three minutes.

Don't dwell on any one question for too long. You should aim to look at every question on the test. It would be unfortunate to not earn the points for a question you could have easily answered because you did not get a chance to look at it. If you are still in the first half of the test and find yourself spending more than a minute on one question and don't see yourself getting closer to solving it, it is better to move on. It will be more productive if you come back to this question with a fresh mind at the end of the test. You do not want to lose points because you were stuck on one or a few questions and did not get a chance to work with other questions that are easy for you.

Nail the easy questions quickly. Each student has their strong and weak topics, and you might be a master on a certain type of questions that are normally considered difficult. Skip the questions you are struggling with and nail the easy ones.

Skip the unfamiliar. If you come across a question that is totally unfamiliar to you, skip it. Do not try to figure out what is going on or what they are trying to ask. At the end of the test, you can go back to these questions if you have time. If you are encountering a question that you have no clue about, most likely you won't be able to answer it through analysis. The better strategy is to leave such questions to the end and use the guessing strategy on them at the end of the test.

Understanding the Question

It is important that you know what the question is asking before you select your answer choice. This seems obvious, but it is surprising how many students don't read a question carefully because they rush through the test and select a wrong answer choice.

A successful student will not just read the question but will take a moment to understand the question before even looking at the answer choices. This student will be able to separate the important information from distracters and will not get confused by the questions that are asking to identify a false statement (which is the correct answer).

Once you've identified what you're dealing with and what is being asked, you should be able to spend less time picking the right answer. If the question is asking for a general concept, try to answer the question before looking at the answer choices, then look at the choices. If you see a choice that matches the answer you thought of, most likely it is the correct choice.

Correct Way to Guess

Random guessing won't help you on the test, but educated guessing is the strategy you should use in certain situations if you can eliminate at least one (or even two) of the four possible choices.

If you randomly entered responses for the first 20 questions, there is a 25% chance of guessing correctly on any given question. Therefore, the odds are you would guess right on 5 questions and wrong on 15 questions.

However, if for each of the 20 questions you can eliminate one answer choice because you know it to be wrong (wrong order of magnitude, wrong units, etc.), you will have a 33% chance of being right and your odds would move to 7 questions right and 13 questions wrong. Correspondingly, if you can eliminate 2 wrong answers, you can increase your odds to 50%.

Guessing is not cheating and should not be viewed that way. Rather it is a form of "partial credit" because while you might not be sure of the correct answer, you do have relevant knowledge to identify one or two choices that are wrong.

AP Physics 1 Tips

Tip 1: Know the formulas

Since 70–80% of the test requires that you know how to use the formulas, it is imperative that you memorize and understand when to use each one. It is not permitted to bring any papers with notes to the test, but you will be given a sheet with formulas allowed by the College Board.

As you work with this book, you will learn the application of all the important physical formulas and will use them in many different question types.

Tip 2: Know how to manipulate the formulas

You must know how to apply the formulas in addition to memorizing them. Questions will be worded in ways unfamiliar to you to test whether you can manipulate equations to calculate the correct answer. Knowing that $F = ma$ is not helpful without understanding that $a = F/m$ because it is unlikely that a question will ask to calculate the force acting on an object with a given mass and acceleration. Rather you are likely to be asked to calculate the acceleration of an object of a given mass with force acting on it.

Tip 3: Estimating

This tip is only helpful for quantitative questions. For example, estimating can help you choose the correct answer if you have a general sense of the order of magnitude. This is especially applicable to questions where all answer choices have different orders of magnitude, and you can save time that you would have to spend on calculations.

Tip 4: Draw the question

Don't hesitate to write, draw or graph your thought process once you have read and understood the question. This can help you determine what kind of information you are dealing with.

Draw the force and velocity vectors, ray/wave paths, or anything else that may be helpful. Even if a question does not require a graphic answer, drawing a graph (for example, a sketch of a particle's velocity) can allow a solution to become obvious.

Tip 5: Eliminating wrong answers

This tip utilizes the strategy of educated guessing. You can usually eliminate one or two answer choices right away in many questions.

In addition, there are certain types of questions for which you can use a particular elimination method.

By using logical estimations for qualitative questions, you can eliminate the answer choices that are unreasonably high or unreasonably low.

Last helpful tip: fill in your answers carefully

This seems like a simple thing, but it is extremely important. Many test takers make mistakes when filling in answers whether it is a paper test or computer-based test.

Make sure you pay attention and check off the answer choice you actually chose as correct.

We want to hear from you

Your feedback is important to us because we strive to provide the highest quality prep materials. Email us any comments or suggestions.

info@sterling–prep.com

Customer Satisfaction Guarantee
Contact us to resolve any issues to your satisfaction.

*We reply to all emails – **check your spam folder***

Thank you for choosing our products to achieve your educational goals!

CHAPTER 1

Kinematics and Dynamics

- **Introduction: The Nature of Science**

- **Units and Dimensions**

- **Vectors, Components**

- **Vector Addition**

- **Speed, Velocity**

- **Acceleration**

- **Freely falling bodies**

Introduction: The Nature of Science

Observation is the first step toward scientific discovery. Observations recognize patterns and anomalies in unexplained phenomena. From objective observation, a hypothesis is advanced to propose the reason for the observation.

A *hypothesis* is a proposed explanation for an observation. The testing of a hypothesis involves experiments and additional observations (i.e., recording and collecting data). By manipulating discrete variables, such as how long the plant is exposed to sunlight per twenty-four hours, additional observations are made. The additional observations are the data collected about the proposed explanation (hypothesis).

Observations either 1) support the hypothesis (i.e., not the same as proves) or 2) refute the hypothesis. The hypothesis can then be modified by narrowing or expanding its proposed application to explain additional data. More experiments are performed, and the results either support (not prove) or refute the hypothesis. This is an iterative process.

Principles are the initially proposed explanations that are specific and apply to a narrow range of phenomena.

A *theory* is proposed to account for the observations if the hypothesis is valid over a range of variables (e.g., sunlight, temperature, or humidity). Theories are proposed to explain the phenomena and to predict what will happen under other conditions with different variables. Further observations determine whether the predictions were accurate.

Research (re-search; again search) continues as these many observations support hypotheses and theories. When theories are accurate over a broad scope of scenarios and experiments, Laws are developed based on these repeatedly replicated results.

Laws are brief descriptions of how nature behaves in a broad set of circumstances. A Law is the consolidation of several theories. They are the products of multiple theories that have been tested and proven, culminating in a broad claim regarding those predictions. Laws are simple explanations that are widely applicable. Laws that make broad and straightforward claims are more robust than those who make claims on a narrower, more specific set of variables and parameters.

The relative number of Laws to describe physical phenomena is minuscule compared to the number of theories and many magnitudes less than the number of supported hypotheses. The number of refuted (unsupported) hypotheses may be several magnitudes larger.

A *failed experiment* does not typically refer to the physical process, such as the researcher made a human error during the experiment, but that the data does not support the hypothesis. Therefore, after additional trials to validate the "failed" results, the hypothesis must be modified to predict the results of either future experiments or objective observations in the physical world.

Theories, Models, and Laws

Theories emerge from a hypothesis that has been repeatedly supported by experimental data and observations. Theories are detailed statements that provide testable predictions of the behavior of natural phenomena. They are established to explain observations and then tested (supported or refuted) based on their predictions. Tested theories can articulate the boundaries of the tested hypothesis. Theories are more specific than hypothesis but vaguer and more encompassing than models.

A *model* is constructed to explain in detail the observed behavior if a hypothesis accurately predicts a phenomenon. Models are far more specific in their application than theories. The data collected to develop the theories provide the conceptual foundation upon which models are constructed. The model creates mental pictures (e.g., complicated weather patterns display as visual pictures for the viewer), of the physical phenomena.

The model should be consistent with the predictions of scientific theories and are useful in the process of a comprehensive understanding of a phenomenon. Models allow for predictive outcomes under specific theories (e.g., when the wind speed reaches x, then y will occur). Multiple models are constructed to explain a portion, or the entire scope, of a theory.

Understand the limitations of a model and do not apply it dogmatically unless its applicability is evaluated. A model is an underlying representation of a part of a theory; it is not intended to provide a complete picture of every occurrence of a phenomenon under that theory. Instead, it provides a familiar and understandable way of envisioning the fundamental aspects of the theory.

Units and Dimensions

Measurement and Uncertainty: Significant Figures

No measurement is exact; there will always be some uncertainty due to limited instrument accuracy and precision.

The *accuracy* of an instrument depends on how well-calibrated that instrument is concerning the actual quantitative value of a measurement. For example, an empty scale holding no objects that are initially calibrated to 0 grams of mass is more accurate than the same empty scale calibrated to 1 gram of mass.

An instrument's *precision* is based upon the scale of the measurement, with measurements on a smaller scale being more precise than measurements on a larger scale.

A meter stick that includes millimeter markings (0.001 m) is more precise than a meter stick with only centimeter markings (0.01 m). The estimated uncertainty of a measurement is written with a ± sign. For example, 8.8 ± 0.1 cm reads as "8.8 centimeters, *give or take* 0.1 centimeters."

The *percent uncertainty* is the ratio of the uncertainty to the measured value, multiplied by 100. For example, the percent uncertainty in the measurement is:

$$\frac{0.1}{8.8} \times 100 \approx 1\%$$

The number of *significant figures* is the number of reliably known digits in an expressed value. The number is written to indicate the number of significant figures:

- 22.41 cm has four significant figures.

- 0.058 cm has two significant figures because the initial zeroes before the significant digits are ignored. If it has three significant figures, it is written as 0.0580 cm.

- 70 km has one significant figure (zeroes that serve as placeholders without a decimal point are not considered significant). If it has two significant figures, it is written as 70. km (notice that the decimal point changes the significance of the trailing zero). If it has three significant figures, the value is written as 70.0 km.

When multiplying or dividing numbers, the result should have as many significant figures as the number with the fewest significant figures used in the calculation.

12.5 cm × 5.5 cm = 68.75 cm, but because 5.5 cm has two significant figures, the value 68.75 cm must be rounded to 69 cm.

When adding or subtracting numbers, the answer is no more precise than the least precise value used. In this case, round the quantity with higher precision to the same decimal place as the quantity with lower precision. For example:

68.75 cm - 32.1 cm = 36.65 cm, but 32.1 cm has three significant figures.

Therefore, 36.65 cm must be rounded to 36.7 cm with three significant figures.

Calculators may not display the correct number of significant figures. Calculators often displaying too many digits, depending on the setting of the instrument.

Order of Magnitude: Rapid Estimating

A quick way to estimate a calculated quantity is to round numbers to one significant figure. The calculated result should be the proper *order of magnitude*.

This estimate is expressed by rounding it to the nearest power of 10.

$3{,}321 \times 401 = 1{,}331{,}721$

$1{,}331{,}721 \approx 13.3 \times 10^5$

The result can be estimated by rounding:

3,321 is rounded to 3×10^3

401 is rounded to 4×10^2

Calculate:

$(3.0 \times 10^3) \times (4.0 \times 10^2) = 12 \times 10^5$

Compare: 13×10^5 (calculated) to 12×10^5 (estimated)

This estimated value is close to the accurate solution (e.g., the difference in the value from estimating compared to the actual calculated value) and of the same order of magnitude. This application of rounding is invaluable because 1) estimating saves time when solving questions, and 2) ensures that the proposed solution is the proper approach to produce a valid answer.

The percent error introduced from estimating:

$$(1.0 \times 10^5) / (12 \times 10^5) \times 100$$

$$= 8.3 \times 10^{-5} \% \text{ (or } 0.000083\%)$$

Dimensions and Dimensional Analysis

The dimensions of a quantity are the base units and are expressed using square brackets around the base units (e.g., [m/t] or meters/second).

speed = distance / time

dimensions of speed: [m/t]

Quantities that added or subtracted must have the same dimensions.

Dimensional analysis is useful for checking the approach for solving calculations. A quantity calculated as the solution should have the correct dimensions, so:

- One dimension only contains the magnitude of quantities.

- Two dimensions contain quantities on a 2D plane (*x*- and *y*-coordinates).

- Three dimensions contain quantities in 3D space (*x*-, *y*-, and *z*-coordinates).

- Four dimensions contain quantities in 3D space at a given time (*x*-, *y*-, and *z*-spatial coordinates, plus a time coordinate *t*).

Units, Standards, and the SI System

Quantity	Unit	Standard
Length	Meter (m)	Length of the path traveled by light (in a vacuum) in 1/299,792,458 seconds
Time	Second (s)	Time required for 9,192,631,770 periods of radiation emitted by cesium atoms
Mass	Kilogram (kg)	A platinum cylinder in the International Bureau of Weights and Measures, Paris

Properties of Units in Different Dimensions

A unit is a label for a quantity; like the quantities, units have similar properties:

- unit + unit = unit

- unit − unit = unit

- unit × unit = unit^2

    unless multiplying the quantities of different units (e.g., meter × second = m·s)

- unit / unit = no unit

    unless dividing the quantities of different units (e.g. meter / second = m/s)

- Powers of units represent dimensions:

    o unit = one dimension

    o unit^2 = two dimensions

    o unit^3 = three dimensions

- The product of operations involving International System of Units (SI) units is in SI units.

In the SI system, the basic units are meters, kilograms, and seconds.

Complex units (e.g., for velocity, force, power) are derived from basic SI units.

Basic Translational Motion SI Units		
Quantity	SI Unit	Name
Length	m	meter
Mass	kg	kilogram
Time	s	second

Complex Translational Motion SI Units		
Speed or Velocity	m/s	meter per second
Acceleration	m/s^2	meters per second squared
Area	m^2	square meter
Volume	m^3	cubic meter
Density	kg/m^3	kilogram per cubic meter
Force	N (kg·m/s^2)	Newton
Energy	J (N·m)	Joule
Power	W (J/s)	Watt

$$Volume = \frac{kg}{1} \times \frac{m^3}{kg}$$

The kilogram terms cancel because they are on opposite sides of the division bar.

Thus, the units for volume are:

$$Volume = m^3$$

As problems become more complex, first check the units to ensure that the solution represents the proper units and that no errors have been introduced.

SI prefixes for indicating powers of 10

Metric (SI) Prefixes		
Prefix	**Abbreviation**	**Value**
peta	P	10^{15}
tera	T	10^{12}
giga	G	10^{9}
mega	M	10^{6}
kilo	k	10^{3}
deci	d	10^{-1}
centi	c	10^{-2}
milli	m	10^{-3}
micro	μ	10^{-6}
nano	n	10^{-9}
pico	p	10^{-12}

Many of these prefixes are familiar, while some are rarely used.

Converting Units

Converting between metric units involves powers of 10.

$$1 \text{ kg} = 10^3 \text{ g}$$

$$1 \text{ mm} = 10^{-6} \text{ km}$$

$$5 \text{ s} = 5 \times 10^3 \text{ ms}$$

Converting to and from imperial (SI) units is considerably more involved.

$$1 \text{ m} = 3.28084 \text{ ft}$$

$$1 \text{ kg} = 2.204 \text{ lbs.}$$

$$1 \text{ km} = 0.621 \text{ mile}$$

Use dimension analysis to ensure the conversion is evaluated correctly. Write the conversion factor, and then cancel units during the calculations.

Convert 2.6 kg to grams. (use the conversion of $1 \text{ kg} = 10^3 \text{ g}$)

$$2.6 \text{ kg} \times (10^3 \text{ g} / \text{kg})$$

$$2.6 \, \cancel{\text{kg}} \times (10^3 \text{ g} / \cancel{\text{kg}})$$

$$2.6 \times (10^3 \text{ g}) = 2.6 \times 10^3 \text{ g}$$

Convert 3.0 miles to km. (use the conversion of 3.28 ft = 1.00 m)

$$3.0 \text{ miles} \times (1 \text{ km} / 0.621 \text{ mile})$$

$$3.0 \, \cancel{\text{miles}} \times (1 \text{ km} / 0.621 \, \cancel{\text{miles}})$$

$$3.0 \times (1 \text{ km} / 0.621) = 4.83 \text{ km}$$

Convert 3.0 km to ft. (use the conversion of 3.28 ft = 1 m and $1 \text{ km} = 10^3 \text{ m}$)

$$3 \text{ km} \times (1000 \text{ m} / 1 \text{ km}) \times (3.28 \text{ ft} / 1 \text{ m})$$

$$3 \, \cancel{\text{km}} \times (1000 \text{ m} / 1 \, \cancel{\text{km}}) \times (3.28 \text{ ft} / 1 \text{ m})$$

$$3000 \text{ m} \times (3.28 \text{ ft} / 1 \text{ m})$$

$$3000 \, \cancel{\text{m}} \times (3.28 \text{ ft} / 1 \, \cancel{\text{m}})$$

$$3000 \times (3.28 \text{ ft}) = 9,840 \text{ ft}$$

Vectors and Vector Components

Kinematics in One Dimension: Reference Frames and Displacement

Any measurement of position, distance, or speed must be made with respect to a reference frame. For example, if a person walks down the aisle of a moving train, the person's speed with respect to the train is a few miles per hour. The person's speed with respect to the ground outside is much higher; it is the combined speed of both the train and the person walking on the train.

Kinematics describes how objects move with respect to a reference frame.

Within a reference frame, the displacement (movement in position) signifies an object's change in position. There is a difference between *displacement* and *distance*.

The *displacement* (a solid line as shown on the graph below) is how far the object is from its starting point, regardless of how it got there.

The *distance* traveled (a dashed line) is measured along the path (*magnitude* of displacement and the *direction* of travel) of the object.

The distance traveled is 100 meters, but the displacement is 40 meters:

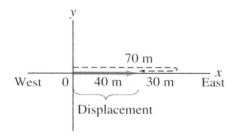

The displacement is expressed as $\Delta x = x_2 - x_1$. Since displacement involves direction, it can be positive or negative about the coordinate directions.

$\Delta x = x_2 - x_1$

$\Delta x = 30\ \text{m} - 10\ \text{m}$

$\Delta x = 20\ \text{m}$

An example of negative displacement:

$$\Delta x = x_2 - x_1$$

$$\Delta x = 10\ m - 30\ m$$

$$\Delta x = -20\ m$$

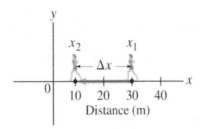

The choice of direction is arbitrary and is selected when choosing a coordinate system. The answer will be correct if the vector components are labeled and computed consistently concerning the chosen coordinate system direction.

Vectors and Vector Components

Scalar quantities represent a magnitude without a direction.

Length, time, and mass are quantities without an associated direction.

Vector quantities include both magnitude and direction.

The displacement, acceleration, and force all inherently contain a direction in which they are applied.

Three trigonometric rules apply when calculating vector components.

A mnemonic is SOH CAH TOA

- **SOH**: *sin* θ = **o**pposite / **h**ypotenuse

- **CAH**: *cos* θ = **a**djacent / **h**ypotenuse

- **TOA**: *tan* θ = **o**pposite / **a**djacent

"Opposite," "adjacent," and "hypotenuse" refer to the vectors about the angle θ.

For example (diagram below):

the vector adjacent to θ_x is v_x

the vector opposite θ_x is the vertical dotted line (equivalent to v_y)

the hypotenuse is v.

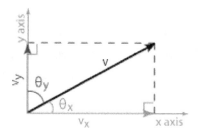

Axis-vector components

Another method to memorize the relationship expressed in "SOH CAH TOA" is from the phrase "Some **O**ld **H**airy **C**amels **A**re **H**airier **T**han **O**thers **A**re."

Vector components are portions of the vector in each direction.

Typically, the components are calculated along the axis directions in a coordinate system.

A vector may have a horizontal component and a vertical component in a two-dimensional (2D) coordinate system (i.e., x-component and y-component):

$$v_x = \vec{v}\cos\theta_x = \vec{v}\sin\theta_y$$

$$v_y = \vec{v}\cos\theta_y = \vec{v}\sin\theta_x$$

The Pythagorean Theorem calculates the magnitude of the resulting vector:

$$\vec{v}^2 = v_x^2 + v_y^2$$

Examples of vectors and vector components in a 2D coordinate system:

Gravity components on slope

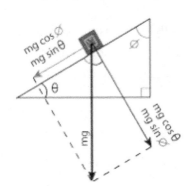

Vector-vector components

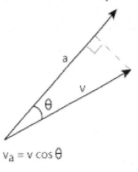

$v_a = v \cos \theta$

In a 3D coordinate system (i.e., *x*-, *y*- and *z*-axis) a third *z*-component of the vector is included:

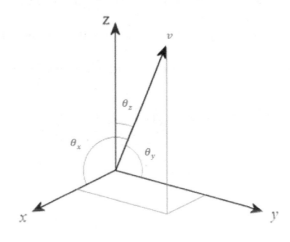

$$v_x = \vec{v} \cos \theta_x$$

$$v_y = \vec{v} \cos \theta_y$$

$$v_z = \vec{v} \cos \theta_z$$

$$\vec{v}^2 = v_x^2 + v_y^2 + v_z^2$$

Vector Addition

Vector addition is performed either graphically or by using the vector components. Vectors can be added if they are in the same dimension (direction). Otherwise, the separate addition of each of the vector's x-, y- and z-components must be calculated.

The sum of all components of a vector equals the vector itself. Therefore, the added components make up the resultant vector.

Operations involving two vectors may or may not result in a vector.

For example, kinetic energy derived from the square of two velocity vectors results in a scalar quantity.

Operations involving a vector and a scalar always result in a vector.

Operations involving a scalar and a scalar always result in a scalar.

For vectors in one dimension, merely addition and subtraction are needed.

The figure below demonstrates vector addition in one dimension (same):

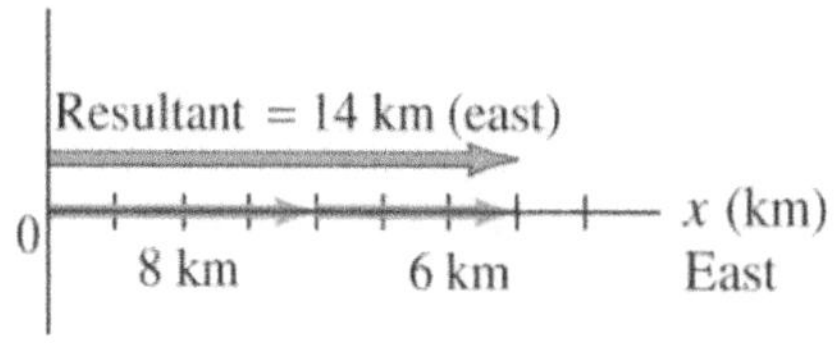

$$8 \text{ km}_{East} + 6 \text{ km}_{East} = 14 \text{ km}_{East}$$

The figure below demonstrates vector subtraction in one dimension (opposite):

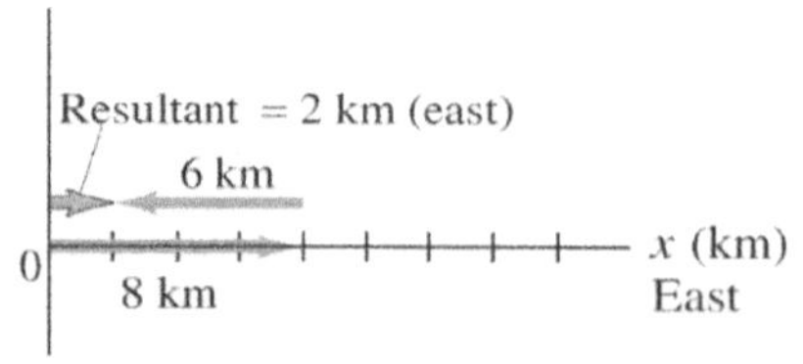

$$8 \text{ km}_{East} - 6 \text{ km}_{East} = 2 \text{ km}_{East}$$

Addition of Vectors — Graphical Methods

If there is motion in two dimensions, the analysis is more complicated.

If the travel paths are at right angles, the displacement (*d*) is calculated by using the Pythagorean Theorem:

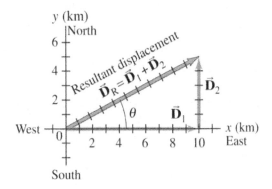

Adding the vectors in the other sequence gives the same result:

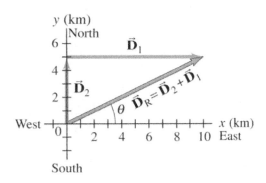

$$|\vec{D}_R| = \sqrt{\vec{D}_1{}^2 + \vec{D}_2{}^2}$$

If the vectors are not at right angles, add using the "tail-to-tip" method.

To use the "tail-to-tip" method, graphically place the tail of each vector at the tip of the arrow of the vector before it.

After the vectors are arranged tail-to-tip, draw the resultant vector from the tail of the original vector to the tip of the last vector.

An example using the "tail-to-tip" method for resolving three vectors:

$$\vec{V}_1 \quad + \quad \vec{V}_2 \quad + \quad \vec{V}_3 \quad = \quad \vec{V}_R$$

If there are two vectors, use the "parallelogram" method. For the parallelogram method, arrange the two vectors such that their tails are connected. Starting from the tips of the two vectors, draw two dashed lines that complete the parallelogram. The resultant vector is drawn from the tails of the original vectors to the corner of the drawn parallelogram.

An example using the "tail-to-tip" and parallelogram method with two vectors:

$$\vec{V}_1 \quad + \quad \vec{V}_2 \quad = \quad \vec{V}_R \qquad \text{Tail-to-tip}$$

$$= \qquad \vec{V}_R \qquad \text{Parallelogram}$$

$$\neq \qquad \text{INCORRECT} \qquad \text{Wrong}$$

Resolving two vectors using the tail-to-tip and parallelogram method

Subtraction of Vectors and Multiplication of a Vector by a Scalar

To subtract vectors, define the negative direction of a vector that has the same magnitude, but points in the opposite direction.

Then add the negative vectors:

$$\vec{V}_2 \quad - \quad \vec{V}_1 \quad = \quad \vec{V}_2 \quad + \quad -\vec{V}_1 \quad = \quad \vec{V}_2 - \vec{V}_1$$

A vector, $\vec{V}$, can be multiplied by a scalar c.

The result is a vector that has the same direction, but a magnitude of $c\vec{V}$.

If c is negative, the resultant vector points in the opposite direction.

An example of a vector, $\vec{V}$ being multiplied by different scalars:

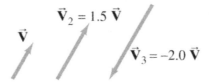

Adding Vectors by Components

A vector can be expressed as the sum of its component vectors.

The component vectors are usually chosen so that they are perpendicular:

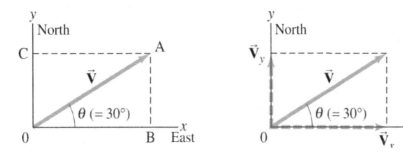

For perpendicular components, calculate the values using trigonometric functions.

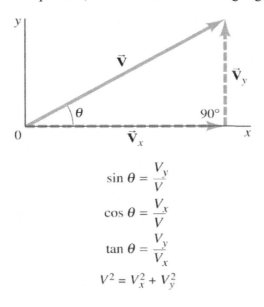

$$\sin \theta = \frac{V_y}{V}$$

$$\cos \theta = \frac{V_x}{V}$$

$$\tan \theta = \frac{V_y}{V_x}$$

$$V^2 = V_x^2 + V_y^2$$

The components are effectively one-dimensional, so add algebraically:

$V_{Ry} = V_{1y} + V_{2y}$

$V_{Rx} = V_{1x} + V_{2x}$

$|\vec{V}_R| = \sqrt{\vec{V}_{Rx}^{\,2} + \vec{V}_{Ry}^{\,2}}$

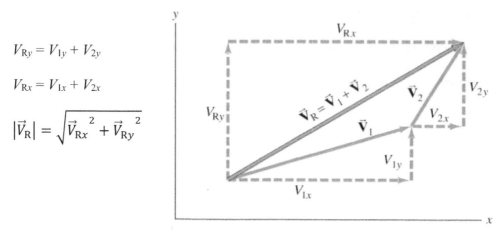

Resolving vectors from component vectors

Five rules for adding vectors:

1. Draw a diagram of the vectors on a coordinate system.

2. Establish the *x* and *y*-axes.

3. Resolve each vector into *x* and *y* components.

4. Calculate each component using sines and cosines.

5. Add the components in each direction to determine the resultant vector.

To find the magnitude and direction of the resultant vector, use:

$$\vec{v} = \sqrt{v_x^2 + v_y^2} \qquad\qquad tan\ \theta = \frac{v_y}{v_x}$$

Speed and Velocity

Speed is the quantity of how far an object travels in each time interval.

Speed is the rate of change in the *distance*; it does not include a direction and is a scalar quantity.

Average speed is the distance (scalar) traveled divided by the time elapsed:

$$\text{Average speed: } speed_{average} = v_{avg} = \frac{d}{t} = \frac{distance\ traveled}{time\ elapsed}$$

The *velocity* quantifies the speed of an object in a direction.

Velocity is the rate of change in *displacement*. Since velocity includes direction, it is a vector quantity (unlike speed, which is a scalar quantity).

Average velocity is the displacement (vector) divided by the elapsed time:

$$velocity_{average} = \vec{v}_{avg} = \frac{s}{t} = \frac{displacement}{time\ elapsed} = \frac{final\ position - initial\ position}{time\ elapsed}$$

Instantaneous speed is the speed at a point in time (infinitesimal time interval).

Instantaneous velocity is the velocity at a point in time (infinitesimal time).

Instantaneous velocity is the mathematical limit (i.e., time becomes infinitesimally small) of the displacement over this imperceptible time interval:

$$\vec{v}_{inst} = \lim_{\Delta t \to 0} \frac{\Delta x}{\Delta t}$$

The instantaneous velocity is a vector and has a direction.

The instantaneous speed is not a vector and does not indicate a direction.

The *direction of instantaneous velocity* is tangent to the path at that point. Its magnitude is equal to that of the instantaneous speed at that point.

The graphs show *constant velocity* (left) and *varying velocity* (right):

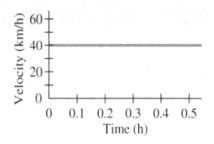
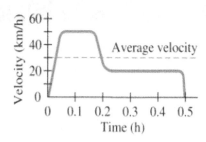

Relative Velocity

The relative speed moves in two dimensions and is calculated by adding or subtracting their magnitudes.

The velocities are vectors that must be added and subtracted accordingly.

Each component velocity is 1) labeled with the object and 2) with the reference frame in which it has this velocity.

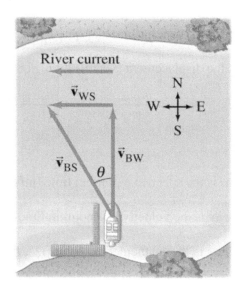

$\vec{v}_{BS}$ is the velocity of the boat relative to the shore

$\vec{v}_{BW}$ is the velocity of the boat relative to the water

$\vec{v}_{WS}$ is the velocity of the water relative to the shore

The relationship between the three velocities is:

$$\vec{v}_{BS} = \vec{v}_{BW} + \vec{v}_{WS}$$

Acceleration

Acceleration is the rate of change in the velocity of an object and is expressed as:

$$average\ acceleration = \vec{a}_{avg}$$

$$\vec{a}_{avg} = \frac{\Delta \vec{v}}{\Delta t}$$

$$\frac{\Delta \vec{v}}{\Delta t} = \frac{\vec{v}_f - \vec{v}_i}{t} = \frac{change\ in\ velocity}{time\ elapsed}$$

From the calculated average acceleration, the instantaneous acceleration of an object can be determined.

The *instantaneous acceleration* is the average velocity over the limit of the time interval as time becomes infinitesimally small:

$$\vec{a}_{inst} = \lim_{\Delta t \to 0} \frac{\Delta \vec{v}}{\Delta t}$$

Like velocity, acceleration is a vector (i.e., magnitude and direction).

In one-dimensional motion (e.g., speed), only a positive or negative sign is needed for the calculation of the resulting motion (e.g., net speed).

If the magnitude of the acceleration is *constant,* and there is *no change in direction*, the values for speed (scalar) and velocity (vector) are interchangeable.

If the magnitude of the acceleration is *constant,* and there is *no change in direction*, the values for distance (scalar) and displacement (vector) are interchangeable.

Reference the direction of the acceleration.

Negative acceleration and deceleration describe different phenomena.

- *Negative acceleration* is an acceleration in the negative direction as defined by the coordinate system (e.g., a booster rocket dislodged from the satellite). The direction of the acceleration is independent of velocity.

- *Deceleration* is relative to the object's velocity; it occurs when the acceleration is opposite in direction to the velocity (e.g., a car skidding to a stop).

If the object is traveling in a positive direction (i.e., the velocity is positive), then deceleration and negative acceleration are the same.

Positive acceleration (i.e.., car advances) is shown:

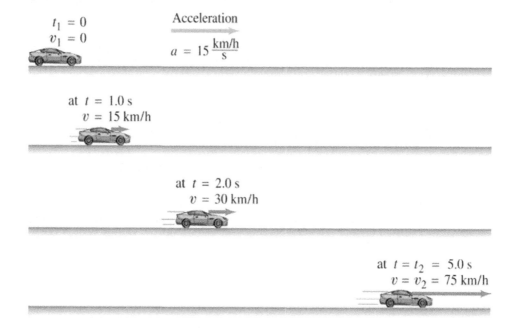

Negative acceleration (i.e., an acceleration in the negative direction) is shown:

Motion at Constant Acceleration

The *average velocity* of an object, during a time interval t is:

$$\bar{v} = \frac{\Delta x}{\Delta t} = \frac{x - x_0}{t - t_0} = \frac{x - x_0}{t}$$

The *constant velocity* expression is:

$$\bar{v} = \frac{v_0 + v}{2}$$

The *constant acceleration* expression is:

$$\vec{a} = \frac{v - v_0}{t}$$

Combine the expressions for *average velocity, constant acceleration,* and *constant velocity*; where x is the position, x_0 is the initial position, v_0 is the initial velocity, t is the time:

$$x = x_0 + \bar{v}t$$

$$x_0 + \bar{v}t = x_0 + \left(\frac{v_0 + v}{2}\right)t$$

$$x_0 + \left(\frac{v_0 + v}{2}\right)t = x_0 + \left(\frac{v_0 + v_0 + at}{2}\right)t$$

or simplified as:

$$x = x_0 + v_0 t + \frac{1}{2}at^2$$

Solve to eliminate t:

$$v^2 = v_0{}^2 + 2a(x - x_0)$$

The equations needed to solve constant acceleration problems:

- $v = v_0 + at$

- $x = x_0 + v_0 t + \frac{1}{2}at^2$

- $v^2 = v_0^2 + 2a(x - x_0)$

- $\bar{v} = \frac{v_0 + v}{2}$

- $s = v_{avg}t$

- $v_{avg} = \frac{v_f + v_i}{2}$

- $a = \frac{\Delta v}{\Delta t} = \frac{v_f - v_i}{t}$

- $v_f^2 = v_i^2 + 2as$

- $s = \frac{1}{2}at^2 + v_i t$

- $l_f = l_i + s$

Learn to rearrange, combine, and apply the equations appropriately.

When solving problems with these equations, assign one direction as positive and the opposite as negative; use this orientation for all subsequent calculations.

In Cartesian coordinates (i.e., horizontal x and vertical y-axes), take upward and rightward motions as positive, and downward and leftward motions as negative.

For free falls, take downward (gravitational acceleration) as positive.

The direction for motion can be assigned arbitrarily, provided that the opposite direction has the opposite sign.

Graphical Analysis of Linear Motion

A graph of the x *vs.* t (i.e., distance *vs.* time) for an object moving with constant velocity is shown below.

Velocity is the slope (rise/run or x- / y-) of the x *vs.* t (i.e., distance *vs.* time) graph.

If the slope is positive, the velocity is positive.

If the slope is negative, the velocity is negative.

The slope of the line is linear (straight line) because the velocity is constant:

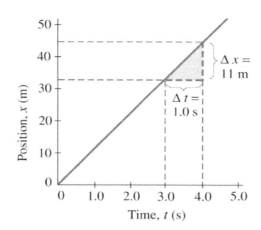

Position vs. time graph shows a linear slope for constant velocity

Freely Falling Bodies

Motion with constant acceleration is an object in *free fall* (e.g., an apple falling to the ground from the tree).

Near the Earth's surface, objects experience approximately the same acceleration due to gravity ($g = 9.8$ m/s^2 or use 10 m/s^2 for ease of calculations).

The differences in acceleration due to gravity between various objects (e.g., feather and marble) are related to air resistance. A larger surface area means higher air resistance (e.g., a flat sheet of paper compared to a crumpled sheet of the same paper).

In a vacuum (i.e., no air resistance), gravity causes all objects to fall with the same acceleration ($g = 9.8$ m/s^2). Acceleration is constant because of no air resistance.

Whenever an object is in the air, it is in free fall, regardless of whether it is tossed upwards, downward, or at an angle. For objects that are dropped, label the downward direction as positive, so g (acceleration) is positive.

For an object thrown downward, both the initial velocity and g are positive.

For an object thrown upward, initial velocity has the opposite sign to acceleration.

Choose either the upward or the downward direction as positive.

Projectiles

A projectile is an object moving in two dimensions under the influence of the Earth's gravity. The projectile's path of travel is a parabola. The object's motion along this path is *projectile motion*, is described through its vertical and horizontal components.

The speed in the horizontal (*x*-direction) is constant.

The speed in the vertical (*y*-direction) is constant acceleration g.

Projectiles are freely falling bodies, so the vertical component of the projectile motion is accelerating toward the Earth at a rate of g. Even when the projectile is traveling upward, the downward acceleration of gravity causes the projectile to decelerate when traveling upward. There is no acceleration due to gravity in the horizontal component.

The *horizontal component* of velocity is constant. The time that elapses while the projectile is in motion is dependent on only the vertical (not horizontal) component of the projectile motion.

The horizontal distance covered by the projectile is determined from the elapsed time during the projectile's path multiplied by its horizontal speed (speed × time).

For an object tossed straight up, and it comes down to where it started, and the total displacement *s* for the trip is zero.

The initial velocity and final velocity are equal and opposite:

$$(\vec{v}_{final} + \vec{v}_{initial} = 0)$$

The acceleration is opposite in sign to the initial velocity.

Two balls that start to fall at the same time are illustrated below. The ball on the right in each figure has an initial velocity in the *x*-direction, while the ball on the left was dropped straight downward (i.e., zero initial velocity in the *x*-direction).

The vertical positions of the two balls are identical at identical times, while the horizontal position of the ball on the right increases linearly.

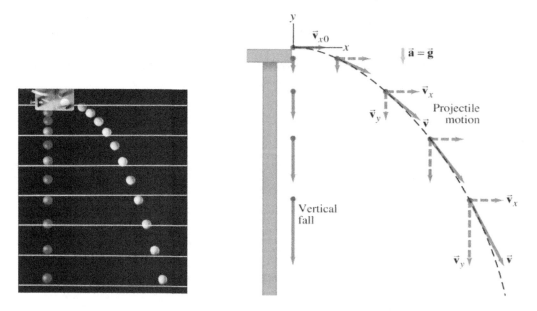

Comparison of a ball dropped vs. projected with a horizontal velocity

The object is launched at an initial angle of θ_0 with the horizontal. The analysis is similar except that the initial velocity has both a *horizontal* and *vertical* component.

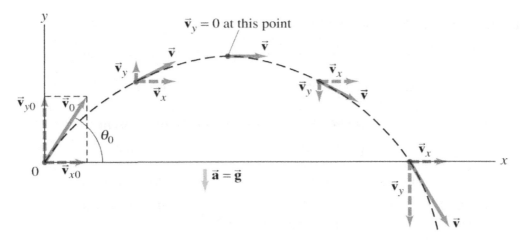

Projectile with both x- and y-component for velocity

Projectile Motion Is Parabolic

To demonstrate that projectile motion is parabolic, write y as a function of x.

A *parabola* is expressed by the equation:

$$y = Ax^2 - Bx + C$$

where A, B, and C are constants.

A is a scalar (magnitude) multiplier of the *object's acceleration*.

B as a scalar multiplier of the *velocity*.

C as a scalar multiplier of the object's *initial position*.

The *direction of the object's acceleration* is determined by the signs associated with these constants for determining the velocity and initial displacement from the origin.

Solving Projectile Motion Problems

Projectile motion is motion with a constant acceleration in one dimension.

For acceleration due to gravity, the direction is downward.

<table>
<tr><td colspan="2" align="center">Kinematic Equations for Projectile Motion
(y positive downward; $a_x = 0$, $a_y = g = 9.8$ m/s^2)</td></tr>
<tr><td align="center">Horizontal Motion
($a_x = 0$, v_x = constant)</td><td align="center">Vertical Motion
($a_y = g$ = constant)</td></tr>
<tr><td>$v_x = v_{x0}$</td><td>$v_y = v_{y0} - gt$</td></tr>
<tr><td>$x = x_0 + v_{x0}\, t$</td><td>$y = y_0 + v_{y0}\, t - (\frac{1}{2})gt^2$</td></tr>
<tr><td></td><td>$v_y^2 = v_{y0}^2 - 2g(y - y_0)$</td></tr>
</table>

Projectile motion problems may be solved by following seven steps:

1. Read the problem carefully and choose the object(s) to be analyzed.

2. Draw a diagram of the described actions.

3. Choose a point of origin and a coordinate system.

4. Determine the time interval;

   the same in both directions, and

   includes only the time the object is moving, with constant acceleration g.

5. Evaluate the x and y-components of the motion separately.

6. List the known and unknown quantities.

   the v_x never changes, and

   the $v_y = 0$ at the highest point.

7. Use the appropriate equations; some of them may have to be combined.

Free Fall *vs.* Non-Free Fall

In free fall, the only force acting on the object is gravity.

Assuming no air resistance, the only resistance to change is the object's inertia.

All objects fall at a *constant acceleration* of 9.8 m/s^2 downward. Since Earth is not a vacuum, air resistance (force opposing the motion downward) is generally accounted for when objects are falling.

In a *non-free fall*, the upward force due to air resistance counteracts the downward force due to gravity. The net force of this interaction is the difference between the force due to gravity and air resistance.

Therefore, the total force on an object in a non-free fall is less than that of the same object in free fall, where the force from air resistance is zero.

As an object falls, the force from air resistance increases with the increased speed of the object, and the force downward decreases until the two opposing forces are equal in magnitude. The acceleration of the object is zero. The *terminal velocity* is the point at which the object is traveling at a constant velocity downward due to the maximum force of air resistance. Terminal velocity is achieved when air resistance equals the weight of the object. Weight is the mass under the influence of gravity. The mass of an object on Earth and the moon are the same. However, the weights are different due to differences in gravity. Gravity is an attractive force between two bodies. Massive objects exert a tremendous attractive force.

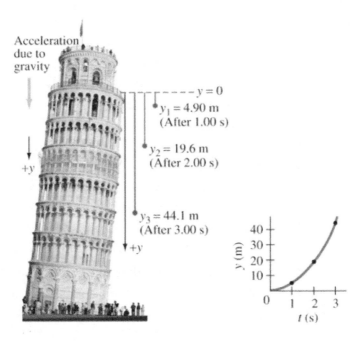

The diagram on the right graphs distance vs. time of the falling object

Satellites and *Weightlessness*

Satellites are routinely put into orbit around the Earth. The tangential speed of the satellite must be enough so that the satellite does not fall to Earth. However, the tangential speed cannot be so high that the satellite escapes Earth's gravity altogether. Satellites orbiting the Earth are in continuous free fall, and their centripetal acceleration equals the acceleration from the Earth's gravity.

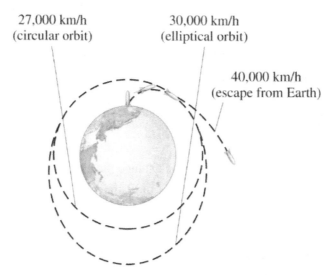

27,000 km/h (circular orbit) 30,000 km/h (elliptical orbit) 40,000 km/h (escape from Earth)

The satellite is kept in orbit around the Earth by its speed. The satellite is continually falling and accelerating toward the Earth. It never crashes into the Earth's surface because the Earth curves away underneath it at the same rate as the satellite falls toward Earth.

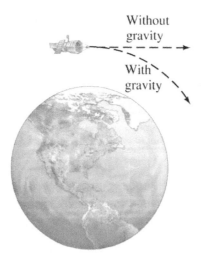

Without gravity

With gravity

Objects in orbit are said to experience weightlessness, even though they do have a gravitational force acting on them. The satellite and all its contents are in free fall, so there is no normal force, leading to the experience of weightlessness. The term to describe this is *apparent weightlessness* because the gravitational force still exists. Apparent weightlessness can be experienced on Earth, but only briefly.

For example, when a roller coaster rushes down a hill, the normal force temporarily goes to zero, and the riders experience apparent weightlessness.

Real weightlessness occurs when there is no net gravitational force acting on an object. Either the object is in outer space:

1) void of the attractive force of gravity when other massive objects are light-years away, or

2) the object does not experience a net gravitational force because it is between two other objects with equal gravitational forces that cancel.

Chapter Summary

Graphs are useful tools to help visualize the motion of an object. They can also help solve problems once the information contained in a graph is translated to describe a physical phenomenon. When working with graphs, consider the following:

- Always look at the axes of the graph first. A common mistake for the velocity *vs.* time graph is thinking about it as a position *vs.* time graph.

- Do not assume one interval is one unit; inspect the numbers on the axis.

- Align the position *vs.* time graphs *directly above* the velocity *vs.* time graphs and *directly above* the acceleration *vs.* time graphs. This way, relationships and the key points among the graphs can be matched.

  The *slope* of a distance *vs.* time (*x vs. t*) graph gives velocity.

  The *slope* of a velocity *vs.* time (*v* vs. *t*) graph gives acceleration.

  The *area* under an acceleration *vs.* time (*a vs. t*) graph gives the change in velocity.

  The *area* under a velocity *vs.* time (*v* vs. *t*) graph gives the displacement.

- The motion of an object in one dimension can be described using Five Equations. Identify what is given, determine what must be calculated, and use the equation that has those variables. Note that sometimes there is hidden (or assumed) information in the problem (e.g., acceleration due to gravity $g = -10$ m/s^2)

		Missing variable
#1*	$\Delta x = vt$	a
#2	$v = v_0 + at$	x
#3	$x = x_0 + v_0 t + \dfrac{1}{2}at^2$	v
#4	$x = x_0 + vt - \dfrac{1}{2}at^2$	v_0
#5	$v^2 = v_0{}^2 + 2a(x - x_0)$	T

* Because the acceleration is uniform: $\Delta x = \frac{1}{2}(v_0 + v)t$

For projectiles, separate the horizontal and vertical components.

Horizontal Motion	Vertical Motion
$x = v_x t$	$y = y_0 + v_0 t + \dfrac{1}{2} g t^2$
$v_x = v_{0x} =$ constant	$v_y = v_{0y} + gt$
$a_x = 0$	$a = g = -10 \dfrac{m}{s^2}$

At any given moment, the relationship between v, v_x and v_y is given by:

$v^2 = v_x{}^2 + v_y{}^2$

$v_x = v \cos \theta$

$v_y = \sin \theta$

$\theta = \tan^{-1}(\dfrac{v_y}{v_x})$

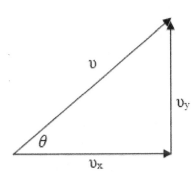

Resolving vectors from the known x- and y-component of the separate vectors

47

Solving Problems

General guidelines for solving problems involving motion:

1. Read the entire problem. Evaluate what is provided and what is asked to be solved for in the problem.

2. Decide which objects are under study and what the time interval is.

3. Draw a diagram and choose coordinate axes.

4. Evaluate all known quantities, then identify the unknown quantities that need to be determined.

5. Determine which equations relate to the known and unknown quantities. Solve algebraically for the unknown quantities and check that the result is sensible (e.g., magnitude and correct dimensions).

6. Calculate the solution and round to the appropriate number of significant figures.

7. Evaluate if the result is reasonable by comparing if it agrees with a rough estimate or approximations (e.g., positive or negative, the order of magnitude).

8. Check that the units on one side of the equation match the units on the other.

Practice Questions

1. Which graph represents a constant non-zero velocity?

I. 　　　II. 　　　III.

    A. I only   **B.** II only   **C.** III only   **D.** I and II only

2. A train starts from rest and accelerates uniformly until it has traveled 5.6 km and has acquired a velocity of 42 m/s. The train then moves at a constant velocity of 42 m/s for 420 s. The train then slows down uniformly at 0.065 m/s^2, until it stops moving. What is the acceleration during the first 5.6 km of travel?

    A. 0.29 m/s^2 **B.** 0.23 m/s^2 **C.** 0.16 m/s^2 **D.** 0.12 m/s^2

3. A cannonball is fired straight up at 50 m/s. Ignoring air resistance, what is the velocity at the highest point it reaches before starting to return towards Earth?

    A. 0 m/s   **B.** 25 m/s   **C.** $\sqrt{50}$ m/s   **D.** 50 m/s

4. The tendency of a moving object to remain in unchanging motion in the absence of an unbalanced force is:

    A. impulse   **B.** acceleration   **C.** free fall   **D.** inertia

5. Which statement is correct when an object that is moving in the $+x$ direction undergoes an acceleration of 2 m/s^2?

    A. It travels at 2 m/s   **C.** It decreases its velocity by 2 m/s every second
    B. It travels at 2 m/s^2 **D.** It increases its velocity by 2 m/s every second

6. What is the increase in speed each second for a freely falling object?

    A. 0 m/s   **B.** 9.8 m/s^2 **C.** 9.8 m/s   **D.** 19.6 m/s

7. A marble is initially rolling up a slight incline at 0.2 m/s and starting at $t = 0$ s, decelerates uniformly at 0.05 m/s^2. At what time does the marble come to a stop?

    A. 2 s   **B.** 4 s   **C.** 8 s   **D.** 12 s

8. An 8.7-hour trip is made at an average speed of 73 km/h. If the first third of the journey was driven at 96.5 km/h, what was the average speed for the rest of the trip?

    A. 54 km/hr   **B.** 46 km/hr   **C.** 28 km/hr   **D.** 62 km/hr

9. The lightning flash and the thunder are not observed simultaneously because light travels much faster than sound. Therefore it can be assumed as instantaneous when the lightning occurs. What is the distance from the lightning bolt to the observer, if the delay between the sound and lightning flash is 6 s? (Use speed of sound in air $v = 340$ m/s)

   A. 2,040 m   **B.** 880 m   **C.** 2,360 m   **D.** 2,820 m

10. If a cat jumps at a 60° angle off the ground with an initial velocity of 2.74 m/s, what is the highest point of the cat's trajectory? (Use acceleration due to gravity $g = 9.8$ m/s^2)

   A. 9.46 m   **B.** 0.69 m   **C.** 5.75 m   **D.** 0.29 m

11. What is the resultant vector AB when vector A = 6 m and points 30° North of East, while vector B = 4 m and points 30° South of West?

   A. 8 m at an angle 45° East of North   **C.** 2 m at an angle 30° North of East
   B. 8 m at an angle 30° North of East   **D.** 2 m at an angle 45° North of East

12. How much farther would an intoxicated driver's car travel before he hits the brakes than a sober driver's car if both cars are initially traveling at 49 mi/h, and the sober driver takes 0.33 s to hit the brakes while the intoxicated driver takes 1 s to hit the brakes?

   A. 38 ft   **B.** 52 ft   **C.** 32 ft   **D.** 48 ft

13. A projectile is fired at time $t = 0$ s from point 0 at the edge of a cliff with initial velocity components of $v_{0x} = 80$ m/s and $v_{0y} = 800$ m/s. The projectile rises, then falls into the sea at point P. The time of flight of the projectile is 200 s. What is the height of the cliff? (Use acceleration due to gravity $g = 10$ m/s^2)

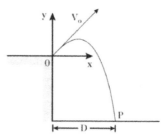

   A. 30,000 m   **C.** 47,500 m
   B. 45,000 m   **D.** 40,000 m

14. Which of the following is a unit that can be used for a measure of weight?

   A. kilogram   **B.** kg·m/s   **C.** Newton   **D.** milligram

15. Which of the following statements about the direction of velocity and acceleration is correct for a ball that is thrown straight up, reaches a maximum height, and falls to its initial height?

   A. Its velocity changes from upward to downward and its acceleration points downward
   B. Its velocity points downward, and its acceleration points upward
   C. Both its velocity and its acceleration point downward
   D. Both its velocity and its acceleration point upward

Solutions

1. B is correct.

Graph I depicts a constant zero velocity process.

Graph II depicts a constant non-zero velocity.

Graph III depicts non- constant velocity.

2. C is correct.

$$v_f^2 = v_i^2 + 2ad$$

$$a = (v_f^2 - v_i^2) / 2d$$

$$a = [(42 \text{ m/s})^2 - (0 \text{ m/s})^2] / [2(5,600 \text{ m})]$$

$$a = (1,764 \text{ m}^2/\text{s}^2) / 11,200 \text{ m}$$

$$a = 0.16 \text{ m/s}^2$$

3. A is correct.

At the maximum height, the velocity = 0 and the cannonball stops moving up and begins to come back.

4. D is correct. An object's inertia is its resistance to change in motion.

5. D is correct.

$$v = v_0 + at$$

If $a = 2 \text{ m/s}^2$ then the object has a 2 m/s increase in velocity every second.

Example:

$$v_0 = 0 \text{ m/s}, a = 2 \text{ m/s}^2, t = 1 \text{ s}$$

$$v = 0 \text{ m/s} + (2 \text{ m/s}^2) \cdot (1 \text{ s})$$

$$v = 2 \text{ m/s}$$

6. C is correct.

The acceleration due to gravity is 9.8 m/s^2. If an object is in freefall, then every second it increases velocity by 9.8 m/s.

$$v = v_0 + at$$

$$v = v_0 + (9.8 \text{ m/s}^2) \cdot (1 \text{ s})$$

$$v = v_0 + 9.8 \text{ m/s}$$

7. B is correct.

To determine the time at which the marble stops:

$$v_2 - v_1 = a\Delta t$$

where $v_1 = 0.2$ m/s and $a = -0.05$ m/s^2

$$\Delta t = (v_2 - v_1) / a$$

$$\Delta t = (0 \text{ m/s} - 0.2 \text{ m/s}) / (-0.05 \text{ m/s}^2)$$

$$\Delta t = (-0.2 \text{ m/s}) / (-0.05 \text{ m/s}^2)$$

$$\Delta t = 4 \text{ s}$$

8. D is correct.

$$v_{avg} = (1/3)v_1 + (2/3)v_2$$

$$73 \text{ km/h} = (1/3) \cdot (96.5 \text{ km/h}) + (2/3)v_2$$

$$73 \text{ km/h} = (32 \text{ km/h}) + (2/3)v_2$$

$$(2/3)v_2 = 41 \text{ km/h}$$

$$v_2 = (41 \text{ km/h}) \cdot (3/2)$$

$$v_2 = 62 \text{ km/h}$$

9. A is correct.

The distance to the lightning bolt is calculated by determining the distance traveled by the sound.

$$\text{Distance} = \text{velocity} \times \text{time}$$

$$d = vt$$

$$d = (340 \text{ m/s}) \cdot (6 \text{ s})$$

$$d = 2{,}040 \text{ m}$$

10. D is correct.

Calculate the vertical component of the initial velocity:

$$v_{up} = v(\sin \theta)$$

$$v_{up} = (2.74 \text{ m/s}) \sin 60°$$

$$v_{up} = 2.37 \text{ m/s}$$

Then solve for the upward displacement given the initial upward velocity:

$$d = (v_f^2 - v_i^2) / 2a$$

$$d = [(0 \text{ m/s})^2 - (2.37 \text{ m/s})^2] / 2(-9.8 \text{ m/s}^2)$$

$$d = (-5.62 \text{ m}^2/\text{s}^2) / (-19.6 \text{ m/s}^2)$$

$$d = 0.29 \text{ m}$$

11. C is correct.

30° North of East is the exact opposite direction of 30° South of West, so set one vector as negative, and the direction of the resultant vector will be in the direction of the larger vector between A and B.

Since the magnitude of A is greater than the magnitude of B and vectors were added "tip to tail," the resultant vector is:

$$AB = A + B$$

$$AB = 6 \text{ m} + (-4 \text{ m})$$

$$AB = 2 \text{ m at } 30° \text{ North of East}$$

12. D is correct.

The solution is measured in feet, so first convert the car velocity into feet per second:

$$v = (49 \text{ mi/h}) \cdot (5280 \text{ ft/mi}) \cdot (1 \text{ h}/3600 \text{ s})$$

$$v = 72 \text{ ft/s}$$

The sober driver's distance:

$$d = vt$$

$$d_{sober} = (72 \text{ ft/s}) \cdot (0.33 \text{ s})$$

$$d_{sober} = 24 \text{ ft}$$

The intoxicated driver's distance:

$$d = vt$$

$$d_{drunk} = (72 \text{ ft/s}) \cdot (1 \text{ s})$$

$$d_{drunk} = 72 \text{ ft}$$

The differences between the distances:

$$\Delta d = 72 \text{ ft} - 24 \text{ ft}$$

$$\Delta d = 48 \text{ ft}$$

13. D is correct.

$$d = v_0t + \frac{1}{2}gt^2$$

Set *g* as negative because it is in the opposite direction as +800 m/s:

$$d = (800 \text{ m/s}) \cdot (200 \text{ s}) + \frac{1}{2}(-10 \text{ m/s}^2) \cdot (200 \text{ s})^2$$

$$d = (160,000 \text{ m}) - (200,000 \text{ m})$$

$$d = -40,000 \text{ m}$$

The projectile traveled –40,000 m from the top of the cliff to the sea at point P, which means the cliff is 40,000 m from the base to the top.

14. C is correct.

1 Newton is the force needed to accelerate 1 kg of mass at a rate of 1 m/s^2.

$$F = ma$$

$$W = mg$$

$$N = \text{kg} \cdot \text{m/s}^2$$

15. A is correct.

When the ball is thrown upwards, its velocity is initially upwards but as it falls back down the velocity direction points downward.

The acceleration due to gravity always points down and does not change.

CHAPTER 2

Force, Motion, Gravitation

- **Newton's First Law: Inertia**

- **Newton's Second Law: $F = ma$**

- **Newton's Third Law: Forces Equal and Opposite**

- **Weight**

- **Center of Mass**

- **Friction: Static and Kinetic**

- **Motion on an Inclined Plane**

- **Uniform Circular Motion and Centripetal Force**

- **Law of Gravitation**

- **Concept of a field**

Newton's First Law: Inertia

Newton's First Law of Motion states that *an object at rest remains at rest and an object in motion (with constant velocity) remains in motion (with that same constant velocity) unless acted on by an external force*.

In other terms, nothing changes about an object's motion regarding speed and direction, unless it is acted on by an outside force.

All objects resist changes in their state of motion (even if that motion is zero) until an outside force manipulates them into a new state of motion. This is because all objects have *inertia*.

Inertia is an inherent property of all objects and is the tendency for objects to resist changes in their current state motion.

Inertia cannot be calculated, but it can be measured by an object's *mass*; the more massive the object, the more inertia it has. In the SI system, mass is measured in kilograms (kg).

Mass is not the same value as weight (i.e., $w = mg$); weight (w) depends on gravity (and can change depending on location), the mass (m) of an object is always the same and gravity (g) depends on the attractive force between two objects.

Newton's First Law of Motion is only valid for an inertial reference frame, which is any frame of reference that moves with constant velocity (i.e., no acceleration) relative to the inertial system under observation.

Newton's Second Law: *F = ma*

Newton's Second Law states that force is the vector product of mass and acceleration, and it is expressed as:

$$\Sigma \vec{F} = m\vec{a}$$

(Net force equals mass times acceleration)

The unit for force in the SI system is the Newton, which is the product of the units of mass and acceleration ($N = kg \cdot m/s^2$).

When considering force, it is essential to note the units. A pound is a unit of force, not of mass. Therefore, it can be equated to the Newton, but not to kilograms.

Conventionally, kilograms are used as a measurement of weight (e.g., a person weighs 186 lbs. or 80 kg). This usage can be misleading, as it is not technically correct; a kilogram is a unit of mass, and the weight of an object is a measurement of force.

Remember that this everyday use of kilogram is incorrect and do not mistake kilograms for weight when solving the problems.

Units for Mass and Force		
System	**Mass**	**Force**
SI	kilogram (kg)	Newton ($N = kg \cdot m/s^2$)
CGS	gram (g)	dyne ($= g \cdot cm/s^2$)
Imperial	slug	pound (lb)
Conversion factors: 1 dyne = 10^{-5} N; 1 lb ≈ 4.45 N; 1 slug ≈ 14.6 kg		

Newton's Second Law of Motion can be separated into *x*- and *y*- and *z*-components because the force is a vector:

$$\Sigma F_x = ma_x$$

$$\Sigma F_y = ma_y$$

$$\Sigma F_z = ma_z$$

From the above equations, the force is directly proportional to the mass of the object. This further explains Newton's First Law of Motion (Law of Inertia). Much more force is required to push a boulder up a hill than to push a pebble up a hill because the mass of the boulder is much higher than that of the pebble. If this situation is applied to Newton's First Law, the boulder has higher inertia than the pebble and will, therefore, be more resistant to changes in motion.

By applying Newton's Second Law, the force needed to move (accelerate) the boulder is directly proportional to its mass and thus greater than the force needed to move (accelerate) the pebble.

Rearranging Newton's Second Law ($F = ma$) shows that acceleration is directly proportional to force and inversely proportional to mass:

$$a = F / m$$

The force on an object with a mass of 2 kg is 4 N, therefore:

$$a = \frac{F}{m} \qquad a = \frac{4\,\text{N}}{2\,\text{kg}} \qquad a = 2\,\text{m/s}^2$$

If the force is 8 N and the mass of the object is 2 kg, then:

$$a = \frac{F}{m} \qquad a = \frac{8\,\text{N}}{2\,\text{kg}} \qquad a = 4\,\text{m/s}^2$$

Acceleration is directly proportional to force. By doubling the force, the acceleration of the object is also doubled.

The opposite holds when doubling the mass. Since mass is inversely proportional to acceleration, doubling the mass will halve the acceleration. This intuitively makes sense considering the mass of the boulder and pebble in the previous example. Exerting the same force on both will not give the same acceleration because the mass (which represents inertia, or the resistance to change) of each object is vastly different.

If the pebble has a mass of 5 kg and its acceleration is 20 m/s^2, what force was exerted on it?

$$a = \frac{F}{m} \qquad 20\,\text{m/s}^2 = \frac{F}{5\,\text{kg}} \qquad F = 100\,\text{N}$$

If the boulder has a mass of 20 kg and the same force of 100 N is exerted, what is the acceleration? The boulder has four times the mass of the pebble, so the acceleration is one-fourth that of the pebble: 5 m/s^2 as compared to 20 m/s^2 for the pebble.

Both force and acceleration are vectors because they have a direction. Many physics questions omit the directional attribute because it is usually assumed. For example, when an apple falls to the ground, the force of gravity acts downwards, and the apple, of course, falls downwards. Many questions involve substituting values into the appropriate formula.

However, more difficult questions have directional attributes associated with them. For example, when a bar of soap slides down an inclined plane, the force of gravity acts downwards, but the acceleration is not entirely downwards; instead, it is slanted. Therefore, vector analysis is needed.

Solving problems involving Newton's Second Law

- Visualize, draw a sketch, and always use a free body diagram.

- Clearly define an appropriate coordinate system. This is particularly important when dealing with inclined planes because the angle between the normal force and the gravitational force acting on the object is altered.

- Always apply Newton's Second Law to each mass separately, and when there are forces in two or more directions, apply Newton's Second Law to each direction separately.

- "Translational equilibrium" implies two equations: $\Sigma F_x = 0$ and $\Sigma F_y = 0$

- When $\Sigma F = 0$, $a = 0$ and vice versa.

- Solve the component equations. If the acceleration of x or y is known, or the object is moving at constant velocity ($a = 0$), then the component equations can be used to solve for unknown forces.

- Use the unit circle to calculate trigonometric functions and make sure to use degrees if the angles are given in degrees or radians if the angles are given in radians.

Newton's Third Law: Forces are Equal and Opposite

For Newton's Third Law, it is essential to understand how forces work. A force must have a source object (i.e., any force exerted on one object that is caused by another object). When a person interacts with an object by exerting a force on it, that object exerts the same amount, or magnitude, of force back on them. This is often simplified into the dogma:

Newton's Third Law: *Every action has an equal and opposite reaction.*

If body A exerts a force F_A on body B, then B exerts a force F_B on body A:

$$F_B = -F_A$$

To correctly apply Newton's Third Law, it is essential to understand that the forces are exerted on different objects, and they should not be treated as if they were acting on the same object. These matched forces are *action and reaction pairs*.

As a helpful notation, the first subscript is the object that the force is being exerted on. The second subscript is the source object. For example, a person (P) walking forward exerts a force on the ground (G), which exerts an equal and opposite force to move them forward. This can be expressed as:

$$\vec{F}_{GP} = -\vec{F}_{PG}$$

$\vec{F}_{GP}$ $\vec{F}_{PG}$

$\vec{F}_{GP}$ is the horizontal force exerted *on* the ground by the woman's foot and $\vec{F}_{PG}$ is the horizontal force exerted on the woman's foot *by* the ground.

Using Newton's Third Law for rocket propulsion, when a rocket is in flight, hot gases from combustion spew out of the tail of the rocket at high speeds (*action force*). The *reaction force* is what propels the rocket forward.

It is important to note that the rocket does not need anything to "push" against. Regardless if it is traveling within Earth's atmosphere or in the vacuum of space, the rocket can propel itself forward because of the action-reaction forces from combustion.

To summarize, all three of Newton's Laws of Motion can be extrapolated and observed in almost any situation. A cannon and cannonball provide an example:

- A cannon is initially at rest. It has a large mass and, therefore, large inertia. It remains at rest until a force is applied (Newton's First Law).

- When the cannon is fired, a large force is applied by the cannon to the cannonball to overcome the inertia of the cannonball and cause it to accelerate (Newton's Second Law).

- The tremendous force applied by the cannon is reciprocated by the cannonball back onto the cannon, the cannon recoils (Newton's Third Law).

Why does the cannonball accelerate faster than the recoiling cannon?

Consider all three laws, but the most important component to consider is inertia.

Third Law: the forces exerted on the cannon and cannonball must be the same.

The Second Law states that force and mass (inertia) determine acceleration; since the forces are equal, but the masses are considerably different, the accelerations are considerably different.

The cannonball accelerates faster because of its mass (i.e., inertia) is less than the mass of the cannon: $a = \frac{F}{m}$

Once the cannonball is airborne, it will remain in flight (according to the First Law) unless a force acts upon it to change its motion. In this case, the forces of air resistance and gravity eventually cause the cannonball to slow and fall to the ground.

Solving Problems with Newton's Laws − Free-Body Diagrams

1. Draw a sketch.

2. For every object, draw a free-body diagram showing all the forces acting *on* the object.

    Make the magnitudes and directions as accurate as possible.

    Label each force.

    If there are multiple objects, draw a separate diagram for each object.

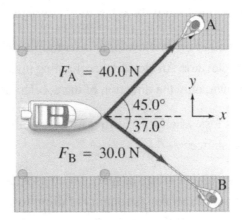

3. Resolve the vectors into components.

4. Apply Newton's Second Law of Motion ($F = ma$) to each component.

5. Solve for the net force in each component direction and combine each component to determine the total net force.

Weight

Weight is the gravitational force (i.e., the force of gravity) that acts on a mass when an object is close to the Earth's surface. The gravitational force changes with substantial increases or decreases in altitude. It is a force, therefore, a vector quantity.

The gravitational force is:

$$\vec{F}_g = m\vec{g}$$

where g is the acceleration due to gravity at 9.8 m/s^2 (sometimes rounded to 10 m/s^2).

An object weighs more on an elevator accelerating up because $F = mg + ma$, where a is the acceleration of the elevator. An elevator accelerating up has the same force as an elevator decelerating on its way down, only the direction of the acceleration changes.

An object weighs less when it is further away from the Earth because the force of gravity decreases with distance.

However, when an object orbits in space (such as an astronaut in a spacecraft), it is not genuinely weightless in space. An astronaut is falling toward the Earth at the same rate as the spacecraft she resides in. If the astronaut's spacecraft falls from space to the surface of the Earth, their weight will increase during the fall due to the increase of gravitational acceleration as they get closer to the Earth's surface.

For a given mass, its weight on Earth is different than it is on the Moon. If a person stands on the Moon, which has a gravitational acceleration of about 1/6 g, that person is 1/6 of their typical weight on Earth. Their mass, however, is the same in both locations.

From Newton's Second Law ($F = ma$), an object at rest must have no net force on it. It is also true, that an object always has a gravitational force acting upon it.

For both Newton's Second and Third Laws, there must be an equal but opposite force. If the object is resting on a flat surface, then the force of the surface pushing up on the object is the *normal force*.

The normal force is always *perpendicular* to the plane of the object.

When an object is lying still on a horizontal surface, the normal force is equal and opposite to the weight (i.e., the force of gravity).

The normal force is precisely as large as needed to balance the downward force from the object (if the required force gets too big, something breaks).

If a statue is placed on a table, the normal force from the table is equal and opposite to the force of gravity.

As a result, the statue experiences no net force and does not move.

$$-\vec{F}_G = \vec{F}_N$$

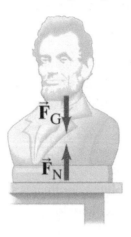

Center of Mass

Every object has a center of mass. The *center of mass* is a single, approximate point at which all an object's mass is concentrated. It is also at this point that external forces can be considered to act on the object. If an object is balanced on its center of mass, it spins uniformly about this axis.

If an object is a uniform along its entire length, the center of mass is the center of the object. If the object is not uniform, the center of mass is the point obtained by taking an average of all the positions weighted by their respective masses:

$$x_{cm} = \frac{\sum x_i m_i}{\sum m_i} \qquad y_{cm} = \frac{\sum y_i m_i}{\sum m_i} \qquad z_{cm} = \frac{\sum z_i m_i}{\sum m_i}$$

It is not necessary to have absolute coordinates when calculating the center of mass. Set the point of reference for a convenient location and use relative coordinates. It is important to understand that the center of mass need not be within the object. For example, a doughnut's center of mass is in the center of its hole. For two objects, the center of mass lies closer to the one with the most mass.

Imagine two balls of an unequal mass attached to a massless stick. The equation and image below describe the situation and the center of mass calculation:

$$m_A > m_B$$

$$x_{CM} = \frac{m_A x_A + m_B x_B}{m_A + m_B} = \frac{m_A x_A + m_B x_B}{\sum M}$$

If the difference in mass between two objects is substantial, then the center of mass can be assumed to be that of the more massive object.

For example, the center of mass of the Earth and a man in space is going to be almost at the Earth's center because the man is comparatively tiny, and therefore his coordinate, weighted with respect to his mass, is almost negligible.

Translational Motion using Center of Mass

When problems involve directional forces on an object and the subsequent path that the object takes, these directions and paths are based on the object's center of mass.

The object is effectively treated as a point or particle that has the same mass as the object but is located at the object's center of mass.

The sum of all forces acting on a system is equal to the total mass of the system multiplied by the acceleration of the center of mass:

$$ma_{CM} = F_{net}$$

This simplifies calculations because calculating the motion of an irregularly shaped object involves complex mathematics.

Center of Gravity

The center of gravity (CG) is the average location of the weight of an object, and it is the point at which the gravitational force is considered to act. The center of gravity is the same as the center of mass only if the gravitational force does not vary between different parts of the object.

The center of gravity is found experimentally (see image below) by suspending an object from different points. A piece of string about the length of the object is securely attached to a point near the object's edge. The object is then held by the string near the point of connection, and a line is traced along the hanging string. The string hangs straight down, perpendicular to the ground, because gravitational force acts purely in the *y*-direction.

The object is then rotated, and the steps are repeated.

The point at which the drawn lines cross is the center of gravity.

If hundreds of lines are drawn onto the object, all lines intersect at this point.

Like the center of mass, an object rotates perfectly around its center of gravity.

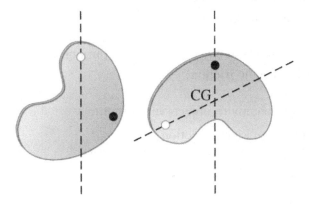

Drawing imaginary lines to determine the center of gravity (CG)

Friction: Static and Kinetic

Friction is a force that always opposes the direction of motion. Like other forces, friction is a vector (i.e., has both magnitude and direction). A dog can walk, and cars can drive because of friction. Lubricants (e.g., oil, grease) reduce friction because they change surface properties and decrease the coefficient of friction. Heat is produced as a by-product of the force of friction.

What is friction? Friction has to do with multiple factors, and it changes depending on the surface of contact. On a microscopic scale, most surfaces are rough. As one surface moves over the other, the crevices of the two surfaces catch and release. This is where the force resisting motion (i.e., friction) comes from.

In the figure below, the block is moving to the right, and as its rough surface moves over the rough surface of the table, the force of friction acts to the left. Friction always acts in the *direction opposing the motion*.

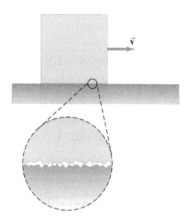

The frictional force is calculated as the product of the normal force of an object and a dimensionless value for the *coefficient of friction*. The coefficient of friction is determined empirically and is intrinsic to the material properties of the surface and the object. Friction occurs in two types: static and kinetic.

Static friction pertains to objects sitting still (an object can remain stationary on an inclined plane because of static friction).

Kinetic friction pertains to objects in motion (a vase sliding across a table has its motion resisted by a force of kinetic friction).

Both the force and the coefficient of static friction are always greater than the force and coefficient of kinetic friction. It takes a greater force to start an object moving on a rough surface than it does to keep the object moving on the same surface.

Equations to determine friction:

Static friction: $F_s = \mu_s F_N$

Kinetic friction: $F_k = \mu_k F_N$

where μ is the coefficient of friction, and F_N is the normal force.

$$F_s > F_k$$

$$\mu_s > \mu_k$$

This table lists the typical values of coefficients of friction. The coefficients depend on the characteristics of both surfaces.

Coefficients of Static and Kinetic Friction		
Surface	**Coefficient of Static Friction μ_s**	**Coefficient of Kinetic Friction μ_k**
Wood on wood	0.4	0.2
Ice on ice	0.1	0.03
Steel on steel (unlubricated)	0.7	0.6
Rubber on dry concrete	1.0	0.8
Rubber on wet concrete	0.7	0.5
Rubber on other solid surfaces	1 – 4	1
Teflon® on Teflon® in air	0.04	0.04
Teflon® on steel in air	0.04	0.04
Lubricated ball bearings	< 0.01	< 0.01
Synovial joints (in human limbs)	0.01	0.01
Values are approximate and intended only as an illustration of the concepts.		

An object at rest on a frictional surface has the force of static friction acting on it.

The force of this friction is $F_s \leq \mu_s F_N$, and it is only equal when the object is just about to move, meaning that the static friction is on the verge of changing over to kinetic friction.

For an object that starts at rest and then has a force applied to it, the force of static friction increases as the applied force increases, until the applied force is enough to overcome the maximum value of static friction.

Then the object starts to move, and the force of kinetic friction takes over.

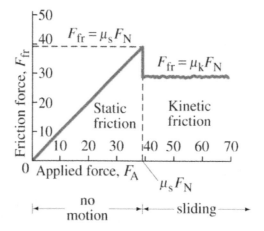

Note: the normal force of an object on a horizontal surface is equal to the weight ($w = mg$) of the object.

However, on an inclined plane, the normal force is perpendicular to the inclined plane, and its magnitude is equal to the weight of the object times the cosine of the incline angle ($F_N = w \cos \theta$; see the chapter on inclined planes).

Motion on an Inclined Plane

When an object is on an inclined plane, the force of gravity is divided into two components: one component is normal (i.e., perpendicular) to the plane surface, and the other component is parallel to the plane surface. The image and equations describe this:

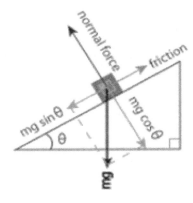

Parallel Force: $F_\parallel = mg \sin \theta$

Perpendicular Force: $F_\perp = F_N$

$$F_N = mg \cos \theta$$

where θ is the angle between the horizontal axis and the surface on which the object rests.

How does the force of gravity affect the force of friction? An object on an incline has three forces acting on it: the normal force, the gravitational force, and the frictional force:

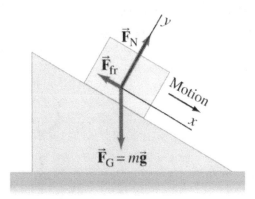

However, the gravitational force is split into parallel and perpendicular components concerning the incline. For an object moving down the inclined plane at a constant velocity, the parallel component of gravity is equal and opposite to the force of kinetic friction:

$$F_{\parallel} = F_k$$

$$F_{\parallel} = \mu_k F_N$$

$$mg \sin \theta = \mu_k mg \cos \theta$$

If the object is not moving, the parallel component of gravity is equal to and opposite to the force of static friction:

$$F_{\parallel} = Fs$$

$$F_{\parallel} = \mu_s F_N$$

$$mg \sin \theta = \mu_s mg \cos \theta$$

Note: frictional forces are always less than or equal to the forces causing an object to move; they are never greater than the forces causing movement. If a frictional force exceeds the other forces involved, it causes the object to move in the opposite direction. Friction does not produce movement; it only inhibits it.

When an object is pushed or pulled up an inclined plane, the parallel component of gravity and the force of friction must be overcome; these forces need to be broken up into their x and y components to perform calculations.

Only the force component parallel to the plane contributes to the motion.

For example, if a block of mass m is accelerating down an inclined plane of angle θ with friction present, what is its acceleration along the x-axis?

$F_{\parallel} = mg \sin \theta$
$\cos \theta$

$F_x = F_{\parallel} - F_{fr}$

$\sin \theta - \mu_k mg \cos \theta$

$\theta - \mu_k g \cos \theta$

$F_N = mg$

$F_{fr} = \mu_k F_N$

$ma_x = mg$

$a_x = g \sin$

Uniform Circular Motion and Centripetal Force

An object moving in a circle at constant speed is in a *uniform circular motion*; this is an example of simple harmonic motion.

The *instantaneous velocity* is always tangent to the circle, and the *centripetal* (or radial) acceleration points inward along the radius.

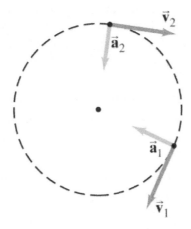

The equation for centripetal (radial) acceleration for uniform circular motion is:

$$a_c = \frac{v^2}{r}$$

Distinguishing between velocity and speed is essential.

Velocity is displacement over time, while speed is the distance over time.

For uniform circular motion, displacement is the shortest straight-line distance between two points on the perimeter of a circle (i.e., a *chord*).

However, distance is the path that the object travels and can be calculated as the product of the radius and arc angle:

$$s = \theta r$$

When working with circular motion problems, the instantaneous velocity is almost always given and equal to the speed.

Some typical issues for circular motion:

- For displacements and distances that approach zero, the instantaneous velocity equals the speed.

- For a quarter of a circle ($\pi/2$ radians or 90°), displacement is the hypotenuse of a right-angled triangle with the radius as the other two sides.

  Using the Pythagorean Theorem, the displacement is $\sqrt{2r^2}$. The distance is the length of the arc or ¼ of the circumference.

- For halfway around the circle, the displacement is the diameter, and the distance is half the circumference.

- For three-quarters around the circle, the displacement is obtained by the Pythagorean Theorem. The magnitude of the displacement is the same as that for a quarter of a circle ($\sqrt{2r^2}$), but the direction is different. The distance is ¾ of the circumference.

- Going around the circle entirely has a displacement of zero, which means that the average velocity is also zero. The distance is equal to the circumference.

- The velocity is always less than or equal to the speed. The displacement is always less than or equal to the distance.

Displacement and velocity are vectors.

Distance and speed are scalars.

Frequency (*f*) is the number of times an object makes a revolution in one second, measured in Hertz (Hz = s^{-1}).

The *period* (*T*) of an object in a circular motion is the time it takes the object to make one revolution, measured in seconds (s).

The frequency and period of an object are inversely related:

$$f = 1 / T$$

Formulas to know:

Centripetal Acceleration: $\quad a_c = \dfrac{v^2}{r}$

Circumference: $\quad C = 2\pi r$

Arc: $\quad arc = \dfrac{\theta}{2\pi} \times C = r\theta$

Area of a Circle: $\quad A = \pi r^2$

Note that theta (θ) is in radians and that 2π radians = 360 degrees.

Centripetal Force ($F = \frac{mv^2}{r}$)

In some situations, more forces are acting on an object than in others.

For example, a puck gliding across an air table experiences almost no frictional force and no pushing force.

A block being pulled up a rough incline experiences both a frictional force and a force of tension. Both objects experience a normal force and a gravitational force.

For circular motion, the number of forces (and whether they are changing or constant) depends on the situation.

Consider circular motion: centripetal force is due to centripetal acceleration.

Centripetal acceleration is due to changes in velocity for an object revolving around a circle. Changes in velocity (vector) are due to a constant change in direction.

The diagrams demonstrate a change in velocity due to change in direction, and the resulting centripetal acceleration.

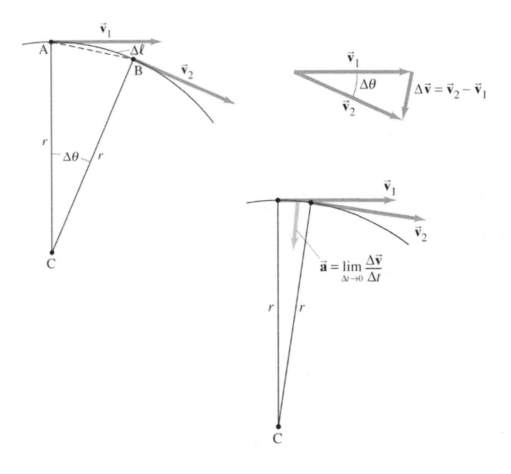

The centripetal force is found when the mass is multiplied by the centripetal acceleration. The centripetal force may be provided by friction, gravity, tension, the normal force, or other forces.

$$\text{Centripetal force: } F = ma_c = \frac{mv^2}{r}$$

$$\text{Centripetal acceleration: } a_c = \frac{v^2}{r}$$

A negative sign is used for the centripetal force to indicate that the direction of the force is toward the center of the circle.

In centripetal motion, the acceleration is always inward. Since the force is always in the same direction as the acceleration, the direction of both the acceleration and the force is toward the center of the circle.

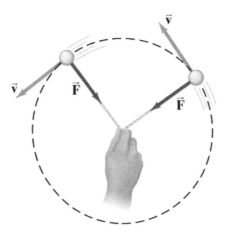

Suppose a ball attached to a string is spun around, and suddenly the string breaks. The ball flies off, following a line of motion tangent to its previous circular path. Why is this true? For an object to be in a uniform circular motion, there must be a net force (string) acting on it in the same direction as the acceleration (inward).

If gravity is ignored, the centripetal force is the only force acting on the ball and keeping it the same distance from the center. If the centripetal force vanishes (the string breaks), the object retains its instantaneous velocity at the point in time at which the string broke (following Newton's laws) and flew off, tangent to the circle.

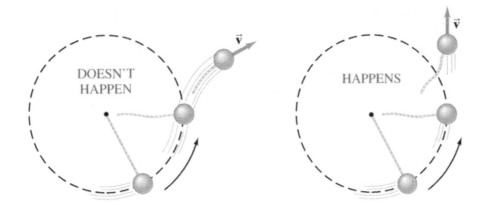

Banked curves (sloped inwards) provide another example of centripetal force. When a car goes around a curve, there must be a net force pointing toward the center of the circle, of which the curve is an arc. If the road is flat, that force is supplied by friction. If the frictional force is insufficient, the car tends to move more closely in a straight line.

If the tires do not slip, the friction is static. If the tires do start to slip, the friction is kinetic. This loss of static friction is bad in two ways:

1.   The kinetic frictional force is smaller than the static frictional force, and the tires have less grip on the road.

2.   The static frictional force can point toward the center of the circle. However, the kinetic frictional force opposes the direction of motion, making it difficult to regain control of the car and continue around the curve.

Banking the curve on the road can help keep cars from skidding. In fact, for every banked curve, there is one speed where the entire centripetal force is supplied by the horizontal component of the normal force, and no friction is required.

This occurs when:

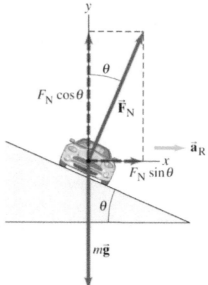

$$F_N \sin \theta = \frac{mv^2}{r} = ma_c$$

Non-uniform Circular Motion

It is important to note that uniform circular motion is usually an idealized scenario, and most systems exhibit some degree of non-uniform circular motion.

An object experiencing non-uniform circular motion has varying speeds. It has an instantaneous velocity tangent to its circular motion, but the acceleration will not point inward along the radius. Because of changing speed, it has a tangential component to its acceleration (and to its force) as well as a radial one.

The direction of net acceleration, and thus net force, depends on the combination of these two components.

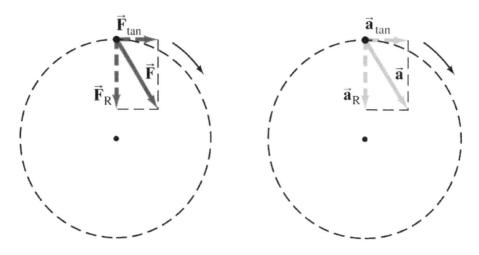

Law of Gravitation

Newton's Third Law of Motion states that every force has an equal and opposite reaction force, indicating that every object pulls on every other object. If the force of gravity is being exerted on objects on Earth, what is the origin of that force? Newton realized that the force must come from the Earth itself and that this force must be what keeps the Moon in its orbit.

Newton developed the *Law of Gravitation* to explains this relationship.

The Law of Gravitation states that any two bodies in the universe attract with force related to the square of the distance between them, the product of their two masses, and the gravitational constant *G*.

Force, for the Law of Gravitation, is defined as:

$$F_G = G \times \frac{m_1 m_2}{r^2}$$

The force of gravity on an object acts through its center of gravity.

How did Newton derive this equation?

The gravitational force is one half of an action-reaction pair: Earth exerts a downward force on a person, and they exert an upward force on the Earth. The reaction force that they exert on the Earth is undetectable because the mass of a person is negligible compared to the mass of the Earth.

However, for bodies with less disparity in mass (such as the Earth and the Moon), the reaction force can be significant.

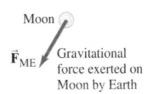

Moon

$\vec{\mathbf{F}}_{ME}$ Gravitational force exerted on Moon by Earth

$\vec{\mathbf{F}}_{EM}$ Gravitational force exerted on Earth by the Moon

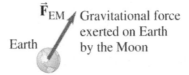

Earth

Therefore, the gravitational force must be proportional to both masses. By observing planetary orbits, Newton also concluded that the gravitational force must decrease as the inverse of the square of the distance between the masses.

How was the constant G derived?

Earlier in this chapter, the acceleration of an object toward the Earth's surface due to the force of Earth's gravity equaled 9.8 m/s^2 and was represented by the variable *g*.

The Law of Gravitation uses the variable *G*, which is different from lowercase *g*.

G is a constant of proportionality, as the *universal gravitational constant*. Note the term "universal" because all objects in the universe are pulling on all other objects. Examine the value of *G* and how it affects the equation.

$$F_G = G \times \frac{m_1 m_2}{r^2}$$

Since Newton could measure force, he was able to assign a value for *G* by rearranging the equation and using known values. For two 1 kg masses, 1 m apart of known force:

$$G = 0.000000000067 \ \text{N·m}^2/\text{kg}^2$$
$$G = 6.67 \times 10^{-11} \ \text{N·m}^2/\text{kg}^2$$

The magnitude of the gravitational constant *G* can also be measured in the laboratory through the Cavendish experiment (1797-1798), pictured below:

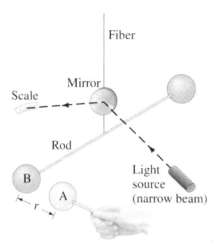

G is an exceedingly small value; it minimizes the value for the term: $\frac{m_1 m_2}{r^2}$

For example, a person pulls on the stars and vice versa. The sheer fact that the stars are a considerable distance away makes $m_1 m_2 / r^2$ a small value (mainly since the distance is squared in this equation).

Multiplying this value by G makes it infinitely small, to the point of approaching zero. Even when considering a person's pull on their neighbor's house, where the value of "r" is relatively small, G diminishes the value.

If that person weighs 0.7 kg, the house weighs 700 kg, and the distance between them is 70 m, then:

$$\frac{m_1 m_2}{r^2} = \frac{(0.7 \text{ kg}) \cdot (700 \text{ kg})}{(70 \text{ m})^2} = 0.1 \text{ kg}^2/\text{m}^2$$

Multiplied by $6.67 \times 10^{-11}\,\text{N·m}^2/\text{kg}^2$ (G), the resulting force equals $6.67 \times 10^{-12}\,\text{N}$, an undetectable value.

The only real gravitational force felt on Earth is that which is caused by the Earth. The concept of G was used to determine the mass of the Earth mathematically. The force of gravity at the Earth's surface was known (9.8 N), and the radius of the Earth was known (which approximates the distance between the center of the Earth and the center of a person standing on the surface). An object can be substituted for m and solved for the Earth's mass as m_E:

On the surface of the Earth, F = ma, so:

$$F_G = mg = G\frac{mm_E}{r_E^2}$$

Solving for g gives:

$$g = G\frac{m_E}{r_E^2}$$

Knowing g and the radius of the Earth ($r_E = 6.38 \times 10^6$ m), the mass of the Earth is:

$$m_E = \frac{gr_E^2}{G} = \frac{(9.8 \text{ m/s}^2) \cdot (6.38 \times 10^6 \text{ m})^2}{6.67 \times 10^{-11} \text{ N} \cdot \text{m}^2/\text{kg}^2}$$

$$m_E = 5.98 \times 10^{24}\text{kg}$$

The Earth has a mass of about 6×10^{24} kg. Since this is a large number, multiplying it by G does not decrease it to a negligible amount. The resulting value is the gravitational force felt by objects on Earth.

Like the value of G, the value of r has a significant impact on the calculations.

There are two essential aspects to note about the distance component, r, of this equation:

$$F_G = G\frac{m_1 m_1}{r^2}$$

First, it refers to the distance between the centers of mass of the two objects (this becomes critical in the discussion of the Earth's pull on objects). The two objects are treated as *point masses*; that is, as if they were the size of one-dimensional points at the locations of their centers of mass, but with the same amount of mass.

Second, the distance is squared, which means that small changes in distance result in substantial changes in *F*, as will be demonstrated with the *inverse square law*.

According to the Law of Gravitation equation, the force is inversely proportional to the square of the distance. Therefore, by increasing the distance between two objects, the force between those two objects is decreased by the inverse square.

If distance increases by a factor of two (i.e., doubles), the force of gravity decreases by a factor of $2^2 = 4$.

This is the primary reason why the gravitational forces of other planets are not felt on Earth, even though they have large masses that are equal to or greater than Earth's mass.

The distance between Earth and another planet is considerable. The distance is squared in the calculating gravitational force. Therefore, the force felt on Earth due to another planet is negligible and essentially eliminated.

For example, Mars is 2.25×10^{11} m away, and it has a mass of 6.4×10^{23} kg.

For a 1 kg mass on Earth, how much force would it exert on Mars?

$$F_G = G \frac{m_1 m_1}{r^2}$$

$$F = (6.67 \times 10^{-11} \, \text{Nm}^2/\text{kg}^2) \times \frac{(1 \, \text{kg}) \cdot (6.4 \times 10^{23} \, \text{kg})}{(2.25 \times 10^{11} \text{m})^2}$$

$$F = 6.83 \times 10^{-10} \, \text{N}$$

In most calculations thus far, a gravitational acceleration value of 9.8 m/s^2 has been used. For most calculations, this is value of 9.8 m/s^2 is acceptable.

The actual acceleration due to gravity varies over the Earth's surface because of altitude, local geology, and the nonspherical shape of the Earth.

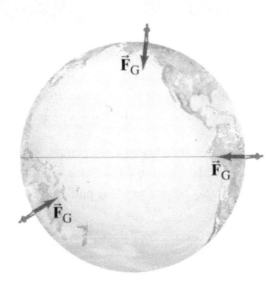

The force of gravitational acceleration points to the Earth's core

Acceleration Due to Gravity at Specific Locations		
Location	**Elevation (m)**	**g (m/s^2)**
New York	0	9.803
San Francisco	0	9.800
Denver	1,650	9.796
Mount Everest	8,800	9.770
Sydney	0	9.798
Equator	0	9.780
North Pole (calculated)	0	9.832

Concept of a Field

Forces often act on a body act in a single direction, like a car that accelerates in a straight-line path. However, the forces can act in a multitude of directions, either from a singular point outward or all directions inward towards a point (e.g., gravitational force).

On Earth, people experience gravity in a single direction (downward) because people are so small relative to the size of the Earth that the Earth is a flat surface below them. Since the Earth is an approximate sphere, its gravitational pull comes from all directions towards its center of mass.

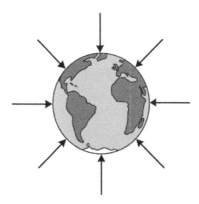

Gravitational field lines radiate towards the Earth's core

These are field lines, more specifically, gravitational field lines. Field lines are often used to depict situations in which multiple vectors are acting in a plane or 3D space.

Notice above that only eight arrows is used to depict the gravitational field around the Earth, even though gravity acts continuously all around the Earth. It would be impossible to draw enough field lines to represent the continuity of Earth's gravitational pull accurately, so it suffices to draw enough lines to show that Earth's gravity acts from all directions.

The arrows are closer to each other the closer they are to the Earth and farther apart, the farther away they are from the Earth. Field lines that are drawn close together represent a stronger field, and field lines drawn farther apart represent a weaker field.

From the figure above, the field lines are closer nearer to Earth, signifying the stronger gravitational force closer to the surface of the Earth. This supports the Law of Gravitation, which was discussed in-depth in the previous section.

In general, the gravitational field lines represent a field of vectors, typically these are force vectors.

The force vectors used in calculations, such as projectile motion, a mass-pulley system, or a mass on a pendulum, are usually single arrows that indicate the direction of a single force. This is because the masses involved in these problems are treated as point masses or masses that have an infinitesimally small size, which reduces the complexity of the calculations.

A boulder-sized projectile or car-sized object on a pendulum would have a force vector field acting on its entire volume, with all the vectors pointing in the same direction.

For example, when a car accelerates in a straight-line path, typically, this action is represented by a single force vector originating from the center of the car's mass in the direction of motion.

More accurately, a force vector would be drawn from every point in the car in the direction of motion, creating a force vector field. Since this creates a far more complex calculation to determine a negligibly more accurate value of the force involved, the vector field is simplified to a single vector originating from the object's center of mass.

Chapter Summary

- Newton's First Law: *An object at rest will remain at rest, and an object in motion (with constant velocity) will remain in motion (with that same constant velocity) unless acted upon by an external force.*

- Newton's Second Law: *Force is the vector product of mass and acceleration*:

$$F = ma$$

- Newton's Third Law: *For every action, there is an equal and opposite reaction.*

When a person interacts with an object by exerting a force on it, that object exerts the same amount, or magnitude, of force back on them.

- Solving Problems with Newton's Laws – Free-Body Diagrams

    1. Sketch the scenario described in the problem.

    2. For every object, draw a free-body diagram showing all the forces acting *on* the object.

       Make magnitudes and directions representative to the scenario.

       Label each force.

       If there are multiple objects, draw separate diagrams.

    3. Resolve vectors into directional components.

    4. Apply Newton's Second Law to each component.

    5. Solve for the net force in each component direction and combine each component to determine the total net force.

- Gravitational force: $F_g = mg$, where g is the acceleration due to gravity at 9.8 m/s^2.

- Equations to find friction, the force that always opposes the direction of motion:

  Static friction: $F_s = \mu_s F_N$

  Kinetic friction: $F_k = \mu_k F_N$

where μ is the coefficient of friction, and F_N is the normal force.

- Motion on an Inclined Plane:

  Parallel Force: $F_\parallel = mg \sin \theta$

  Perpendicular Force: $F_\perp = F_N$

  $F_N = mg \cos \theta$

where θ is the angle between the horizontal axis and the surface the object rests.

- An object moving in a circle at constant speed is in *uniform circular motion*, an example of simple harmonic motion.

  The instantaneous velocity is always tangent to the circle, and the *centripetal* acceleration (or radial acceleration) points inward along the radius.

- Centripetal acceleration for the uniform circular motion:

  $a_c = v^2 / r$

- Centripetal force:

  $$F = ma_c = \frac{mv^2}{r}$$

- Law of Gravitation:

  $$F_G = G \times \frac{m_1 m_2}{r^2}$$

Practice Questions

1. Two bodies of different masses are subjected to identical forces. Compared to the body with a smaller mass, the body with a greater mass experiences:

A. less acceleration, because the ratio of force to mass is smaller
B. greater acceleration, because the ratio of force to mass is greater
C. less acceleration, because the product of mass and acceleration is smaller
D. greater acceleration, because the product of mass and acceleration is greater

2. An object is propelled along a straight-line path by force. If the net force were doubled, the object's acceleration would:

A. halve   **C.** double

B. stay the same   **D.** quadruple

3. A 500 kg rocket ship is firing two jets at once. The two jets are at right angles with one firing with a force of 500 N and the other with a force of 1,200 N. What is the magnitude of the acceleration of the rocket ship?

A. 1.4 m/s^2 **B.** 2.6 m/s^2 **C.** 3.4 m/s^2 **D.** 5.6 m/s^2

4. Assume the strings and pulleys in the diagram below have negligible masses and the coefficient of kinetic friction between the 2 kg block and the table is 0.25. What is the acceleration of the 2 kg block? (Use acceleration due to gravity $g = 9.8$ m/s^2)

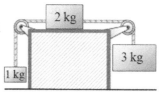

A. 3.2 m/s^2 **B.** 4 m/s^2 **C.** 0.3 m/s^2 **D.** 2.5 m/s^2

5. Which of the following statements must be true for an object moving with constant velocity in a straight line?

A. The net force on the object is zero
B. There are no forces acting on the object
C. A constant force is being applied in the direction opposite of motion
D. A constant force is being applied in the direction of motion

6. A person gives a shopping cart an initial push along a horizontal floor to get it moving and then releases the cart. The cart travels forward along the floor, gradually slowing as it moves. Consider the horizontal force on the cart while it is moving forward and slowing. Which of the following statements is correct?

    A. Only a forward force is acting, which diminishes with time

    B. Only a backward force is acting; no forward force is acting

    C. Both a forward and a backward force are acting on the cart, but the forward force is larger

    D. Both a forward and a backward force are acting on the cart, but the backward force is larger

7. A truck is using a hook to tow a car whose mass is one quarter that of the truck. If the force exerted by the truck on the car is 6,000 N, then the force exerted by the car on the truck is:

    A. 1,500 N   **B.** 24,000 N   **C.** 6,000 N   **D.** 12,000 N

8. How large is the force of friction impeding the motion of a bureau when the 120 N bureau is being pulled across the sidewalk at a constant speed by a force of 30 N?

    A. 0 N   **B.** 30 N   **C.** 120 N   **D.** 3 N

9. An object maintains its state of motion because it has:

    A. mass   **B.** acceleration   **C.** speed   **D.** weight

10. The Earth and the Moon attract with the force of gravity. The Earth's radius is 3.7 times that of the Moon, and the Earth's mass is 80 times greater than the Moon's. The acceleration due to gravity on the surface of the Moon is 1/6 the acceleration due to gravity on the Earth's surface. If the distance between the Earth and the Moon decreases by a factor of 4, how would the force of gravity between the Earth and the Moon change?

    A. Remain the same   **C.** Decrease by a factor of 16

    B. Increase by a factor of 16   **D.** Decrease by a factor of 4

11. Two forces acting on an object have magnitudes $F_1 = -6.6$ N and $F_2 = 2.2$ N. Which third force causes the object to be in equilibrium?

    A. 4.4 N at 162° counterclockwise from F_1

    B. 4.4 N at 108° counterclockwise from F_1

    C. 7 N at 162° counterclockwise from F_1

    D. 7 N at 108° counterclockwise from F_1

12. What are the readings on the spring scales when a 17 kg fish is weighed with two spring scales if each scale has negligible weight?

   A. The top scale reads 17 kg, and the bottom scale reads 0 kg

   B. Each scale reads greater than 0 kg and less than 17 kg, but the sum of the scales is 17 kg

   C. The bottom scale reads 17 kg, and the top scale reads 0 kg

   D. The sum of the two scales is 34 kg

13. Two forces of equal magnitude are acting on an object as shown. If the magnitude of each force is 2.3 N and the angle between them is 40°, which third force causes the object to be in equilibrium?

   A. 1.8 N pointing to the right   **C.** 3.5 N pointing to the right

   B. 2.2 N pointing to the right   **D.** 4.3 N pointing to the right

14. An object at rest on an inclined plane starts to slide when the incline is increased to 17°. What is the coefficient of static friction between the object and the plane? (Use acceleration due to gravity $g = 9.8$ m/s^2)

   A. 0.37   **B.** 0.43   **C.** 0.24   **D.** 0.31

15. What is the force exerted by the table on a 2 kg book resting on it? (Use acceleration due to gravity $g = 10$ m/s^2)

   A. 100 N   **B.** 20 N   **C.** 10 N   **D.** 0 N

Solutions

1. A is correct.

Newton's Second Law ($F = ma$) is rearranged:

$$a = F / m$$

If F is constant, then a is inversely proportional to m.

A larger mass implies a smaller F / m ratio; the ratio is the acceleration.

2. C is correct.

$F = ma$, so doubling the force doubles the acceleration.

3. B is correct.

Pythagorean Theorem ($a^2 + b^2 = c^2$) to calculate the net force:

$$F_1^2 + F_2^2 = F_{net}^2$$

$$(500 \text{ N})^2 + (1{,}200 \text{ N})^2 = F_{net}^2$$

$$250{,}000 \text{ N}^2 + 1{,}440{,}000 \text{ N}^2 = F_{net}^2$$

$$F_{net}^2 = 1{,}690{,}000 \text{ N}^2$$

$$F_{net} = 1{,}300 \text{ N}$$

Newton's Second Law:

$$F = ma$$

$$a = F_{net} / m$$

$$a = 1{,}300 \text{ N} / 500 \text{ kg}$$

$$a = 2.6 \text{ m/s}^2$$

4. D is correct.

The acceleration of the 2 kg block is the acceleration of the system because the blocks are linked together. Balance forces and solve for acceleration:

$$F_{net} = m_3 g - m_2 g \mu_k - m_1 g$$

$$(m_3 + m_2 + m_1)a = m_3 g - m_2 g \mu_k - m_1 g$$

$$a = (m_3 - m_2 \mu_k - m_1)g / (m_3 + m_2 + m_1)$$

$$a = [3 \text{ kg} - (2 \text{ kg}){\cdot}(0.25) - 1 \text{ kg}]{\cdot}(9.8 \text{ m/s}^2) / (3 \text{ kg} + 2 \text{ kg} + 1 \text{ kg})$$

$$a = 2.5 \text{ m/s}^2$$

5. A is correct.

Objects are moving at constant velocity experience no acceleration and therefore no net force.

6. B is correct.

The cart decelerates, which is an acceleration in the opposite direction caused by the force of friction in the opposite direction.

7. C is correct.

Newton's Third Law states that when two objects interact by a mutual force, the force of the first on the second is equal in magnitude to the force of the second on the first.

8. B is correct.

If the bureau moves in a straight line at a constant speed, its velocity is constant. Therefore, the bureau is experiencing zero acceleration and zero net force.

The force of kinetic friction equals the 30 N force that pulls the bureau.

9. A is correct.

Newton's First Law states that an object at rest tends to stay at rest, and an object in motion tends to maintain that motion unless acted upon by an unbalanced force.

This law depends on a property of an object called inertia, which is inherently linked to the object's mass. More massive objects are more difficult to move and manipulate than less massive objects.

10. B is correct.

$$F_g = Gm_{\text{Earth}}m_{\text{moon}} / d^2$$

d is the distance between the Earth and the Moon.

If d decreases by a factor of 4, F_g increases by a factor of $4^2 = 16$

11. C is correct.

Find equal and opposite forces:

$$F_{Rx} = -F_1$$

$$F_{Rx} = -(-6.6 \text{ N})$$

$$F_{Rx} = 6.6 \text{ N}$$

$$F_{Ry} = -F_2$$

$$F_{Ry} = -2.2 \text{ N}$$

Pythagorean Theorem ($a^2 + b^2 = c^2$) to calculate the magnitude of the resultant force:

The magnitude of F_R:

$$F_R^2 = F_{Rx}^2 + F_{Ry}^2$$

$$F_R^2 = (6.6 \text{ N})^2 + (-2.2 \text{ N})^2$$

$$F_R^2 = 43.6 \text{ N}^2 + 4.8 \text{ N}^2$$

$$F_R^2 = 48.4 \text{ N}^2$$

$$F_R = 7 \text{ N}$$

The direction of F_R:

$$\theta = \tan^{-1} (-2.2 \text{ N} / 6.6 \text{ N})$$

$$\theta = \tan^{-1} (-1 / 3)$$

$$\theta = 342°$$

The direction of F_R with respect to F_1:

$$\theta = 342° - 180°$$

$$\theta = 162° \text{ counterclockwise of } F_1$$

12. D is correct.

Each scale weighs the fish at 17 kg, so the sum of the two scales is:

$$17 \text{ kg} + 17 \text{ kg} = 34 \text{ kg}$$

13. D is correct.

If θ is the angle with respect to a horizontal line, then:

$$\theta = \tfrac{1}{2}(40°)$$

$$\theta = 20°$$

Therefore, in order for the third force to cause equilibrium, the sum of all three forces' components must equal zero. Since F_1 and F_2 mirror each other in the y direction:

$$F_{1y} + F_{2y} = 0$$

In order for F_3 to balance the forces in the y direction, its y component must equal zero:

$$F_{1y} + F_{2y} + F_{3y} = 0$$

$0 + F_{3y} = 0$

$F_{3y} = 0$

Since the y component of F_3 is zero, the angle that F_3 makes with the horizontal is zero:

$\theta_3 = 0°$

The x component of F_3:

$F_{1x} + F_{2x} + F_{3x} = 0$

$F_1 \cos \theta + F_2 \cos \theta + F_3 \cos \theta = 0$

$F_3 = -(F_2 \cos \theta_2 + F_3 \cos \theta_3)$

$F_3 = -[(2.3 \text{ N}) \cos 20° + (2.3 \text{ N}) \cos 20°]$

$F_3 = -4.3 \text{ N}$

$F_3 = 4.3 \text{ N}$ to the right

14. D is correct.

At $\theta = 17°$, the force of static friction is equal to the force due to gravity:

$F_f = F_g$

$\mu_s mg \cos \theta = mg \sin \theta$

$\mu_s = \sin \theta / \cos \theta$

$\mu_s = \tan \theta$

$\mu_s = \tan 17°$

$\mu_s = 0.31$

15. B is correct.

The force of the table on the book, the normal force (F_N), is a result of Newton's Third Law of Motion, which states for every action there is an equal and opposite reaction.

A book sitting on the table experiences a force from the table equal to the book's weight:

$W = mg$

$F_N = W$

$F_N = mg$

$F_N = (2 \text{ kg}) \cdot (10 \text{ m/s}^2)$

$F_N = 20 \text{ N}$

CHAPTER 3

Equilibrium and Momentum

- **Concept of Equilibrium**

- **Concept of Force and Linear Acceleration, Units**

- **Translational Equilibrium ($Fi = 0$) Σ**

- **Torques, Lever Arms**

- **Rotational Equilibrium**

- **Analysis of Forces Acting on an Object**

- **Momentum**

- **Conservation of Linear Momentum**

- **Elastic Collisions**

- **Inelastic Collisions**

- **Impulse**

- **Chapter Summary**

Concept of Equilibrium

The concept of equilibrium is related to Newton's First Law of Motion.

Newton's *First Law of Motion* (Law of Inertia) states that *an object at rest tends to stay at rest, and an object in motion will remain in motion at a constant velocity unless acted upon by an external force.*

The object is in equilibrium until an outside force is applied, upon which the object begins to accelerate. Acceleration is the change in the rate of velocity; this change may be just for the direction of motion).

The concept of equilibrium is linked to acceleration; objects undergoing an acceleration are not in equilibrium, while those with zero acceleration are in equilibrium.

There are two forms of equilibrium: translational equilibrium and rotational equilibrium. These two forms of equilibrium may exist concurrently or separately.

Objects in *translational equilibrium* have no linear acceleration.

Objects in *rotational equilibrium* have no angular acceleration.

For example, an object with zero linear acceleration and zero angular acceleration is in both translational and rotational equilibrium.

However, an object with zero linear acceleration but non-zero angular acceleration is only in translational equilibrium.

Both types of equilibrium can be separated into static and dynamic equilibrium.

Static equilibrium refers to objects with zero velocity (linear or angular).

Dynamic equilibrium refers to objects with constant non-zero velocity (linear or angular).

Concept of Force and Linear Acceleration & Units

Force causes objects to accelerate (i.e., change speed), change direction, or both.

Newton's *Second Law of Motion* states that *the acceleration of an object is directly proportional to the applied force and inversely proportional to the mass of the object*:

$$\vec{a} = \frac{F}{m} \qquad \text{or} \qquad F = m\vec{a}$$

An arrow above a symbol indicates a force with the arrowhead pointing in the direction of the force.

The *magnitude of the force* is labeled near the arrow and is measured in the units of Newtons (N).

A typically labeled force vector:

F = 20 N

The concept of force is essential when discussing equilibrium, as force imparts linear or angular acceleration to an object.

Linear acceleration is measured in units of m/s^2 and is the rate of change of the linear velocity of an object over time:

$$\vec{a} = \frac{\Delta \vec{v}}{\Delta t}$$

Angular acceleration is measured in units of rad/s^2 and is the rate of change of the angular velocity of an object over time:

$$\vec{\alpha} = \frac{\Delta \vec{\omega}}{\Delta t}$$

Translational Equilibrium

Translational equilibrium refers to an object undergoing zero linear acceleration.

In translational equilibrium, either 1) no forces are acting upon the object, and the linear acceleration is zero, or 2) all the forces acting upon the object cancel, and the object experiences zero linear acceleration in any direction.

Most typical situations refer to the latter scenario where the forces acting upon the object cancel; thus, translational equilibrium is achieved when the sum of all forces along each coordinate axis sum to zero.

Force is expressed by the equation: $\Sigma\vec{F} = 0$ N

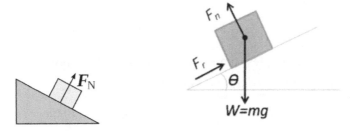

For example, a book, shown below, lies at rest on a table in translational equilibrium. The equal and opposite normal upward force of the table cancels the force due to gravity. The normal force is the component of the contact force that is perpendicular to the surface that an object contacts.

The book experiences a zero net linear acceleration and remains stationary.

The book has zero velocity and is an example of a static system.

$$\Sigma F_y = F_N + F_G$$

$$\Sigma F_y = 0 \text{ N}$$

$$\vec{v} = 0 \text{ m/s}$$

Below is another system in static translational equilibrium. A two-coordinate axis (*x*- and *y-axis*) is presented, and the forces along each axis sum to zero. Like the previous example, no velocity vector is labeled (no movement of the object).

Therefore, the system is *static* and has no velocity.

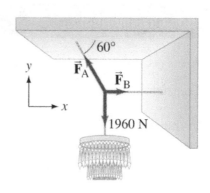

$$F_{Ax} = F_A \cos 60°$$

$$F_{Ay} = F_A \sin 60°$$

$$\Sigma F_x = F_{Ax} + F_B = 0 \text{ N}$$

$$\Sigma F_y = F_{Ay} + 1,960 \text{ N} = 0 \text{ N}$$

$$\vec{v} = 0 \text{ m/s}$$

The skydiver below presents an example of dynamic translational equilibrium.

A skydiver has achieved terminal velocity, and therefore the force of gravity (weight) is balanced by the equal and opposite force from air resistance.

Unlike the previous examples, the skydiver has a constant non-zero velocity and is therefore considered a *dynamic translational* system.

$$\Sigma F_y = F_G + F_{Air\ Resistance} = 0 \text{ N}$$

$$\vec{v} = constant$$

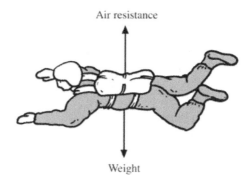

Translational equilibrium *vs.* non-equilibrium

Scenario	Type of Equilibrium	Translational non-equilibrium
An apple at rest	Static Translational	An apple falling toward the Earth with an acceleration of g
A car moving at a constant velocity	Dynamic Translational	A car either accelerating or decelerating
A skydiver falling at terminal velocity	Dynamic Translational	A skydiver before reaching terminal velocity

Torques, Lever Arms

Force applied to an object or system that induces rotation is torque.

Torque is the angular equivalent of force; it causes objects to rotate, have angular acceleration and change angular velocity. The *position and direction of the force* applied to the rotating body, about the axis of rotation, determines the magnitude of the torque.

The torque is the product of the applied force and the lever arm. Torque is directly proportional to the magnitude of the applied force and the length of the lever arm, expressed in the unit of the Newton-meter (N·m).

$$\vec{\tau} = r_\perp \vec{F} = r \sin \theta \vec{F}$$

The lever arm is a distance from the axis of rotation to the line along which the perpendicular component of the force acts. The force of the lever arm from the angle between the applied force and the distance to the axis of rotation:

$r_\perp = r \sin \theta$

$\theta \leq 90$

$r_\perp \leq r$

The *maximum torque* on an object occurs when the force is applied entirely perpendicular to the radius. For maximum torque, the angle $\theta = 90°$ between the force vector and the radius:

$\vec{\tau}_{max} = r \sin (90)\vec{F} = r_\perp \vec{F})$, where $\sin 90° = 1$

The *minimum torque* occurs when the force applied to the rotational body is directed toward the center of that body:

$\vec{\tau}_{min} = r \sin (0)\vec{F} = 0$ N·m., where $\sin \theta = 0°$

For a door with two forces (A and B) applied at different points along its length:

$\vec{F}_A = \vec{F}_B$

$\theta_A = \theta_B = 90°$

$\vec{\tau} = r_\perp \vec{F}$

$r_{\perp A} > r_{\perp B}$

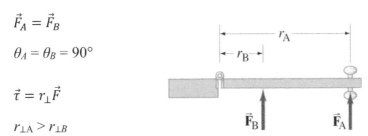

$$\vec{\tau}_A > \vec{\tau}_B$$

In the diagram above, both F_A and F_B are equal in magnitude, and each is applied perpendicularly to the door (i.e., $\theta = 90°$). Moving the door by F_A is easier than by using F_B because the lever arm for F_A is longer than the lever arm for F_B (torque = r sin θ F).

The torque produced by F_A is larger than the torque produced by F_B, and the door can be opened more easily with this larger torque.

Imagine a door with force applied at various angles concerning the doorknob:

$$\vec{F}_A = \vec{F}_C = \vec{F}_D$$

$$90° = \theta_A > \theta_C > \theta_D$$

$$\vec{\tau} = r_\perp \vec{F} = r \sin \theta \vec{F}$$

$$r_{\perp A} > r_{\perp C} > r_{\perp D}$$

$$\vec{\tau}_A > \vec{\tau}_C > \vec{\tau}_D$$

The forces A, C, and D are equal in magnitude and are applied at the same point from the axis of rotation (the length from the doorknob to the hinge).

The torques produced by forces A, C, and D are not the same because the forces are applied at different angles.

Force A produces the maximum torque because it is applied perpendicular (i.e., sin (90°) = 1) to the door, and thus has the largest lever arm.

Force C is applied at a non-perpendicular angle to the door; it has a smaller lever arm and produces a smaller torque.

Force D is applied parallel to the door and produces no torque because the force and its lever arm are equal to zero (sin (0°) = 0).

Rotational Equilibrium

The Conditions for Rotational Equilibrium

When objects are in rotational equilibrium, they have zero angular acceleration.

For *rotational equilibrium*, either no torques are applied, or the sum of all torques around every rotational axis equals zero.

Rotational equilibrium is expressed as:

$$\sum \vec{\tau} = 0 \text{ N} \cdot \text{m}$$

The object either does not rotate (static rotational equilibrium), or it rotates at a constant rate (dynamic rotational equilibrium).

Positive torques act counterclockwise, while negative torques act clockwise.

Positive Convention +   Negative Convention -

A pulley system demonstrates static rotational equilibrium. Force 1 and force 2 are equal and applied at opposite ends tangent to the pulley. The resulting torque 1 and torque 2 are equal and opposite. The sum of all torques along the pulley's rotational axis is zero. The pulley experiences no angular velocity and is a static system.

$\vec{F}_1 = \vec{F}_2$ and $\theta_1 = \theta_2 = 90°$

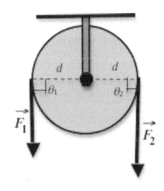

$r_\perp = d$

$\vec{\tau}_1 = \vec{F}_1(d \sin \theta_1)$

$\vec{\tau}_2 = \vec{F}_2(d \sin \theta_2)$

$\sum \vec{\tau} = \vec{\tau}_1 + \vec{\tau}_2 = 0 \text{ N} \cdot \text{m}$

$\vec{\omega} = 0 \text{ rad/s}$

A system in static rotational equilibrium involves a mass attached to a cable-supported beam. The mass hangs perpendicularly from the beam at distance L, creating a clockwise torque from the gravitational force. The cable attached at a distance d produces its torque from the tension force and cancels the torque from the mass.

The sum of all torques about the axis of rotation is zero, and the system is static because it has no angular velocity.

$$\vec{F}_G \neq \vec{F}_T$$

$$\vec{\tau}_G = \vec{F}_1 (L \sin 90°)$$

$$\vec{\tau}_T = \vec{F}_T (d \sin \theta)$$

$$\sum \vec{\tau} = \vec{\tau}_G + \vec{\tau}_T = 0 \text{ N} \cdot \text{m}$$

$$\vec{\omega} = 0 \text{ rad/s}$$

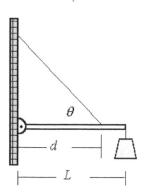

Rotational equilibrium *vs.* non-equilibrium

Scenario	Equilibrium Type	Rotational Non-Equilibrium
Equal masses on a balance	*Static* rotational	Unequal masses on a balance causing an angular acceleration
Propeller spinning at a fixed frequency	*Dynamic* rotational	Propeller spinning faster and faster
Asteroid rotating at a constant velocity	*Dynamic* rotational	Asteroid rotation slowing down

Analysis of Forces Acting on an Object

Solving Problems

1. Identify the objects and draw *free-body diagrams* of all forces acting on them and where they act.

2. Choose a coordinate system and determine the negative and positive directions for each axis.

3. Resolve forces into components (the normal and parallel components for inclined planes).

4. Add the force components; the resulting *x*-, *y*- and *z*-components determine the net force acting on the object.

5. Choose any axis perpendicular to the plane of the forces and select the equilibrium equations for the forces and torques. A smart choice here can simplify the problem enormously.

6. Determine the type of equilibrium (refer to the table below).

7. Use the Pythagorean Theorem to determine the magnitude of the net force from its components. Use trigonometry to solve for the angles. Angles are measured in radians, a whole circle = 2π radians.

Acceleration	Velocity	Equilibrium Type
$a = 0$ m/s^2	$v = 0$ m/s	Static Translational
	$v \neq 0$ m/s	Dynamic Translational
$\alpha = 0$ rad/s^2	$\omega = 0$ rad/s	Static Rotational
	$\omega \neq 0$ rad/s	Dynamic Rotational

Solved example 1 for a *static equilibrium* system

A 15,000 kg printing press is set upon a 1,500 kg table, as shown. Assuming the center of gravity of the table contains all its mass, what are the reaction forces from the table legs A and B?

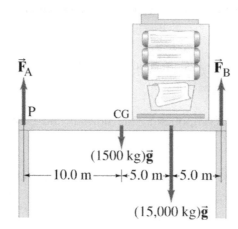

Sum all the forces in *y*-axis:

$$\Sigma F_y = F_A + F_B - (1{,}500 \text{ kg}) \cdot (9.8 \text{m/s}^2) - (15{,}000 \text{ kg}) \cdot (9.8 \text{m/s}^2) = 0$$

$$F_A + F_B = 161{,}700 \text{ N}$$

Sum all the torques about point P:

$$\Sigma \tau_P = [-(1{,}500 \text{ kg}) \cdot (9.8 \text{m/s}^2) \cdot (10 \text{ m}) - (15{,}000 \text{ kg}) \cdot (9.8 \text{ m/s}^2) \cdot (15 \text{ m})] + F_B (20 \text{ m}) = 0$$

$$F_B (20 \text{ m}) = 2{,}352{,}000 \text{ N} \cdot \text{m}$$

$$F_B = 117{,}600 \text{ N}$$

Solve for the remaining forces:

$$F_A + 117{,}600 \text{ N} = 161{,}700 \text{ N}$$

$$F_A = 44{,}100 \text{ N}$$

If the calculated force is negative, it is in the opposite direction of the direction initially chosen to be positive.

There is no "correct" way to choose which direction is positive. The requirement is that it is kept consistent throughout the problem.

Solved example 2 for a *static equilibrium* system

A beam with a mass of 500 kg located at the center of gravity is attached to two supporting legs. According to the diagram, what are the reaction forces from leg A and leg B? (Use the acceleration due to gravity, $g = 9.8$ m/s^2)

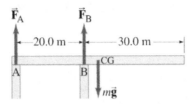

Sum the forces in the y-axis:

$$\Sigma F_y = F_A + F_B - (500 \text{ kg}) \cdot (9.8 \text{ m/s}^2)$$

$$\Sigma F_y = 0$$

$$F_A + F_B = 4,900 \text{ N}$$

Sum the torques about point A (center of gravity is at the midpoint of the beam):

$$\Sigma \tau_A = -(500 \text{ kg}) \cdot (9.8 \text{m/s}^2) \cdot (25 \text{ m}) + F_B (20 \text{ m})$$

$$\Sigma \tau_A = 0$$

$$F_B (20 \text{ m}) = 122,500 \text{ N} \cdot \text{m}$$

$$F_B = 6,125 \text{ N}$$

Solve for the remaining forces:

$$F_A + 6,125 \text{ N} = 4,900 \text{ N}$$

$$F_A = -1,225 \text{ N}$$

For a cable attached, it can support tension forces (F_T) only along its length.

Force applied perpendicular to F_T would cause it to bend.

107

Solved example 3 for a *static equilibrium* system

A sign support consists of a beam attached to a hinge with a sign attached at the opposite end, and a cable supports the load. The beam has a length of 10 m, a mass of 500 kg and the center of gravity is at the 5 m point. The sign has a mass of 1,000 kg and is located 10 m from the hinge. If the support cable forms an angle of 45° with the beam, what are the reaction forces labeled in the diagram?

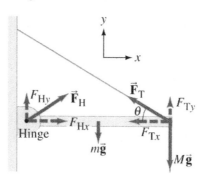

Sum the forces in the *y*-axis:

$$\Sigma F_v = F_{Hy} + F_{Ty} - (500 \text{ kg}) \cdot (9.8 \text{ m/s}^2) - (1,000 \text{ kg}) \cdot (9.8 \text{ m/s}^2)$$

$$\Sigma F_v = 0$$

$$F_{Hy} + F_{Ty} = 14,700 \text{ N}$$

Sum the forces in the *x*-axis:

$$\Sigma F_x = F_{Hx} - F_{Tx} = 0$$

$$F_{Hx} = F_{Tx}$$

Sum the torques about hinge H (center of gravity is at the beam's midpoint):

$$\Sigma \tau_H = -(1,000 \text{ kg}) \cdot (9.8 \text{ m/s}^2) \cdot (10 \text{ m}) - (500 \text{ kg}) \cdot (9.8 \text{ m/s}^2) \cdot (5 \text{ m}) + F_T (10 \text{ m}) \, sin \, (45°)$$

$$\Sigma \tau_H = 0$$

$$F_T (10 \text{ m}) \, sin \, (45°) = 122,500 \text{ N·m}$$

$$F_T = 17,324 \text{ N}$$

Solve for the remaining forces:

$F_{Ty} = F_T \sin (45°)$ N $\qquad$ and $\qquad$ $F_{Hx} = F_{Tx} = F_T \cos (45°)$ N

$F_{Ty} = (17{,}327$ N$) \sin (45°)$ $\qquad$ and $\qquad$ $F_{Hx} = F_{Tx} = (17{,}327$ N$) \cos (45°)$

$F_{Ty} = 12{,}250$ N $\qquad$ and $\qquad$ $F_{Hx} = F_{Tx} = 12{,}250$ N

$F_{Hy} + 12{,}250$ N $= 14{,}700$ N

$F_{Hy} = 2{,}450$ N

These principles of force and torque can be used to understand the human body. In the diagram below of an arm, the elbow is acting as a fulcrum, and the forearm is acting as the lever arm. The biceps can be modeled as a cable containing tension.

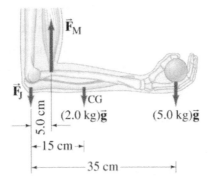

Sum the forces in the y-axis:

$\Sigma F_y = F_M - F_J - (2$ kg$) \cdot (9.8$ m/s$^2) - (5$ kg$) \cdot (9.8$ m/s$^2)$

$\Sigma F_y = 0$

$F_M - F_J = 69$ N

Sum the torques about point J:

$\Sigma \tau_J = F_M(0.05$ m$) - (2$ kg$) \cdot (9.8$ m/s$^2) \cdot (0.15$ m$) - (5$ kg$) \cdot (9.8$ m/s$^2) \cdot (0.35$ m$)$

$\Sigma \tau_J = 0$

$F_M = 402$ N

Solve for the remaining forces:

402 N $- F_J = 69$ N

$F_J = 333$ N

Stability and Balance

Stable equilibrium is when the forces on an object return the object to its equilibrium position. A hanging ball connected to a string is an example of stable equilibrium. If the ball were to be momentarily disturbed, the net force returns the ball to its original equilibrium position.

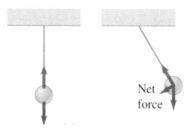

Unstable equilibrium is when the forces tend to move an object away from its equilibrium point. A pencil balanced on its tip is in unstable equilibrium. When disturbed from its equilibrium position, the net force will not return the pencil to its original equilibrium position (i.e., pencil resting on the tip), but cause it to settle in a new equilibrium position (e.g., lying on its side).

An object in stable equilibrium may transition to an unstable equilibrium if it is disturbed, so its center of gravity (CG) is outside the pivot point.

A resting refrigerator is in stable equilibrium, while its center of gravity (CG) is vertically positioned over the pivot point. If the refrigerator's center of gravity deviates from being vertically above the pivot point, it transitions to an unstable equilibrium, and the net force causes it to settle in a new equilibrium position (e.g., on its side).

Momentum

Newton's *First Law of Motion* (Law of Inertia) states that *an object at rest tends to stay at rest, and an object in motion will remain in motion at a constant velocity unless acted upon by an external force.*

This is due to the object's *inertia* (resistance to change). Inertia is directly related to an object's mass, so more massive objects have more resistant to a change in motion.

When an object is in motion (i.e., it has a non-zero velocity), this inertia translates into the object's momentum.

Momentum (*p*) is the vector product of mass and velocity:

$$\vec{p} = m\vec{v}$$

where *m* is mass measured in kg, $\vec{v}$ is the velocity measured in m/s and the momentum $\vec{p}$ is measured in units of kg·m/s or N·s (Newton·seconds)

Total momentum is the vector sum of individual momenta (note the velocity directions of individual momenta).

The *Law of Conservation of Momentum* states that *in an isolated system of objects, the total momentum of the objects is conserved.* The conservation of momentum has important implications in understanding and predicting the behavior of natural phenomena. A classic example for the Law of Conservation of Momentum is the predictable behavior of colliding objects (e.g., bumper cars or pool balls).

Conservation of Linear Momentum

In an isolated system, the total momentum for any collision is conserved.

An *isolated system* is a collection of two (or more) objects free from any net external force. The only forces present within the isolated system are those supplied by the objects.

If two balls collide on a frictionless surface, it is considered an isolated system since no external forces are present, and the conservation of momentum applies.

If non-negligible friction is present, then the balls experience an external force (force of friction), and their momentum changes according to the force supplied by friction (the force of friction is in the direction opposite to the motion).

The Law of Conservation of Momentum does not apply if:

1) an external force is supplied, and

2) the motion is not within an isolated system.

The conservation of momentum in a collision (within isolated systems), is when the total momentum (p) before a collision equals the total momentum after the collision.

$$\vec{p}_{initial} = \vec{p}_{final}$$

Momentum (p) is a vector, so assign one direction as positive and the opposite direction as negative when adding the component momenta vectors.

The momentum of a bomb at rest equals the vector sum of the momenta of all shrapnel from the explosion. Because shrapnel tends to travel in all directions, the momenta of individual pieces cancel, and the total momentum is conserved.

The conservation of momentum applies to a rocket in flight if the rocket and its fuel are considered as one system to accounts for the mass loss of the rocket's fuel.

When a rocket fires in space, it does not need air to push against, because the momentum of the combustion gasses must be conserved. Thus, the rocket moves in the opposite direction.

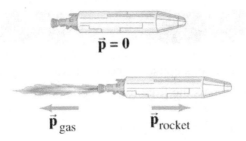

Momentum before = Momentum after = 0 N·s

$$m_{Gas}\vec{v}_{Gas} = m_{Rocket}\vec{v}_{Rocket}$$

For elastic collisions and inelastic collisions, *momentum is conserved.*

For elastic collisions, the kinetic energy (KE) *is conserved* (e.g., pool balls bounce after collision)

For inelastic collisions, the kinetic energy (KE) *is not conserved* (e.g., bullet embeds into the wooden block).

Elastic Collisions

Perfectly elastic collisions conserve both kinetic energy and momentum so that the initial total kinetic energy equals the final total kinetic energy ($KE_{Before} = KE_{After}$).

Kinetic energy is a scalar quantity (not a vector):

$$KE = \frac{1}{2}mv^2$$

The unit for energy is the Joule (J), and since energy is scalar (no direction is specified), there are no associated positive or negative signs for KE.

In a perfectly elastic collision, a dropped ball bounces back to its original height (e.g., ignoring gravity and air resistance).

A ball strikes a wall and bounces at about the same speed it struck the wall.

For elastic collisions, use the conservation of kinetic energy and the conservation of momentum.

The example below has two objects, with known masses and initial speeds, colliding elastically. The top diagram below is before impact, and the bottom diagram is after the collision. Since both *momentum and kinetic energy* are conserved, both equations can be written to solve for the two unknown final speeds via substitution:

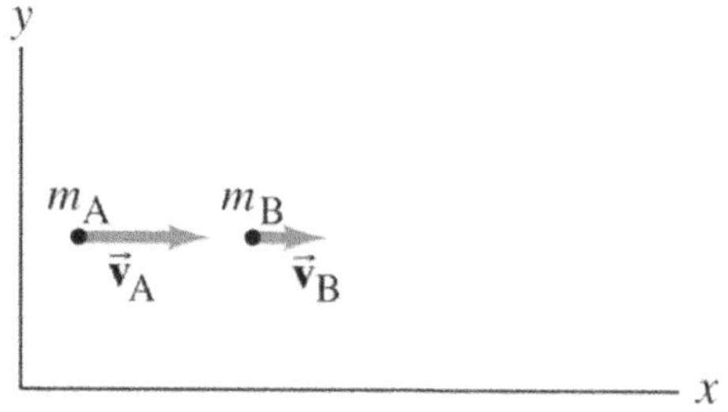

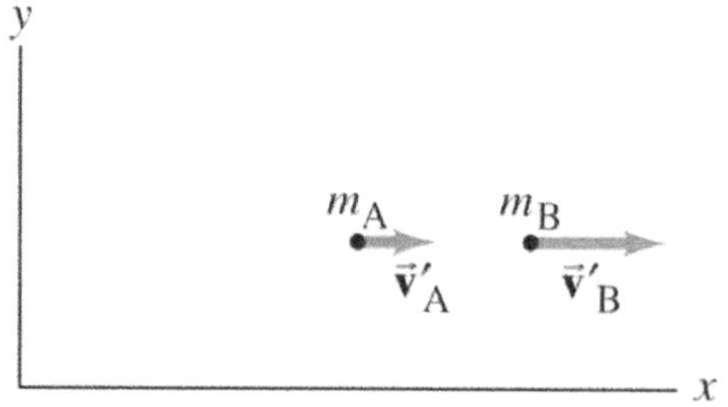

$$\vec{p}_A + \vec{p}_B = \vec{p}'_B + \vec{p}'_A$$

$$m_A\vec{v}_A + m_B\vec{v}_B = m_A\vec{v}'_A + m_B\vec{v}'_B$$

$$KE_{Before} = KE_{After}$$

$$KE = \tfrac{1}{2}mv^2$$

$$\frac{1}{2}m_A\vec{v}_A{}^2 + \frac{1}{2}m_B\vec{v}_B{}^2$$
$$= \frac{1}{2}m_A\vec{v}'_A{}^2$$
$$+ \frac{1}{2}m_B\vec{v}'_B{}^2$$

For the *elastic collision* of objects traveling in opposite directions:

initial momentum equals the final momentum.

initial kinetic energy equals the final kinetic energy (the signs of the velocity changes, depending upon the coordinate axis).

$$\vec{p}_A + \vec{p}_B = \vec{p}_B' + \vec{p}_A'$$

$$m_A \vec{v}_A + m_B \vec{v}_B = m_A \vec{v}_A' + m_B \vec{v}_B'$$

$$KE_{Before} = KE_{After}$$

$$KE = \frac{1}{2} m v^2$$

$$\frac{1}{2} m_A \vec{v}_A{}^2 + \frac{1}{2} m_B \vec{v}_B{}^2$$
$$= \frac{1}{2} m_A \vec{v}_A'{}^2$$
$$+ \frac{1}{2} m_B \vec{v}_B'{}^2$$

Inelastic Collisions

Inelastic collisions *conserve momentum* but do not conserve kinetic energy ($KE_{initial}$ > KE_{final}). This does not violate the Law of Conservation of Energy because the lost kinetic energy is converted into another form of energy during the collision.

Collisions in everyday life are often, to varying extents, inelastic. If a ball is dropped from a person's hand, the ball does not reach the same height as it was released from after bouncing off the ground. This is because the collision was not elastic, but inelastic. The momentum was conserved, but the kinetic energy was not. Some of the ball's kinetic energy was converted to other forms (e.g., acoustic, thermal, vibrational).

This diagram illustrates two objects that experience elastic collision (conserves both momentum and kinetic energy) and inelastic collision (conserves momentum only; not kinetic energy).

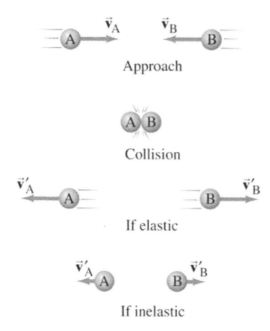

Objects that stick after a collision are typically inelastic collision.

Below, a bullet with a known velocity and mass is shot into a hanging block of known mass. To solve for the height attained by the block + bullet (inelastic collision), apply the conservation of momentum to find the velocity after the collision.

After collision, the kinetic energy of the system is converted to potential energy.

The conservation of energy is applied, and the height can be calculated.

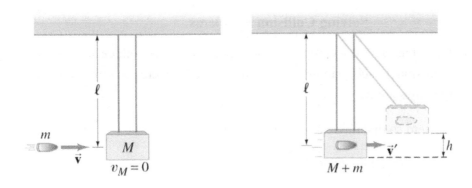

$$\vec{p}_{Bullet} + \vec{p}_{Block} = \vec{p}'_{Bullet+Block}$$

$$m\vec{v} + M\vec{v}_M = (M + m)\vec{v}'$$

$$KE_{Bullet\ Before} \neq KE_{System\ After}$$

$$KE_{System\ After} = PE_{System\ After}$$

$$KE = \frac{1}{2}mv^2$$

$$PE = mgh$$

$$\frac{1}{2}(M + m){\cdot}(\vec{v}')^2 = (M + m)gh$$

Collisions in Two or Three Dimensions

Conservation of kinetic energy and momentum can also be used to analyze collisions in two or three dimensions. A moving object m_A collides with an object m_B initially at rest. Determining the final velocities requires 1) the masses, 2) the initial velocities, and 3) the angles of the object's post-collision trajectory.

$$\Sigma\vec{p}_x = \vec{p}_{Ax} + \vec{p}_{Bx} = \vec{p}'_{Bx} + \vec{p}'_{Ax}$$

$$m_A\vec{v}_A = m_A\vec{v}'_A \cos\theta'_A + m_B\vec{v}'_B \cos\theta'_B$$

$$\Sigma\vec{p}_y = \vec{p}_{Ay} + \vec{p}_{By} = \vec{p}'_{By} + \vec{p}'_{Ay}$$

$$0 = m_A\vec{v}'_A \sin\theta'_A + m_B\vec{v}'_B \sin\theta'_A$$

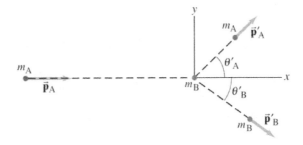

Solving Collision Problems

1. Choose the system. If it is a complex system (e.g., involves both elastic and inelastic collisions), subsystems should be chosen where one or more conservation laws apply.

2. Choose a system so that no external forces are present.

3. Draw diagrams of the initial and final situations, with the momentum vectors labeled.

4. Choose a coordinate system. If an object's momentum is at an angle to the axis, separate the motion into the *x*- and *y*- components:

$$p_x = \vec{p} \cos \theta \qquad \text{and} \qquad p_y = \vec{p} \sin \theta$$

5. Apply conservation of momentum with a separate equation for motion in each dimension.

   The total initial momentum in the *x*-direction must equal the total final momentum in the *x*-direction ($\Sigma p_{xi} = \Sigma p_{xf}$).

   The total initial momentum in the *y*-direction must equal the total final momentum in the *y*-direction ($\Sigma p_{yi} = \Sigma p_{yf}$).

6. Do not assume the type of collision (elastic or inelastic) if unknown. The type may be given or determine if kinetic energy is conserved.

   If the KE is conserved, the collision is elastic.

   If the KE is not conserved, the collision is inelastic.

7. For elastic collisions, use substitution between the conservation of kinetic energy and the conservation of momentum; for inelastic collisions, only use momentum conservation.

$$\vec{p} = \sqrt{p_x^2 + p_y^2} \text{ , and the angle is given by } \theta = tan^{-1}\left(\frac{p_y}{p_x}\right)$$

8. Check the units and the magnitudes to evaluate if they make sense.

Example of an Inelastic Collision

Train car A (m =1,000 kg) collides inelastically with train car B of equal mass. After the collision, the train cars stick (inelastic collision that conserves momentum, but not kinetic energy). What is the final velocity of the attached train cars?

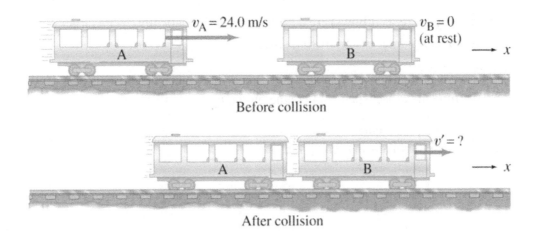

Before collision

After collision

Apply the Law of Conservation of Momentum:

$$\vec{p}_A + \vec{p}_B = \vec{p}'_{A+B}$$

$$m_A\vec{v}_A + m_B\vec{v}_B = (m_A + m_B)\vec{v}'$$

Solve for the final velocity:

$$(1{,}000 \text{ kg}) \cdot (24 \text{ m/s}) + (1{,}000 \text{ kg}) \cdot (0 \text{ m/s}) = (1{,}000 \text{ kg} + 1{,}000 \text{ kg})\vec{v}'$$

$$\vec{v}' = 12 \text{ m/s}$$

Determine the magnitude of the difference in kinetic energy:

$$KE = \frac{1}{2}mv^2$$

$$KE_{\text{Before}} = \frac{1}{2}(1{,}000 \text{ kg}) \cdot (24 \text{ m/s})^2 = 288 \text{ kJ}$$

$$KE_{\text{After}} = \frac{1}{2}(2{,}000 \text{ kg}) \cdot (12 \text{ m/s})^2 = 144 \text{ kJ}$$

$$KE_{\text{Before}} \neq KE_{\text{After}}$$

Impulse

During a collision, objects are deformed to varying degrees due to the large forces involved.

Softer objects (e.g., pillows) are deformed more dramatically over a larger time frame than objects made of harder materials (e.g., metal).

The *impulse* (*J*) relates the extent to which an object deforms due to an impact, regarding the time the object spends in contact with another mass.

Impulse (i.e., the change in momentum, *p*), is represented as *F*Δ*t*, where *F* is a force, and Δ*t* is the time interval during which the force acts:

$$\Sigma \vec{F} = \frac{\Delta \vec{p}}{\Delta t}$$

$$\vec{F}\Delta t = \Delta \vec{p}$$

The total force equals the change in momentum divided by the time interval:

$$\Sigma \vec{F} = \frac{\Delta \vec{p}}{\Delta t}$$

Impulse ($\vec{J} = \vec{F}\Delta t$) can be derived using the equation $\vec{F} = m\vec{a}$.

$$\vec{F} = m\vec{a} = m\frac{\Delta \vec{v}}{\Delta t} \quad \rightarrow \quad \vec{F}\Delta t = m\Delta \vec{v} = \Delta \vec{p} = \vec{J}$$

The impulse determines if a change in momentum occurs by either:

1) a large force acting for a short time, or

2) a small force acting for a long time.

Automobile airbags are effective because they increase the length of time between the initial impact of the two objects (the airbag and the person) and the moment both objects come to rest. Without an airbag, this time interval would be shorter (smaller impulse), and therefore the force of impact is greater and more harmful.

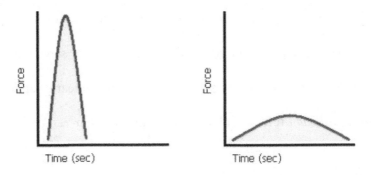

For the force *vs.* time diagrams, the magnitude of the force changes with time.

The area under the curve represents the impulse. For the above diagram on the right, the magnitude of the force is less because the impulse is extended over a greater range of time.

In practice, the time of the collision is often short, and the exact time dependence of the force is less relevant.

Since the time interval is relatively short, the average force, rather than the time-dependent force, can be used when calculating impulse (diagrams below).

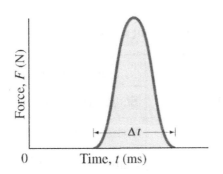
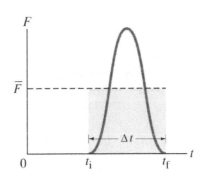

Chapter Summary

- Objects in *translational equilibrium* have no linear acceleration

- Objects in *rotational equilibrium* have no angular acceleration.

  These two forms of equilibrium may exist concurrently or separately.

- *Static equilibrium* refers to objects with zero velocity (linear or angular)

- *Dynamic equilibrium* refers to objects with constant non-zero velocity (linear or angular).

- In translational equilibrium, either 1) no forces are acting upon the object, and linear acceleration is zero, or 2) all the forces acting upon the object cancel, and the object experiences no linear acceleration in any direction.

- Force applied to an object or system that induces rotation is *torque*.

- Torque can be expressed as:

$$\vec{\tau} = r_\perp \vec{F} = r \sin \theta \vec{F}$$

- When objects are in rotational equilibrium, the angular acceleration is zero.

  Therefore, either

    1) no torques are applied, or

    2) the sum of all torques around every rotational axis equals zero.

Acceleration	Velocity	Equilibrium Type
$a = 0$ m/s^2	$v = 0$ m/s	Static Translational
	$v \neq 0$ m/s	Dynamic Translational
$\alpha = 0$ rad/s^2	$\omega = 0$ rad/s	Static Rotational
	$\omega \neq 0$ rad/s	Dynamic Rotational

- Momentum (p) is the vector product of mass × velocity, represented by the equation:

$$\vec{p} = m\vec{v}$$

- According to the Law of Conservation of Momentum, in an isolated system of objects, the total momentum is conserved.

$$\vec{p}_{initial} = \vec{p}_{final}$$

- For an elastic collision, the momentum and total kinetic energy are conserved:

$$\frac{1}{2}m_A\vec{v}_A{}^2 + \frac{1}{2}m_B\vec{v}_B{}^2 = \frac{1}{2}m_A\vec{v}_A'{}^2 + \frac{1}{2}m_B\vec{v}_B'{}^2$$

- For an inelastic collision, the momentum is conserved (not the kinetic energy.

$$(KE_{initial} > KE_{final})$$

This does not violate the Law of Conservation of Energy because the lost kinetic energy is converted into another form of energy (e.g., light, heat, sound) during the collision.

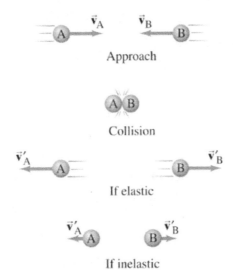

- The object's *impulse* (J), the time the object spends in contact with another mass, determines the extent to which an object deforms (e.g., airbags) due to an impact.

- Impulse, the change in momentum, is represented as $F\Delta t$, where F is a force, and Δt is the time interval during which the force acts:

$$\sum \vec{F} = \frac{\Delta\vec{p}}{\Delta t}$$

Practice Questions

1. A 1.2 kg asteroid is traveling toward the Orion Nebula at a speed of 2.8 m/s. Another 4.1 kg asteroid is traveling at 2.3 m/s in a perpendicular direction. The two asteroids collide and stick. What is the change in momentum from before to after the collision?

   A. 0 kg·m/s   **B.** 2.1 kg·m/s   **C.** 9.4 kg·m/s   **D.** 12 kg·m/s

2. A 1,120 kg car experiences an impulse of 30,000 N·s during a collision with a wall. If the collision takes 0.43 s, what was the speed of the car just before the collision?

   A. 12 m/s   **B.** 64 m/s   **C.** 42 m/s   **D.** 27 m/s

3. Does the centripetal force acting on an object do work on the object?

   A. No, because the force and the displacement of the object are perpendicular
   B. Yes, since a force acts and the object moves, and work is force times distance
   C. Yes, since it takes energy to turn an object
   D. No, because the object has a constant speed

4. Cars with padded dashboards are safer in an accident than cars without padded dashboards, because a passenger hitting the dashboard has:

        I. increased time of impact
        II. decreased impulse
        III. decreased impact force

   A. I only   **B.** II only   **C.** III only   **D.** I and III only

5. The acceleration due to gravity on the Moon is only one-sixth of that on Earth, and the Moon has no atmosphere. If a person hit a baseball on the Moon with the same effort (and therefore at the same speed and angle) as on Earth, how far would the ball travel on the Moon compared to on Earth? (Ignore air resistance on Earth)

   A. The same distance as on Earth   **C.** 1/6 as far as on Earth
   B. 6 times as far as on Earth   **D.** 36 times as far as on Earth

6. A uniform meter stick weighing 20 N has a weight of 50 N attached to its left end and a weight of 30 N attached to its right end. The meter stick is hung from a rope. What is the tension in the rope and how far from the left end of the meter stick should the rope be attached so that the meter stick remains level?

   A. 100 N placed 37.5 cm from the left end of the meter stick
   B. 50 N placed 40 cm from the left end of the meter stick
   C. 80 N placed 37.5 cm from the left end of the meter stick
   D. 100 N placed 40 cm from the left end of the meter stick

7. To catch a ball, a baseball player extends her hand forward before impact with the ball and then lets it ride backward in the direction of the ball's motion upon impact. Doing this reduces the force of impact on the player's hand principally because the:

    A. time of impact is decreased   **C.** relative velocity is less

    B. time of impact is increased   **D.** force of impact is reduced by $\sqrt{2}$

8. A 1,200 kg car, moving at 15.6 m/s, collides with a stationary 1,500 kg car. If the two vehicles lock together, what is their combined velocity immediately after the collision?

    A. 12.4 m/s   **B.** 5.4 m/s   **C.** 6.9 m/s   **D.** 7.6 m/s

9. A 0.05 kg golf ball, initially at rest, has a velocity of 100 m/s immediately after being struck by a golf club. If the club and ball were in contact for 0.8 ms, what is the average force exerted on the ball?

    A. 5.5 kN   **B.** 4.9 kN   **C.** 11.8 kN   **D.** 6.3 kN

10. Which of the following is an accurate statement for a rigid body that is rotating?

    A. All points on the body are moving with the same angular velocity

    B. Its center of rotation is its center of gravity

    C. Its center of rotation is at rest and therefore not moving

    D. Its center of rotation must be moving with a constant velocity

11. Cart 1 (2 kg) and Cart 2 (2.5 kg) run along a frictionless, level, one-dimensional track. Cart 2 is initially at rest, and Cart 1 is traveling 0.6 m/s toward the right when it encounters Cart 2. After the collision, Cart 1 is at rest. Which of the following is true concerning the collision?

    A. The collision is completely elastic   **C.** Momentum is conserved

    B. Kinetic energy is conserved   **D.** Total momentum is decreased

12. What is the reason for using a long barrel in a gun?

    A. Allows the force of the expanding gases from the gunpowder to act for a longer time

    B. Increases the force exerted on the bullet due to the expanding gases from the gunpowder

    C. Exerts a larger force on the shells

    D. Reduces frictional losses

Questions **13-15** are based on the following:

A 5-gram bullet is fired horizontally into a 2 kg block of wood suspended from the ceiling by 1.5 m strings. The bullet becomes embedded within the block of wood, and they move together at a speed of 1.5 m/s. Gravity can be ignored during the time of the bullet's impact with the block. Then, the wood block with the bullet swings upward by height h.

13. What best describes the energy flow as the bullet impacts the block of wood?

    A. Kinetic to heat and kinetic   **C.** Kinetic to potential

    B. Potential and kinetic to heat   **D.** Potential to heat

14. What is the velocity of the bullet just before it enters the block?

    A. 30 m/s   **B.** 60 m/s   **C.** 600 m/s   **D.** 90 m/s

15. Immediately after the bullet embeds itself in the wood, what is the kinetic energy of the block and bullet?

    A. 2.26 J   **B.** 4.5 J   **C.** 9 J   **D.** 18 J

Solutions

1. A is correct.

Since the momentum is conserved during the collision, the change is $p = 0$.

$$p_{\text{initial}} = p_{\text{final}}$$

$$m_1v_1 + m_2v_2 = (m_1 + m_2)v_3$$

2. D is correct.

$$J = \Delta p = m\Delta v$$

$$\Delta v = J \, / \, m$$

$$\Delta v = (30{,}000 \text{ N·s}) \, / \, (1{,}120 \text{ kg})$$

$$\Delta v = 27 \text{ m/s}$$

$$\Delta v = v_f - v_i$$

$$27 \text{ m/s} = 0 - v_i$$

$$v_i = 27 \text{ m/s}$$

3. A is correct. In uniform circular motion, the centripetal force does no work because the force and displacement vectors are at right angles.

$$W = Fd$$

The work equation is only applicable if force and displacement direction are the same.

4. D is correct.

$$J = F\Delta t$$

Impulse remains constant, so the time of impact increases and the impact force decreases.

5. B is correct.

Consider a dropped baseball on Earth:

$$d_E = -\tfrac{1}{2}gt^2$$

On the Moon:

$$d_M = -\tfrac{1}{2}(g \, / \, 6)t^2$$

$$d_E \, / \, d_M = (-\tfrac{1}{2}gt^2) \, / \, (-\tfrac{1}{2}(g \, / \, 6)t^2)$$

$$d_E \, / \, d_M = 1/6, \text{ so the distance is 6 times greater on the Moon}$$

6. D is correct. The total downward force on the meter stick is:

$$20 \text{ N} + 50 \text{ N} + 30 \text{ N} = 100 \text{ N}$$

The total upward force on the meter stick – which is provided by the tension in the supporting rope – must be 100 N to keep the meter stick in static equilibrium.

Let x be the distance from the left end of the meter stick to the suspension point.

From the pivot point, balance the torques.

The counterclockwise (CCW) torque due to the 50 N weight at the left end is 50 x.

The total clockwise (CW) torque due to the weight of the meter stick and the 30 N weight at the right end is:

$$(50 \text{ N})x = (20 \text{ N}){\cdot}(50 \text{ cm} - x) + (30 \text{ N}){\cdot}(100 \text{ cm} - x)$$

$$(50 \text{ N})x = [1{,}000 \text{ cm} - (20 \text{ N})x] + [3{,}000 \text{ cm} - (30 \text{ N})x]$$

$$(50 \text{ N})x = 4{,}000 \text{ cm} - (50 \text{ N})x$$

$$(100 \text{ N})x = 4{,}000 \text{ cm}$$

$$x = 40 \text{ cm}$$

7. B is correct.

$J = F\Delta t$ is constant

increased t = decreased F

8. C is correct.

$$m_1 v_1 = (m_1 + m_2)v_2$$

$$v_2 = (m_1 v_1) / (m_1 + m_2)$$

$$v_2 = (1{,}200 \text{ kg}){\cdot}(15.6 \text{ m/s}) / (1{,}200 \text{ kg} + 1{,}500 \text{ kg})$$

$$v_2 = (18{,}720 \text{ kg}{\cdot}\text{m/s}) / (2{,}700 \text{ kg})$$

$$v_2 = 6.9 \text{ m/s}$$

9. D is correct.

$$F\Delta t = m\Delta v$$

$$F = (m\Delta v) / \Delta t$$

$$F = [(0.05 \text{ kg}){\cdot}(100 \text{ m/s} - 0 \text{ m/s})] / (0.0008 \text{ s})$$

$$F = (5 \text{ kg}{\cdot}\text{m/s}) / (0.0008 \text{ s})$$

$$F = 6{,}250 \text{ N} = 6.3 \text{ kN}$$

10. A is correct.

In circular motion, all points along the rotational body have the same angular velocity regardless of their radial distance from the center of rotation.

11. C is correct.

In both elastic and inelastic collisions, momentum is conserved.

However, in an ideal elastic collision, KE is conserved, but not in an inelastic collision.

To determine if the collision is elastic or inelastic, compare the KE before and after the collision.

Initial KE:

$$KE_i = \tfrac{1}{2}m_1v_1{}^2$$

$$KE_i = \tfrac{1}{2}(2 \text{ kg}) \cdot (0.6 \text{ m/s})^2$$

$$KE_i = 0.36 \text{ J}$$

Conservation of momentum:

$$m_1v_1 + m_2v_2 = m_1u_1 + m_2u_2$$

$$m_1v_1 = m_2u_2$$

$$(m_1 / m_2)v_1 = u_2$$

$$u_2 = (2 \text{ kg} / 2.5 \text{ kg}) \cdot (0.6 \text{ m/s})$$

$$u_2 = 0.48 \text{ m/s}$$

Final KE:

$$KE_f = \tfrac{1}{2}m_2u_2{}^2$$

$$KE_f = \tfrac{1}{2}(2.5 \text{ kg}) \cdot (0.48 \text{ m/s})^2$$

$$KE_f = 0.29 \text{ J}$$

KE_i does not equal KE_f and thus KE is not conserved.

The collision is therefore inelastic, and only momentum is conserved.

12. A is correct.

A longer barrel gives the expanding gas more time to impart a force upon the bullet and thus increase the impulse upon the bullet.

$$J = F\Delta t$$

13. A is correct.

The energy starts as kinetic. Initially, there is no change in the potential energy.

Upon impact, most of the bullet's kinetic energy is converted into heat, some are transferred into kinetic energy of the block, and a small amount remains as kinetic energy for the bullet.

Since gravity is being ignored, the increase in the height of the block does not lead to potential energy.

14. C is correct.

Conservation of momentum:

$$m_1 v_1 = (m_1 + m_2)v_2$$

$$(0.005 \text{ kg})v_1 = (0.005 \text{ kg} + 2 \text{ kg}) \cdot (1.5 \text{ m/s})$$

$$v_1 = 600 \text{ m/s}$$

15. A is correct.

$$KE = \tfrac{1}{2}mv^2$$

$$KE = \tfrac{1}{2}(m_1 + m_2)v^2$$

$$KE = \tfrac{1}{2}(2.005 \text{ kg}) \cdot (1.5 \text{ m/s})^2$$

$$KE = 2.2556 \text{ J} \approx 2.26$$

CHAPTER 4

Work and Energy

- **Concept of Work**

- **Derived Units, Sign Conventions**

- **Work Done by a Constant Force**

- **Mechanical Advantage**

- **Conservative Forces**

- **Path Independence of Work Done in Gravitational Field**

- **Concept of Energy**

- **Kinetic Energy**

- **Work-Kinetic Energy Theorem**

- **Potential Energy**

- **Conservation of Energy**

- **Power, Units**

The Concept of Work

Work is the relationship between a force and the distance traveled by an object acted upon by force, in a direction parallel to the force.

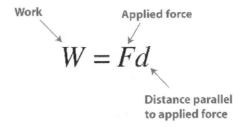

The above equation is for an applied force and a displacement parallel to the force.

If the distance traveled is not parallel to the force, but at an angle, the angle must be accounted for by the formula:

$$W = \vec{F}d \cos \theta$$

Where $\vec{F}$ is force, d is the distance over which the force is applied, and θ is the angle between the applied force and the distance.

Essentially, this formula divides the forces into components, and the only value used in the work calculation is the force parallel (*cos θ*) to displacement.

There are some instances in which the work done is zero:

- When the displacement is zero ($W = \vec{F} \cdot 0 = 0$)

- When the displacement is perpendicular to the applied force (the object moves at 90° to the applied force)

$$W = \vec{F}d \cos (90°) = \vec{F} \cdot 0 = 0$$

- When an object is moving at a constant velocity, with no forces acting in

    the direction of movement ($W = 0 \cdot d = 0$)

Derived Units & Sign Conventions

The units of work are:

$$W = \vec{F}\vec{d}$$

$$W = m\vec{a}\vec{d} = (\text{kg}) \cdot \left(\frac{\text{m}}{s^2}\right) \cdot (\text{m})$$

$$W = \frac{\text{kg} \times \text{m}^2}{s^2} = \text{N} \cdot \text{m} = \text{J}$$

The Newton-meter represents the combined units of force and distance.

The magnitude of work (W) is generally expressed in *Joules* (J) since the Newton-meter is the unit of measurement for torque.

The Joule is named after English physicist James Prescott Joule (1818-1898), is also the unit for the measurement for energy.

If the applied force and the displacement are in the same direction, the work is positive. For example, pushing a crate across a rough terrain involves doing positive work (pushing forward as the crate moves forward).

If the force opposes the direction of motion (e.g., friction), the work is negative.

Work Done by a Constant Force

As noted earlier, the work done by a constant force is defined as *the distance moved multiplied by the component of the force in the direction of displacement*:

$$W = \vec{F}\vec{d}\cos\theta$$

For example, a crate on the ground has a rope attached to the side, which a woman pulls to move the crate a distance *d*. If she pulls with a constant force, and the rope forms an angle θ with the crate, how much work did she perform?

$$W = \vec{F_{\parallel}}\vec{d}$$

$$\vec{F_{\parallel}} = \vec{F}\cos\theta$$

$$W = \vec{F}\vec{d}\cos\theta$$

The following five steps can be useful in solving work problems:

1. Draw a free-body diagram.

2. Choose a coordinate system.

3. Apply Newton's Laws to determine any unknown forces.

4. Find the work done by a specific force.

5. To find the net work done:

> find the net force and then find the work it does, or

> find the work done by each force and add them together.

If the force and displacement are perpendiculars, the work done is zero.

The centripetal force does no work.

In a uniform circular motion, the centripetal force is constant when an object moves in a circle at a constant speed.

The centripetal force is directed toward the center of a circular path and is perpendicular to the linear movement of the object.

For a circular motion at a constant speed, the velocity is tangent to the direction of motion.

If a ball attached to a string is spun in a circle, how much work is performed?

$$W = \vec{F}_{\parallel}\vec{d}$$

$$\vec{F_{\parallel}} = \vec{F} \cos(90°) = 0 \text{ N}$$

$$W = 0 \text{ J}$$

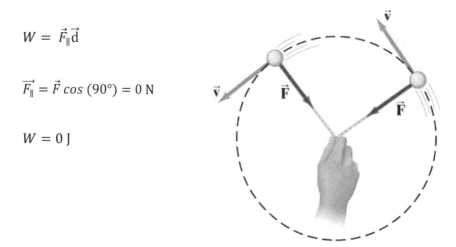

The centripetal force points toward the center and velocity is tangent to the circle

Mechanical Advantage

A mechanical advantage takes an input force of little effort and results in an output of a much larger force.

A *lever arm* or a *pulley* achieves such a mechanical advantage. Mechanical advantages are useful in the construction and movement of large objects, which are otherwise too heavy to manipulate.

Simple machines are any mechanical device that is used to apply a force. The premise of a simple machine is that the work put in is equal to the work put out. This refers to the amount of force multiplied by a ratio of distances.

Examples of simple machines:

– Pulleys

– Inclined planes

– Wedges

– Screws

– Levers

– Wheels and axles

Pulley systems are conventional simple machines. Like all simple machines, a pulley system does not reduce the amount of work done on an object, but it does reduce the amount of the force needed to manipulate it; the distance over which the force acts is increased.

The work equation shows that the force and distance are inversely related and that the distance of pulling increases by the same factor the force decreases.

$$\frac{W}{\vec{d}} = \vec{F}$$

A method for solving pulley problems is to realize that the ropes on either side of a moving pulley contribute to pulling the load. A stationary pulley, however, does not contribute to the load. The above rules apply to problems with simple pulleys. Complicated pulleys have additional ropes that contribute to pulling the load.

In the example below, a pulley is attached to the ceiling and is used to lift a box. The pulley is stationary, so no mechanical advantage is imparted to the system. Therefore, if the weight of the box is 100 N, the force needed to pull the box up is 100 N. For every 1 meter pulled, the box moves up 1 meter.

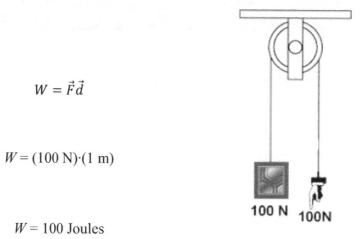

$$W = \vec{F}\vec{d}$$

$$W = (100 \text{ N}) \cdot (1 \text{ m})$$

$$W = 100 \text{ Joules}$$

As stated, moving pulleys impart a mechanical advantage to the system.

In the diagrams below, there is one moving pulley in each system. When there is one moving pulley, the force needed to pull is halved because the rope on each side of the pulley contributes equally. The 50 N force is transmitted to the right-hand rope, while the left-hand rope contributes the other 50 N.

However, for a moving pulley system, the distance required to pull the rope is not the same as for a simple pulley system.

If the box is to be pulled up one meter (e.g., previous example), the distance of the rope required to pull the box is doubled because the force is halved.

In the diagram below, the pulley system on the right is an equivalent system to the pulley system on the left.

Although there are two pulleys on the right, only the mobile pulley halves the force needed to pull the box.

For any system, the work required to lift the box a specific distance is the same regardless of the reduction in force.

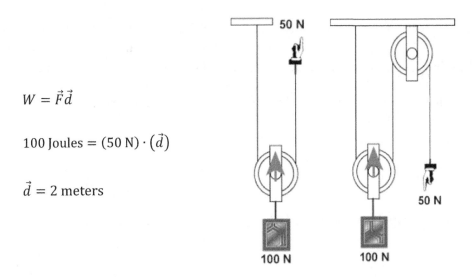

$$W = \vec{F}\vec{d}$$

$$100 \text{ Joules} = (50 \text{ N}) \cdot (\vec{d})$$

$$\vec{d} = 2 \text{ meters}$$

In the diagrams below, two equivalent systems are shown. Although the pulley arrangement is different, each system has two mobile pulleys, which reduce the force needed to lift the box. If each mobile pulley reduces the force by half, then the total force needed to lift the box will be reduced to a quarter of the original value.

Thus, the 100 N box can be lifted with only 25 N. Again, the work required to lift the box one meter must always be the same, so for every 1 m the box moves, 4 m of the rope must be pulled.

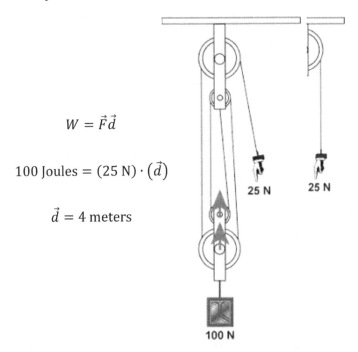

$$W = \vec{F}\vec{d}$$

$$100 \text{ Joules} = (25 \text{ N}) \cdot (\vec{d})$$

$$\vec{d} = 4 \text{ meters}$$

Below is an example of a complex pulley system. Like the simple pulleys, the ropes on both sides of the moving pulley contribute. However, the left-most rope also contributes. This makes three contributing ropes, which reduces the effort required by a factor of three.

The distance needed to pull is three times the distance the box travels.

$$W = \vec{F}\vec{d}$$

$$100 \text{ Joules} = (33 \text{ N}) \cdot \left(\vec{d}\right)$$

$$\vec{d} \cong 3 \text{ meters}$$

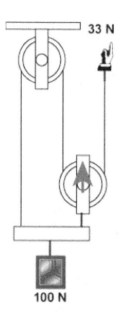

Conservative Forces

A force can be either conservative or non-conservative. Determining how to label a specific force can be slightly confusing. However, there are a few qualifications that can be checked to determine what type of conservation a force follows.

Conservative force does not dissipate heat, sound, or light. Furthermore, if the work done by a force is path independent, then that force is conservative.

Conservative forces are associated with potential energy as potential energy can only be defined for conservative forces.

The force from a spring can be stored as spring potential energy, and gravitational force can be stored as gravitational potential energy. Electromagnetic forces are also conservative. If only conservative forces are acting, mechanical energy is conserved.

A few things to consider when a particle is moving along a path:

- If the work done to move a particle in any round-trip path is zero, the force is conservative.

- If the work needed to move a particle between two points is the same regardless of the path taken, then the force is conservative.

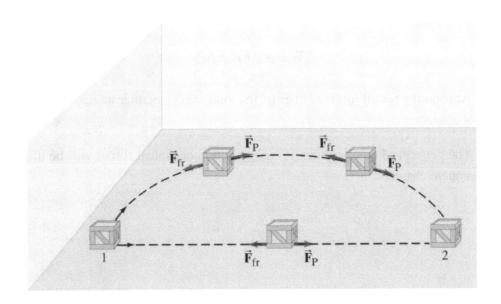

Most forces are conservative, but some non-conservative forces include friction and human exertion. If friction is present, the work done depends not only on the starting and ending points but also on the path taken, as frictional forces directly oppose the course of motion of an object.

As an object encounters friction, heat, and sound energy are released, and the total energy is not conserved. Heat energy is also lost in human exertion.

When muscles are flexed during exercise, the heat from the muscles rises off the skin and cannot be recovered or reabsorbed.

Conservative Forces	Non-conservative Forces
Gravitational	Friction
	Air resistance
Elastic	Tension in a cord
	Motor or rocket propulsion
Electric	Push or pull by a person

Potential energy is defined for conservative forces.

The work done by conservative forces must be distinguished from the work done by non-conservative forces.

The work done by non-conservative forces is equal to the total change in kinetic and potential energies:

$$W_{NC} = \Delta KE + \Delta PE$$

Accounting for all forms of energy, the total energy neither increases nor decreases; energy is conserved.

The concept of conservation of energy with mechanical forces will be discussed in the subsequent chapters.

Path Independence of Work Done in Gravitational Field

The amount of work done in a gravitational field is path-independent since gravitational forces always act downward. Sideward motion, which is perpendicular to the gravitational force, involves no work. For example, a man lifting a bag of groceries is a form of positive work in a gravitational field. The act of lifting a bag of groceries is positive work because a force is exerted (to overcome the force of gravity), and the distance the bag is lifted is in the direction of the force.

However, once the bag is being held up, it is at rest (as in, no longer traveling), and no work is being done on the bag. If the man does not lift or lower the bag, he is doing no work on it because there is no vertical displacement. Walking home with the bag of groceries also does no work on the bag. This is because the displacement (horizontal) is perpendicular to the force of gravity, and the resulting work must be zero.

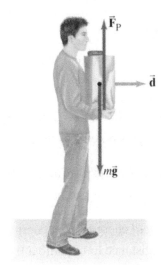

$$\vec{F}_P = m\vec{g}$$

Work to lift the bag: $\quad W = \vec{F}_P \vec{d}_y > 0 \text{ J}$

Work to walk home: $\quad W = \vec{F}_P \vec{d}_x = 0 \text{ J}$

Another example of work in a gravitational field is pushing an object at constant speed up a frictionless, inclined plane. This uses the same amount of work as directly lifting the object to the same height at a constant speed because the displacement perpendicular to the force of gravity contributes no work.

Similarly, sliding an object down a frictionless, inclined plane involves the same gravitational work as the object undergoing a free fall from the same height.

Since the only forces involved in these motions are acting on a vertical plane, the work done is only dependent on the height of the ramp.

The Concept of Energy

Work and energy are closely related concepts. *Energy* is traditionally defined as the ability to do work, and, like work, the unit of energy is the Joule. However, although work and energy have the same units, the two concepts are not always interchangeable. Energy takes many different forms, while mechanical work is limited to the definition above.

For example, energy may be exerted to move a heavy box, but if the box does not budge, then no work has been done.

Another important concept of energy is that the sum of the energy of the universe in its current state is the same amount of energy that was present at the inception of the universe. There is an infinite amount of space for it to go, but it never disappears. This is the Law of Conservation of Energy and is discussed in this chapter.

Energy forms

All the energy that was created from the beginning of the universe is divided into different types of energy.

Mechanical energy—The energy associated with motion and position. It is equal to kinetic plus potential energy.

Electrical energy—The energy made up of the current and potential provided by a circuit. Any charged particle within an electrical field contains electrical energy.

Chemical energy—The energy involved in all chemical reactions. This is the potential of a substance to undergo a transformation or reaction.

Radiant energy—Consists of all the energy from electromagnetic waves. It can be viewed as the energy stored in a photon, or the motion of an electromagnetic wave.

Visible light is a small portion of the full spectrum of electromagnetic waves—there are many other sources of radiant energy that cannot be seen with the human eye.

Nuclear energy—The energy that is released during reactions involving the fusion or fission of the nucleus. Examples are nuclear bombs and nuclear power plants.

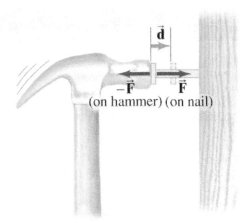

Although energy can take different forms, there are two main types of energy within mechanical physics problems:

- *Kinetic energy*: the energy of motion (energy that is being consumed or released at a given time)

- *Potential energy*: stored energy (energy that could be released for a body)

Kinetic Energy

Kinetic energy (*KE*) is the energy associated with the motion of an object and results from work or a change in potential energy. Kinetic energy is only dependent on the mass of an object as well as its speed.

As with energy, the unit of kinetic energy is a Joule (kg·m^2/s^2).

The equation for kinetic energy is:

$$KE = \frac{1}{2}mv^2$$

An important feature of kinetic energy is its relation to the mass and speed of an object. In the equation above, the *KE* is directly proportional to mass, and *KE* is proportional to the square of the velocity.

If the mass (*m*) of an object is doubled, *KE* is also doubled.

If the velocity (*v*) is doubled, the *KE* is quadrupled (because velocity is squared).

For example, two cars are on the road, but one is twice as heavy as the other.

If both cars are traveling at the same speed, the car with twice the mass has twice as much *KE* as that of the other car.

If two cars of equal mass are on the road, and one is traveling twice as fast as the other, the faster car has a *KE* four times that of the slower car.

The importance of this is that a change in velocity is more significant, regarding kinetic energy than a change in mass because velocity is squared.

For objects of the same mass, the object with the higher velocity always has the greater *KE*, and for objects with the same velocity, the object with a greater mass always has the greater *KE*.

Work-Kinetic Energy Theorem

Work on an object can be transformed into kinetic energy. If the net work on the object is positive, the kinetic energy increases; if the net work is negative, the kinetic energy decreases. Thus, work (W) and kinetic energy (*KE*) are directly related by the equation:

$$|\,W\,| = |\,\Delta KE\,| \quad \text{(change in kinetic energy)}$$

Given that the definition of kinetic energy is:

$$KE = \frac{1}{2}mv^2$$

Work can be written, regarding a change in the kinetic energy, as:

$$W = \Delta KE = \frac{1}{2}mv_2^2 - \frac{1}{2}mv_1^2$$

For example, the force *F* provided by a car's engine moves the car a distance *d*, and thus performs positive work on the car. This work is transformed into kinetic energy and increases the total kinetic energy of the car.

The car has a higher final velocity than before the work was performed.

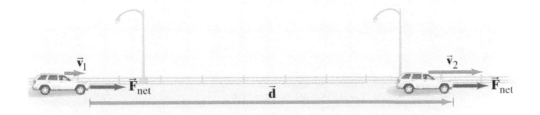

$$+W = +\Delta KE$$

$$v_2 > v_1$$

If the same car applied its brakes at a stop sign, the force provided by friction in the car's brakes does negative work on the car.

In this case, the negative work on the car would reduce its kinetic energy, and the change in kinetic energy would be negative.

As a result, the final velocity of the car would be less than its initial velocity.

$$-W = -\Delta KE$$

$$v_2 < v_1$$

The kinetic energy of an object can also do work when forces are involved.

For example, a moving object on a frictionless surface can convert all of its kinetic energy to work if it slides up an inclined plane before coming to a complete stop. The kinetic energy of the object is converted to work to lift the object a distance against the force of gravity.

$$-\Delta KE = +W$$

In summary, energy can perform work against:

- inertia

- gravity

- friction

- deformation of shape

- combinations of the above

Potential Energy

Potential energy (*PE*) is the energy stored in an object. Regardless if an object is in motion, an object always retains energy. This energy can be stored in many different forms, such as the chemical potential energy of food. The reason living things eat is because food is full of chemically bonded substances. Organisms' bodies store these substances in cells until they are needed. Then the cells will break the bonded substances down into individual parts. This process of breaking bonds releases potential energy.

Unlike chemical potential energy, potential energy in mechanical physics problems depends solely upon the position or configuration of objects. By this definition, an object has potential energy by its surroundings.

Some examples of potential energy:

- An object at some height above the ground

- A wound-up spring

- A stretched elastic band

There are a few types of potential energy: gravitational potential energy (local and general) and spring (elastic) potential energy.

Gravitational, local (*PE = mgh*)

Local gravitational potential energy is the energy stored in an object due to its position (height) above the ground. It only depends upon the mass of the object, its height above the ground, and the acceleration of gravity:

$$PE = mgh$$

As can be seen, by the equation, potential energy is directly proportional to mass and height. If two objects of equal mass are at different heights above the ground, then the higher object has more potential energy. Likewise, if two objects of unequal mass are at the same height, then the object with a larger mass will have higher potential energy.

On Earth, $g = 9.8$ m/s^2 and is assumed constant regardless of the location or height relative to the Earth (unless stated otherwise).

Another important feature of gravitational potential energy is that measuring h requires a reference height. Usually, the reference height is evident in a problem (i.e., the ground). However, if not, a reference height can be established at any arbitrary location if the reference height $h = 0$, and thus the potential energy is zero.

For example, if a rock of mass m is held a height h_1 above a table, its potential energy concerning the table (reference height) is:

$$PE = mgh_1$$

If the surface of the table is a height h_2 above the ground, then the rock's potential energy (PE) concerning the ground (reference height) is:

$$PE = mg(h_2 + h_1)$$

Like kinetic energy, work can be performed to increase or decrease potential energy. If all the work (W) is transformed into potential energy (or vice versa), then work, and the equation can relate potential energy:

$$|W| = |\Delta PE|$$

Work can be written, regarding a change in the potential energy, as:

$$W = \Delta PE = mgh_2 - mgh_1$$

For example, the diagram below shows a block of mass m that is raised a height h from position y_1 to position y_2. The work performed results in a positive change in potential energy because the new position of the block is at a greater height than its original position.

$$+W = +\Delta PE$$

$$y_2 > y_1$$

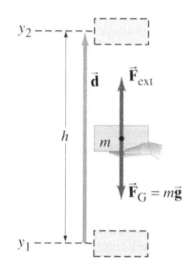

Gravitational, general (*PE = –GmM/r*)

The general formula for gravitational potential energy is found by using Newton's *Law of Universal Gravitation.* This formula was discussed in depth in the previous chapter, but it defines *g* as being:

$$g = \frac{GM}{r^2}$$

where *G* is the universal gravitation constant, *M* is the mass of the attracting object, and *r* is the distance between the two objects in question. The gravitational constant *G* has a value of 6.67×10^{-11} N·m^2/kg^2.

To find the general form of gravitational potential energy *g* is substituted into the equation for local gravitational energy, and the equation results:

$$PE = m \times \frac{GM}{r^2} \times h$$

The height *h* is essentially another measurement of the distance between two objects and is equal to the radius *r*. This cancels an *r* in the denominator, and the equation for general gravitational potential energy is:

$$PE = \frac{GmM}{r}$$

Spring (*PE* $=\frac{1}{2}kx^2$)

Springs can also store potential energy. The potential energy of a spring is dependent upon the spring material and the stretch or compression of the spring:

$$PE = \frac{1}{2}kx^2$$

The spring constant *k* is a measure of the stiffness of the spring; stiffer springs have a larger *k* because they require more energy to stretch or compress.

The compression of the spring from its original equilibrium position is represented as *x*.

The *PE* of a spring is the elastic potential energy (PE) and is sometimes notated as PE_{el}.

The force required to compress a spring is described by the equation:

$$F_s = -kx$$

Notice the negative sign in front of the constant; this is to indicate that the spring force is a restoring force and acts opposite to the direction of the stretch.

This can be observed in the diagram below:

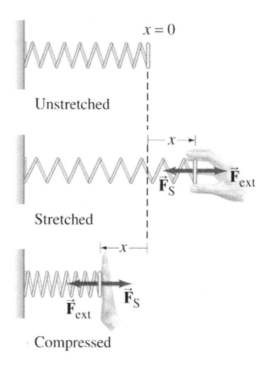

For the figure labeled unstretched, the spring is at equilibrium.

For the figure labeled stretched, if the spring is stretched a distance x from the equilibrium length, then the spring force acts opposite to the direction of the stretch.

For the figure labeled compressed, if the spring is compressed a distance x from the equilibrium length, then the spring force acts opposite to the compression.

Conservation of Energy

The conservative forces include gravity, spring forces, and the electrostatic force. Non-conservative forces include friction and human exertion. Mechanical energy, like all energy, must be conserved. If there are no non-conservative forces, the sum of the changes in the kinetic energy and the potential energy is zero. The kinetic and potential energy changes are equal but opposite in sign.

The total mechanical energy can then be defined as:

$$\Sigma E = KE + PE$$

Moreover, its conservation is:

$$E_2 = E_1 = \text{constant}$$

The total amount of initial energy equals the total amount of final energy. Gravitational potential energy is converted to kinetic energy as an object falls, but the total amount of energy stays the same. When a crate slides to a stop on a rough surface, its kinetic energy is converted into heat and sound energy.

Take the example of a man dropping a rock some distance y. By conservation of energy, the total mechanical energy of the rock at any given instant is:

$$\Sigma E = KE + PE$$

$$KE + PE = \tfrac{1}{2}\, mv^2 + mgh$$

$$\Sigma E = \tfrac{1}{2}\, mv^2 + mgh$$

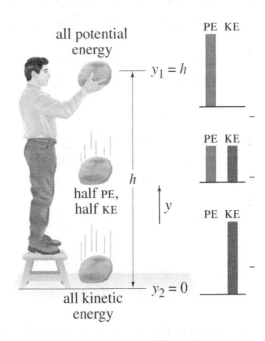

Initially, the rock is held stationary above the ground a distance y, and all its energy is potential energy. When the rock is released, it drops down the ground; at precisely the halfway point of the rock's descent, half of its *PE* has been converted to *KE*.

Finally, right before impact with the ground, all the initial potential energy has been converted to kinetic energy. The energy bar graphs next to the figure show how the energy moves from all potential to all kinetic.

Another example of energy conservation is a rollercoaster. The speed of a roller coaster only depends on its current height compared to its starting height.

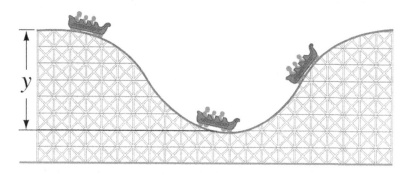

$$PE_{1st\ hill} = KE = PE_{2nd\ hill}$$

At the top of the drop, all the rollercoaster's energy will exist as potential energy. At the bottom, the rollercoaster converted all its energy into kinetic energy. If there is no friction, then all the kinetic energy at the bottom is converted back to potential energy to bring the roller coaster up the second hill of equal height to the first.

Another example of conservation of energy can be seen in the spring. The diagram below depicts a ball being shot using a spring:

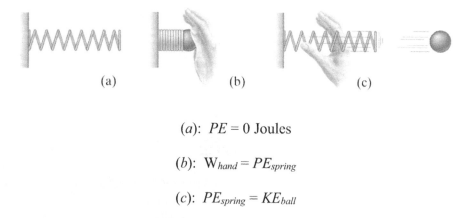

(a) (b) (c)

(a): $PE = 0$ Joules

(b): $W_{hand} = PE_{spring}$

(c): $PE_{spring} = KE_{ball}$

In figure (a), the spring is at its equilibrium length and has no potential energy.

Figure (b) shows that work has been performed against the restoring force of the spring. For an ideal system, the work performed is converted entirely into spring potential energy.

In figure (c), the ball is released, and all the spring's potential energy is converted into the kinetic energy of the ball.

However, if there is a non-conservative force, such as friction, where does the kinetic and potential energy go?

Energy cannot be destroyed, only converted into different forms; in this case, the friction performs work, which transforms the initial energy into heat.

Remember, in the presence of friction:

$$PE_{initial} > PE_{final}$$

$$KE_{initial} > KE_{final}$$

Tips for Problem Solving:

1. Draw a picture

2. Determine the system for which energy will be conserved

3. Determine the initial and final positions

4. Choose a logical reference frame

5. Apply the conservation of energy

6. Solve

Power, Units

Often, problems do not give the total energy or input work, but instead, give the power a system consumes.

Power is the work performed over time, and can be written as:

$$P = \frac{W}{t}$$

Power (watts, W), Work, time

$$W = Pt$$

kWh = energy, kW = power, h = time

Power can be derived as the product of the force on an object times its velocity:

$$P = \vec{F}\vec{v}$$

The SI unit for power is the *watt* (Joules/second).

Another unit for power, more commonly used for high powered objects such as engines, is *horsepower* (hp). One hp is equal to ~745.7 Watts. A key concept of power is the time at which work is performed.

Lifting an object of mass m one meter off the ground always requires the same amount of work. However, lifting the object in one minute requires more power than lifting the object in an hour.

The longer the time interval, the less power is required. The difference between walking and running upstairs is power—the change in gravitational *PE* is the same.

$$P = average\ power\ = \frac{work}{time} = \frac{energy\ transformed}{time}$$

Power is useful for predicting the amount of work that can be performed over a given time. For example, if there are two engines, the more powerful engine can do the same amount of work in less time than the less powerful engine.

Sports cars are described by their engine's horsepower and are compared by how they accelerate from 0 mph to 60 mph. Sports cars have powerful engines that can perform work, which is, in turn, converted into kinetic energy. Electric companies also use power because it describes energy use (work done) over time.

Chapter Summary

- Work is a force applied across a displacement. Work can cause a change in energy. Positive work puts energy into a system, while negative work takes energy out of a system.

  Basic equations for work include:

  $$W = \vec{F}\vec{d}\cos\theta \qquad W = \Delta KE \qquad W = \text{area under an } F \text{ vs. } d \text{ graph}$$

Conservative Forces	Non-conservative Forces
Gravitational	Friction
	Air resistance
Elastic	Tension in a cord
	Motor or rocket propulsion
Electric	Push or pull by a person

- Energy is the ability to do work and is a conserved quantity.

  The total initial energy is equal to the total final energy.

  Basic equations for energy include:

  $$KE = \frac{1}{2}mv^2 \qquad PE_g = mgh \qquad PE_s = \frac{1}{2}kx^2$$

- *Kinetic energy*: the energy of motion (energy that is being consumed or released at a given time)

- *Potential energy*: stored energy (energy that could be released for a certain body)

- Types of energy:

    Mechanical energy—The energy associated with motion and position. It is equal to kinetic plus potential energy.

    Electrical energy—The energy made up of the current and potential provided by a circuit. Any charged particle within an electrical field contains electrical energy.

    Chemical energy—The energy involved in all chemical reactions. This is the potential of a certain substance to undergo a transformation or reaction.

    Radiant energy—Consists of all the energy from electromagnetic waves. It can be viewed as the energy stored in a photon, or the motion of an electromagnetic wave. Visible light is only a small part of the full spectrum of electromagnetic waves—there are many other sources of radiant energy that cannot be seen with the naked eye.

    Nuclear energy—The energy that is released during reactions involving the fusion or fission of the nucleus. Examples include nuclear bombs and nuclear power plants.

- Gravitational energy: $PE = GmM / r$

- Spring energy: $PE = \frac{1}{2}kx^2$

- The Law of Conservation of Energy states that the total amount of initial energy equals the total amount of final energy,

- Often, interactions are limited to mechanical energy with no heat lost or gained.

    In this situation:

    $$KE_i + PE_i \pm W = KE_f + PE_f$$

- Power is the rate at which work is performed, and is given by:

    $$P = \frac{W}{t} \quad \text{or} \quad P = \vec{F}\vec{v}$$

Practice Questions

1. When a pebble is dropped from height h, it reaches the ground with kinetic energy. Ignoring air resistance, from what height should the pebble be dropped to reach the ground with twice the KE?

A. $\sqrt{2}h$ **B.** $2h$ **C.** $4h$ **D.** $8h$

2. Which of the following situations requires the greatest power?

A. 50 J of work in 20 minutes   **C.** 10 J of work in 5 minutes
B. 200 J of work in 30 minutes   **D.** 100 J of work in 10 minutes

3. A kilowatt-hour is a unit of:

I. work   II. force   III. power

A. I only   **B.** II only   **C.** III only   **D.** I and II only

4. A hydraulic press (like a simple lever), properly arranged, is capable of:

I. multiplying energy input
II. multiplying output force
III. exerting force only vertically

A. I only   **B.** II only   **C.** III only   **D.** I and II only

5. 4.5×10^5 J of work are done on a 1,150 kg car while it accelerates from 10 m/s to some final velocity. What is this final velocity? (Use acceleration due to gravity $g = 10$ m/s^2)

A. 30 m/s   **B.** 37 m/s   **C.** 12 m/s   **D.** 19 m/s

6. Which of the following is not a unit of work?

A. N·m   **B.** kw·h   **C.** J   **D.** kg·m/s

7. The Law of Conservation of Energy states that:

I. the energy of an isolated system is constant
II. energy cannot be used faster than it is created
III. energy cannot change forms

A. I only   **B.** II only   **C.** III only   **D.** I and II only

8. A crane lifts a 300 kg steel beam vertically upward a distance of 110 m. Ignoring frictional forces, how much work does the crane do on the beam if the beam accelerates upward at 1.4 m/s²? (Use acceleration due to gravity $g = 9.8$ m/s²)

    A. 2.4×10^3 J   **B.** 4.6×10^4 J   **C.** 3.7×10^5 J   **D.** 6.2×10^5 J

9. Steve pushes twice as hard against a stationary brick wall as Charles. Which of the following statements is correct?

    A. Both do the same amount of positive work
    B. Both do positive work, but Steve does one-half the work of Charles
    C. Both do positive work, but Steve does four times the work of Charles
    D. Both do zero work

10. What is the change in the gravitational potential energy of an object if the height of the object above the Earth is doubled? (Assume that the object remains near the surface)

    A. Quadruple   **B.** Doubled   **C.** Unchanged   **D.** Halved

11. If 1 N is exerted for a distance of 1 m in 1 s, the amount of power delivered is:

    A. 3 W   **B.** 1/3 W   **C.** 2 W   **D.** 1 W

12. A brick is dropped from a roof and falls a distance h to the ground. If h were doubled, how does the maximal KE of the brick, just before it hits the ground, change?

    A. It doubles   **C.** It remains the same
    B. It increases by $\sqrt{2}$ **D.** It increases by 200

13. A helicopter with single landing gear descends vertically to land with a speed of 4.5 m/s. The helicopter's shock absorbers have an initial length of 0.6 m. They compress to 77% of their original length and the air in the tires absorbs 23% of the initial energy as heat. What is the ratio of the spring constant to the helicopter's mass?

    A. 0.11 kN/kg·m   **B.** 1.1 N/kg·m   **C.** 0.8 kN/kg·m   **D.** 11 N/kg·m

14. A 21 metric ton airplane is observed to be a vertical distance of 2.6 km from its takeoff point. What is the gravitational potential energy of the plane with respect to the ground? (Use acceleration due to gravity $g = 9.8$ m/s², metric ton = 1000 kg)

    A. 582 J   **B.** 384 J   **C.** 535 MJ   **D.** 414 MJ

15. A tennis ball bounces on the floor. During each bounce, it loses 31% of its energy due to heating. How high does the ball reach after the third bounce if it is initially released 4 m from the floor?

    A. 55 cm   **B.** 171 mm   **C.** 106 cm   **D.** 131 cm

Solutions

1. B is correct.

When the pebble falls, *KE* at impact = *PE* before.

$$PE = KE$$

$$mgh = KE$$

$$mg(2h) = 2KE$$

$$2PE = 2KE$$

If the mass and gravity are constant, then the height must be doubled.

2. D is correct.

Power = Work / time

A: Power = 50 J / 20 min = 2.5 J/min

B: power = 200 J / 30 min = 6.67 J/min

C: power = 10 J / 5 min = 2 J/min

D: power = 100 J / 10 min = 10 J/min

Typically, power is measured in watts or J/s.

3. A is correct.

kilowatt = unit of power

hour = unit of time

kW·h = power × time

power = work / time

kW·h = (work / time) × time

kW·h = work

4. B is correct.

Mechanical advantage:

$$d_1 / d_2$$

where d_1 and d_2 are the effort arm and load arm, respectively.

If d_1 is greater than d_2, force output is increased.

5. A is correct.

Find the final speed using conservation of energy.

Let the energy added as work be represented by W. Then, conservation of energy requires:

$$E_f = E_i + W$$

$$½mv^2_f = ½mv^2_i + W$$

Solving for v_f:

$$v_f = \sqrt{v^2_i + (2W) / m}$$

$$v_f = \sqrt{[(10 \text{ m/s})^2 + (2) \cdot (4.5 \times 10^5 \text{ J}) / (1150 \text{ kg})]}$$

$$v_f = 29.7 \text{ m/s} \approx 30 \text{ m/s}$$

6. D is correct.

$$\text{Work} = \text{Force} \times \text{distance}$$

$$W = Fd$$

The unit kg·m/s cannot be manipulated to achieve this.

7. A is correct. The Law of Conservation of Energy states that for an isolated system (no heat or work transferred), the energy of the system is constant. Energy can only transform from one form to another.

8. C is correct.

The work done by this force is:

$$W = Fd,$$

where F = force applied by the crane and d = distance over which the force is active.

Solve for F using Newton's Second Law.

There are two forces on the beam – the applied force due to tension in the crane's cable and gravity.

$$F_{net} = ma$$

$$F - mg = ma$$

Therefore:

$$W = m(a + g)d$$

$$W = (300 \text{ kg}) \cdot (1.4 \text{ m/s}^2 + 9.8 \text{ m/s}^2) \cdot (110 \text{ m})$$

$$W = 3.7 \times 10^5 \text{ J}$$

9. D is correct.

Work = Force × displacement × cos θ

$W = Fd \cos \theta$

If $d = 0$, then work = 0

10. B is correct.

Relative to the ground, an object's gravitational PE = mgh, where h is the altitude.

PE is proportional to h; doubling h doubles PE.

11. D is correct.

W = Fd

$P = W / t$

$P = Fd / t$

$P = (1 \text{ N}) \cdot (1 \text{ m}) / 1 \text{ s}$

$P = 1 \text{ W}$

12. A is correct.

$KE = PE$

$KE = mgh$

h is directly proportional to KE.

If h doubles, then the KE doubles.

13. C is correct.

The initial kinetic energy of the helicopter is entirely converted to the potential energy of the landing gear and heat. By conversation of energy:

$\Delta KE = \Delta PE + Q$

Let the equilibrium length of the landing gear's spring be L_0 and the compressed length be L. The change in potential energy of the landing gear is:

$\Delta PE = \frac{1}{2}k(\Delta x)^2$

$\Delta PE = \frac{1}{2}k(L_0 - L)^2$

$\Delta PE = \frac{1}{2}k(L_0 - (0.23)L_0)^2$

$\Delta PE = \frac{1}{2}k(0.77)L_0^2$

The energy lost to heat is 23% of the initial kinetic energy. The final kinetic energy is zero, therefore:

$$Q = (0.23) \, \Delta KE$$

$$Q = (0.23) \, \tfrac{1}{2}mv^2$$

Conservation of energy becomes:

$$\tfrac{1}{2}mv^2 = (0.77)\tfrac{1}{2}kL_0^2 + (0.23)\tfrac{1}{2}mv^2$$

Solving for $k \, / \, m$:

$$k \, / \, m = [(0.77) \, v^2] \, / \, [(0.23)^2 L_0^2]$$

$$k \, / \, m = 819 \text{ s}^{-2}$$

$$k \, / \, m = 0.8 \text{ kN m}^{-1} \text{ s}^{-1}$$

14. C is correct.

$$PE = mgh$$

$$PE = (21 \times 10^3 \text{ kg}) \cdot (9.8 \text{ m/s}^2) \cdot (2.6 \times 10^3 \text{ m})$$

$$PE = 535 \text{ MJ}$$

15. D is correct.

$$h_0 = 3.5 \text{ m}$$

$$PE_0 = mgh$$

$$PE_1 = mgh(0.69) \rightarrow \text{after first bounce}$$

$$PE_2 = mgh(0.69)^2 \rightarrow \text{after second bounce}$$

$$PE_3 = mgh(0.69)^3 \rightarrow \text{after third bounce}$$

Because mass and gravity are constant, the final height is:

$$\text{final height} = h(0.69)^3$$

$$\text{final height} = (4 \text{ m}) \cdot (0.69)^3$$

$$\text{final height} = 1.31 \text{ m} = 131 \text{ cm}$$

CHAPTER 5

Electrostatics

- **Charges, Electrons, Protons, Conservation of Charge**

- **Conductors, Insulators**

- **Coulomb's Law**

- **Electrostatic Induction**

Charges, Electrons and Protons, Conservation of Charge

What is charge?

Like mass, the *charge* is an intrinsic property of all matter. Every particle in the universe has a mass and a charge measured in coulombs (C). Unlike mass, however, three distinct types of charges exist: positive charge, negative charge, and neutral charge. (Neutral charge does NOT mean that the particle has no charge, the net charge is neutral.)

Where does charge come from?

Today, it is known that the basic unit of matter is the atom, which has electrons orbiting a nucleus of protons and neutrons. These subatomic particles, specifically the electron and proton, are the basis of all macroscopically observed charge phenomenon. The electron is negatively charged and has a measured charge of -1.60×10^{-19} coulombs.

Conversely, the proton is positively charged and has an equal but opposite charge of $+1.60 \times 10^{-19}$ coulombs. For macroscopic objects that contain a charge, it is essential to note that only the electrons contribute to the charge because they are mobile. Protons are part of the core nuclei of the atom and are not mobile.

The charge on an atom is either due to an excess of electrons (if the observed charge is negative) or a shortage of electrons (if the observed charge is positive).

Negative charge: # electrons > # protons

Positive charge: # electrons < # protons

Neutral charge: # electrons = # protons

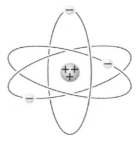

Schematic of an atom with a core of protons and neutron and orbiting electrons

What are the properties of charge?

Charges have several unique properties that govern the laws of nature. Most importantly, charges exhibit force upon each other according to the types of charge. The same charges produce repulsive forces, and opposite charges produce attractive forces.

The figures below show a ruler that is negatively charged (i.e., excess of electrons) and a glass rod that is positively charged (i.e., deficiency of electrons).

In the top diagram, two negatively charged rulers are brought close together and repel due to their like charges.

In the middle diagram, two positively charged rulers are brought close together and repel due to their like charges.

In the bottom diagram, the charged ruler and the glass rod attract each other due to their opposite charges.

Two charged plastic rulers repel

Two charged glass rods repel

Charged glass rod attracts
charged plastic ruler

The charge is always conserved. Like mass and energy, the charge cannot be created nor destroyed. The charge can only be transferred from one source to another.

If a charged object (e.g., the ruler in the above example) is placed on a table for some time, and later found to be neutrally charged, the charge was not destroyed, but instead transferred to the surroundings (e.g., air and table).

Another unique property of charge is that all charge is quantized.

The magnitude of the electron's charge (or proton) is the *fundamental charge* and is the smallest unit of charge that exists.

All macroscopically charged objects have a net charge equal to an integer multiple of the fundamental charge.

The fundamental charge can be expressed as:

$$q = ne$$

where q is the net charge (C), n is the integer multiple (i.e., excess electrons or protons), and e is the magnitude of the fundamental charge (1.60×10^{-19} C).

The quantization of charge enables the calculation for the excess or deficiency of electrons in an object that contributes to the object's net charge.

For example, if the negatively charged ruler from the earlier example is measured to have one coulomb of charge, then the number of excess electrons in the ruler is:

$$n = \frac{q}{e}$$

$$n = \frac{1.00 \text{ Coulomb}}{1.60 \times 10^{-19} \text{ Coulomb}}$$

$$n = 6.25 \times 10^{18} \text{ electrons}$$

Conductors, Insulators

Conductivity is a measure of a material's ability to transmit a charge.

Conductors are materials that have a high conductivity. These types of materials allow electrical charge (electrons) to "flow" through the material.

Copper is a good conductor. In most wires for electrical equipment, the electricity is transferred via copper wires because copper allows the electrical charges to flow easily.

Insulators are materials that do not transmit charge well and are poor conductors. Conventional insulators are wood, glass, and paper.

In the diagram on the left, one sphere has been charged positively (i.e., a deficit of electrons), and the other sphere is neutral.

In the middle diagram, a metal nail is placed on top of both spheres. The metal nail acts as a conductor and allows electrons to flow through it (from the neutral to the positive sphere) until the charge in each sphere is equal.

In the diagram on the right, a piece of wood is placed across the spheres. The piece of wood is an insulator and does not allow the flow of electrons from the neutral sphere to the positive sphere.

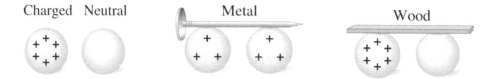

It is the electrons (i.e., negatively charged particles) that move and not the protons (i.e., positively charged particles).

Coulomb's Law

As mentioned earlier, charges either repel or attract one another, depending on if the charges are similar (repel) or opposite (attract).

This resulting force is the *electrostatic force* (Coulomb force) and can be found using *Coulomb's Law*, which describes the interaction between two charged particles:

$$F = \frac{1}{4\pi \, \epsilon_0} \frac{q_1 q_2}{r^2}$$

which simplifies to:

$$F = k \frac{q_1 q_2}{r^2}$$

where F is the electrostatic force between the two charges (N), q is the magnitudes of the charges (C), r is the distance between them (m), ϵ_0 is the permittivity of free space (8.854×10^{-12} $C^2/N \cdot m^2$), and k is Coulomb's constant with a value of 9×10^9 $N \cdot m^2/C^2$.

Coulomb's Law strictly applies only to point charges. If two objects have a net charge, then the objects must be approximated as point charges to calculate the force each exerts on the other.

The electrostatic force is always along the line connecting the charges.

If the charges have the same sign, the force is repulsive.

If the charges have opposite signs, the force is attractive.

To find the electrostatic force on more than two point charges, use the superposition principle and sum the force from each charge in all axial directions.

For example, what is the net force on Q_3 in the example below?

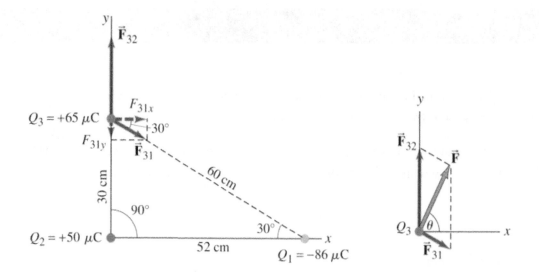

$$F_{32} = k\frac{q_1 q_2}{r^2} = \frac{(9 \times 10^9 \text{Nm}^2)\cdot(65 \times 10^{-6}\text{C})\cdot(50 \times 10^{-6}\text{C})}{(0.3 \text{ m})^2} = 325 \text{ N}$$

$$F_{31y} = \sin\theta\, k\frac{q_1 q_2}{r^2} = \left|\frac{\sin 30\,(9 \times 10^9 \text{Nm}^2)\cdot(65 \times 10^{-6}\text{C})\cdot(-86 \times 10^{-6}\text{C})}{(0.6 \text{ m})^2}\right| = 70 \text{ N}$$

$$F_{31x} = \cos\theta\, k\frac{q_1 q_2}{r^2} = \left|\frac{\cos 30\,(9 \times 10^9 \text{Nm}^2)\cdot(65 \times 10^{-6}\text{C})\cdot(-86 \times 10^{-6}\text{C})}{(0.6 \text{ m})^2}\right| = 121 \text{ N}$$

$$F_{net} = \sqrt{(121 \text{ N})^2 + (325\,N - 70\,N)^2} = 282 \text{ N}$$

Electrostatic Induction

Electrostatic energy is a charge more or less fixed in a single place. However, this charge can be transferred to other objects in two ways.

Conduction is the transfer of energy where there is a point of direct contact between the two objects.

Induction is the transfer of energy where there is no direct contact between the two objects, and the transfer of energy is across an open space between two objects.

Electrostatic induction is where a charged object induces the movement or redistribution of charges in another object. Electrostatic induction occurs when an object is placed in or near an electric field.

Metal objects can be charged by conduction. In the diagram below, the metal rod B is initially neutral. When the neutral rod B touches a charged rod A, negatively charged electrons flow from the neutral rod B to positively charged rod A.

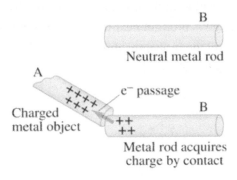

Induction in a neutral metal rod by a charged metal object

The rods can also be charged by induction.

In the figure below, the two rods never touch, and the neutral rod is grounded.

Electrons from the neutral rod can be transferred to the ground and leave the surface of their object.

In the middle diagram, when the negatively charged rod is brought near the neutral rod, the electric field attracts a positive charge. It causes the negatively charged electrons to be repelled and travel into the ground.

In the bottom diagram, if the connection to ground is cut (such that electrons cannot flow back into the system) and the negatively charged rod is removed, the neutral rod has a positive charge evenly distributed across its surface.

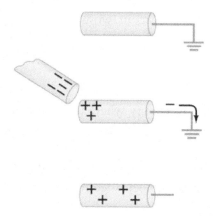

Insulators will not be charged by conduction or induction but experience a charge separation as *polarization*.

Unlike conductors, insulators do not have electrons that can move freely about the material. When a strong charge is brought near the insulator, the molecules become polarized and orient such that charges on the molecule align with the electric field (like electric dipoles in an electric field), as shown below.

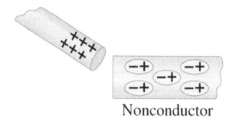

Nonconductor

An *electroscope* detects charge in an object. Below is a schematic of a gold-leaf electroscope. The gold arms in the middle hang together if there is no charge, and the arms spread apart when a charge is present.

In the diagram on the left, an object is held near the metal knob on top.

In the diagram on the right, an object is held near the metal knob on top.

If electrons flow due to induction (no contact) or conduction (contact between objects), the gold leaves become similarly charged and repel.

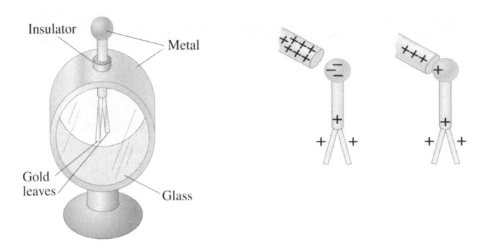

Electroscopes and the leaves that are used determines the sign of an unknown charge

The charged electroscope determines the sign of an unknown charge.

In the middle diagram below, if a negatively charged object is held near the knob and the leaves expand. Additional electrons are trying to get away from the like-charged object, causing an even stronger negative charge in both leaves.

In the diagram on the right, a positively charged object is held near the knob, and the leaves move toward each other. Electrons are moving into the knob to be close to the presence of the opposite charge. The leaves will not be as negatively charged as before, and there is less of a force driving the leaves apart.

Electroscope determines the sign of an unknown charge

Chapter Summary

Charge

- There are two kinds of electric charge—positive and negative.

- Charge is always conserved.

- The charge on an electron is: $e = 1.602 \times 10^{-19}$ C

- Charge is quantized in units of e (how many times greater than the charge on an electron).

- Conductors are materials in which electrons are free to move.

- Insulators are nonconductors, and thus do not allow electrons to move freely.

- Objects can be charged by conduction or induction.

Electric Fields

- Coulomb's Law gives the magnitude of the electrostatic force:

$$F = k \times \frac{Q_1 Q_2}{r^2}$$

- An electric field is a force per unit charge: $\vec{E} = \frac{\vec{F}}{q}$

- An electric field is given by a single point charge:

$$E = \frac{F}{q} = \frac{kqQ/r^2}{q} = k \times \frac{Q}{r^2}$$

- Electric field lines can represent electric fields.

- The static electric field inside a conductor is zero; the surface field is perpendicular to the surface.

- Electric flux (flow of a field through a closed surface):

$$\Phi_E = E_\perp A = EA_\perp = EA \cos(\theta)$$

- Gauss's Law (electric flux through a closed surface):

$$\sum_{\substack{closed \\ surface}} E_\perp \Delta A = \frac{Q_{encl}}{\epsilon_0}$$

Practice Questions

1. In the figure, $Q = 5.1$ nC. What is the magnitude of the electrical force on the charge Q? (Use Coulomb's constant $k = 9 \times 10^9$ N·m²/C²)

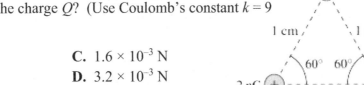

    A. 4.2×10^{-3} N   **C.** 1.6×10^{-3} N

    B. 0.4×10^{-3} N   **D.** 3.2×10^{-3} N

2. Two uncharged metal spheres, A and B, are mounted on insulating support rods. A third metal sphere, C, carrying a positive charge, is then placed near B. A copper wire is momentarily connected between A and B, and then removed. Finally, sphere C is removed. In this final state:

    A. spheres A and B both carry equal positive charges

    B. sphere A carries a negative charge and B carries a positive charge

    C. sphere A carries a positive charge and B carries a negative charge

    D. spheres A and B both carry positive charges, but B's charge is greater.

3. Two charges separated by 1 m exert a 1 N force on each other. What is the force on each charge when they are pulled to a separation distance of 3 m?

    A. 3 N   **B.** 0 N   **C.** 9 N   **D.** 0.11 N

4. One coulomb of charge passes through a 6 V battery. Which of the following is the correct value for the increase of some property of the battery?

    A. 6 watts   **B.** 6 ohms   **C.** 6 amps   **D.** 6 J

5. A Coulomb is a unit of electrical:

    A. capacity   **C.** charge

    B. resistance   **D.** potential difference

6. Two like charges of the same magnitude are 10 mm apart. If the force of repulsion they exert upon each other is 4 N, what is the magnitude of each charge? (Use Coulomb's constant $k = 9 \times 10^9$ N·m²/C²)

    A. 6×10^{-5} C   **C.** 2×10^{-7} C

    B. 6×10^{5} C   **D.** 1.5×10^{-7} C

7. To say that electric charge is conserved means that no case has ever been found where:

A. charge has been created or destroyed

B. the total charge on an object has increased

C. the net negative charge on an object is unbalanced by a positive charge on another object

D. the total charge on an object has changed by a significant amount

8. Two charges $Q_1 = 1.7 \times 10^{-10}$ C and $Q_2 = 6.8 \times 10^{-10}$ C are near. How would F change if the charges were both doubled, but the distance between them remained the same?

A. F increases by a factor of 2   C. F decreases by a factor of $\sqrt{2}$

B. F increases by a factor of 4   D. F decreases by a factor of 4

9. A point charge $Q = -600$ nC. What is the number of excess electrons in charge Q? (Use the charge of an electron $e = -1.6 \times 10^{-19}$ C)

A. 5.6×10^{12} electrons   C. 2.8×10^{11} electrons

B. 2.1×10^{10} electrons   D. 3.8×10^{12} electrons

10. Two charges separated by 1 m exert a 1 N force on each other. What is the force on each charge if the charges are pushed to a 0.25 m separation?

A. 1 N   B. 2 N   C. 4 N   D. 16 N

Solutions

1. C is correct.

$$F_e = kQ_1Q_2 / r^2$$

$$F_e = [(9 \times 10^9 \text{ N·m}^2/\text{C}^2) \cdot (5.1 \times 10^{-9} \text{ C}) \cdot (2 \times 10^{-9} \text{ C})] / (0.1 \text{ m})^2$$

$$F_e = 9.18 \times 10^{-4} \text{ N}$$

$F_e \sin(60°)$ represents the force from one of the positive 2 nC charges.

Double to find the total force:

$$F_{total} = 2F_e \sin(60°)$$

$$F_{total} = 2(9.18 \times 10^{-4} \text{ N}) \sin(60°)$$

$$F_{total} = 1.6 \times 10^{-3} \text{ N}$$

The sine of the angle is used since only the vertical forces are added because the horizontal forces are equal and opposite and therefore they cancel.

2. C is correct.

When the positively charged sphere C is near sphere B, it polarizes the sphere causing its negative charge to migrate towards C and a positive charge to build on the other side of sphere B.

The wire between sphere A and sphere B allows negative charge to flow to B and create a net positive charge on sphere A. Once the wire is removed and sphere C is removed, sphere A will have a net positive charge and B has a net negative charge.

3. D is correct.

Coulomb's Law:

$$F_e = kQ_1Q_2 / r^2$$

If r is increased by a factor of 3:

$$F_{new} = kQ_1Q_2 / (3r)^2$$

$$F_{new} = kQ_1Q_2 / (9r^2)$$

$$F_{new} = (1/9)kQ_1Q_2 / r^2$$

$$F_{new} = F_{original} (1/9)$$

$$F_{new} = (1 \text{ N}) \cdot (1/9)$$

$$F_{new} = 0.11 \text{ N}$$

4. D is correct.

A volt is defined as the potential difference that causes 1 C of charge to increase potential energy by 1 J. Therefore, moving 1 C through 6 V causes the potential energy of the battery to increase by 6 J.

5. C is correct.

The coulomb is the basic unit of electrical charge in the SI unit system.

6. C is correct.

Coulomb's Law:

$$F = kQ_1Q_2 / r^2$$

$$Q_1 = Q_2$$

Therefore:

$$Q_1Q_2 = Q^2$$

$$F = kQ^2 / r^2$$

Rearranging:

$$Q^2 = Fr^2 / k$$

$$Q = \sqrt{(Fr^2 / k)}$$

$$Q = \sqrt{[(4 \text{ N}) \cdot (0.01 \text{ m})^2 / (9 \times 10^9 \text{ N·m}^2/\text{C}^2)]}$$

$$Q = 2 \times 10^{-7} \text{ C}$$

7. A is correct.

Law of Conservation of Charge, charge cannot be created nor destroyed.

8. B is correct.

Coulomb's Law:

$$F = kQ_1Q_2 / r^2$$

If both charges are doubled,

$$F = k(2Q_1) \cdot (2Q_2) / r^2$$

$$F = 4kQ_1Q_2 / r^2$$

F increases by a factor of 4.

9. D is correct.

charge = # electrons × electron charge

$Q = ne^-$

$n = Q / e^-$

$n = (-600 \times 10^{-9}\,C) / (-1.6 \times 10^{-19}\,C)$

$n = 3.8 \times 10^{12}$ electrons

10. D is correct.

Coulomb's Law:

$F_1 = kQ_1Q_2 / r^2$

$F_2 = kQ_1Q_2 / (0.25r)^2$

$F_2 = 16kQ_1Q_2 / r^2$

$F_2 = 16F_1$

F increases by a factor of 16,

$(1\,N)\cdot(16) = 16\,N$

CHAPTER 6

DC Circuits

- **Circuits**

- **Batteries, Electromotive Force, Voltage**

- **Current**

- **Resistance**

- **Power**

CIRCUITS

An *electric circuit* is a series of connections between a voltage source, circuit elements, and conducting wires, which result in a flow of current.

The voltage source is the energy input and is necessary for continuing the flow of energy.

The circuit elements can use some of the energy from the voltage source as heat or light.

The current in a circuit always flows from high potential to low potential through the external circuit.

A complete circuit is one where current can flow in a complete loop.

The top image shows a complete circuit. The battery provides a potential difference, which causes current to flow from its positive terminal, through the light bulb, then to its negative terminal, completing the loop.

The bottom figure is a schematic circuit drawing of the circuit shown above it. Note that the schematic drawing looks different than the photograph of the physical circuit that it represents.

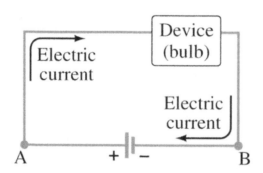

Batteries, Electromotive Force, Voltage

The electric potential difference is important for solving circuit problems.

The *electromotive force* (EMF) describes the measure of energy that causes the flow of current in a circuit. The EMF is defined as the potential difference between two points in a circuit. It is the energy per unit of charge given by an energy source. This value is the same as the amount of work done on one unit of electric charge, given in volts (V).

Batteries are physical devices that produce an electric potential difference and are often used to provide the EMF in electric circuits. These devices operate by transforming chemical energy into electrical energy.

Chemical reactions within the battery cell create a potential difference between the two terminals.

This potential difference can be maintained, even if a current is flowing until, eventually, the chemical reaction has exhausted itself, and the battery can no longer maintain a potential difference.

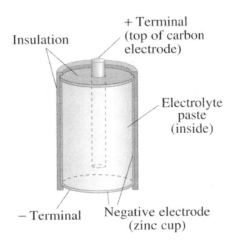

Component of a battery for stored voltage

Internal resistance of a battery

Although batteries are often depicted as having no resistance, all non-ideal batteries will have some internal resistance. The internal resistance of a battery is like a resistor right next to the battery, connected in series.

If the battery in a circuit has no internal resistance (ideal case), the potential difference across the battery equals the EMF. If the battery does have an internal resistance, the potential difference across the battery equals the EMF, minus the voltage drop due to internal resistance.

The *terminal voltage* is given by the equation:

$$V_{ab} = V_0 - IR_{battery}$$

where V_{ab} is the terminal voltage of the battery (V), V_0 is the voltage before internal resistance (V), I is the current through the battery (A), and $R_{battery}$ is the internal resistance of the battery (Ω).

The figure below depicts a non-ideal battery with internal resistance and resulting terminal voltage.

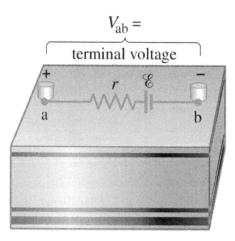

Battery with internal resistance and terminal voltage

Batteries in series and parallel

When two or more batteries are in series, the total potential difference provided is the sum of the EMF provided by each battery. This is only the case if the terminals are aligned such that the batteries' terminals go from positive to negative, or vice versa.

The figure below shows two batteries in series (note that these batteries have internal resistance and the voltage shown is the terminal voltage). The total voltage provided by the two batteries is expressed as:

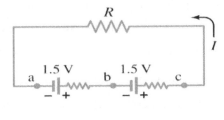

$$V_{total} = 1.5V + 1.5V = 3V$$

When the batteries are in series but aligned such that the positive terminal goes to positive (or negative to negative), the total voltage provided is the difference between the two batteries. In this scenario, the battery with less voltage is being charged:

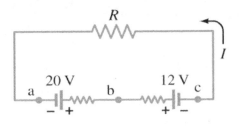

$$V_{total} = 20\ V - 12\ V = 8\ V$$

Batteries in parallel (shown below) produce the same voltage but can support larger current draws depending upon the resistance of the circuit.

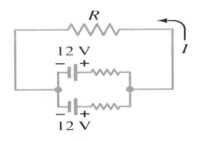

$$V_{total} = 12\ V$$

Current

Current results from the flow of electrons through a conductor. Electrons in a conductor are loosely bound to the nuclei and have large, random speeds dependent upon the temperature of the conductor. Metals are well-known conductors because one electron from each atom is loosely bound and free to move through the metal lattice.

When an electric potential difference is applied across a metal or any conducting material, it creates an electrical field that passes through the conductor at near the speed of light. The free electrons in the conductor are attracted against the line direction of the electric field due to Coulomb attraction forces.

As the electrons pass through the conduction material, these electrons acquire an average drift velocity, which, although considerably smaller than the thermal velocity of the electrons, creates the electric current through the conductor.

The diagram below shows a conductor with an applied potential difference and the resulting electric field.

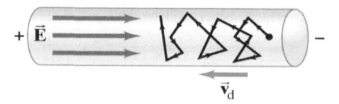

The current through the conductor is calculated as the number of electrons drifting through a unit's volume at the drift velocity:

$$I = nq_eAv_{\mathrm{d}}$$

where I is the current (A), n is the number of electrons per unit volume (electrons/m^3), A is the area of the conductor (m^2), v_{d} is the drift velocity (m/s) and q_e is the charge of an electron (1.6×10^{-19} C).

More generally, the electric current is defined as the rate at which charge flows through a conductor.

Current I is expressed as:

$$I = \frac{\Delta q}{\Delta t}$$

There are two types of current: direct current (DC) and alternating current (AC).

A *direct current* (DC) is when a constant potential difference is applied to the circuit, and the current moves only in one direction. Direct current is characteristic of electronic devices, batteries, and solar cells.

Most generated electricity is *alternating current* (AC) in which the potential difference is cycled between high and low, creating an oscillatory current flow. The alternating current is transmitted from the power source to the consumer over high voltage lines and "stepped down" for use in homes and businesses.

Resistance

Resistivity ($\rho = RA/l$)

Electrical resistance is the loss of current energy (i.e., electron flow) through a material.

There are two sources of electrical resistance:

collisions with other electrons in current, or

collisions with other charges in the material.

The collisions are factors that account for resistance. Resistance is determined by the resistivity of a material (a measure of conductance) and other factors. In most electronic circuit applications, wires transmit current.

The resistance of a wire depends upon the length, the cross-sectional area, the temperature, and the material:

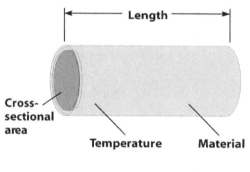

$$R = \rho \frac{\ell}{A}$$

where R is the resistance (Ohms or Ω), ρ is the resistivity ($\Omega \cdot m$), ℓ is the length of the wire (m), and A is the cross-sectional area of the wire (m^2).

The resistivity is directly proportional to the resistance. Therefore, the greater the resistivity, the higher the resistance of the material. Resistance is inversely proportional to the area (inverse square to the radius and diameter).

The greater the diameter of the wire, the lower is the resistance; there is a larger area for electrons to flow.

From the resistance equation above, a wire of low resistance will be short, of large diameter, and made from a material that has low resistivity. Extension cords are made of wires with thicker diameters to keep the resistance low. The resistance of a wire is also dependent upon the temperature of the material.

For any given material, the resistivity increases with temperature:

$$\rho_T = \rho_0[1 + \alpha(T - T_0)]$$

where ρ_T is the resistivity at a temperature T ($\Omega \cdot m$), ρ_0 is the standard resistivity at a standard temperature of T_0 ($\Omega \cdot m$), α temperature coefficient of resistivity (K^{-1}) and T is the temperature (K)

Ohm's Law (I = V/R)

Ohm's Law gives the relationship between the potential difference across resistance and the current through the resistance.

Ohm's Law states that, in electrical circuits, the current through a conductor between two points is directly proportional to the potential difference (or voltage) across the two points. Current is inversely proportional to the resistance between them:

$$I = \frac{V}{R} \quad \text{or} \quad V = IR$$

where V is the potential difference (V), I is the current (A), and R is the resistance (Ω).

Resistors in series

In a circuit, *resistors* are arranged in series or parallel.

For series circuit (shown below), the resistors have current pass through the first resistor, then into the second, into the third and so on:

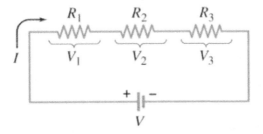

For series circuits, the total resistance of the circuit is the sum of all the resistances of the components. Adding elements to the circuit increases the total resistance and decreases the total current.

The equivalent resistance of resistors in series is found by:

$$R_{\text{equivalent}} = R_1 + R_2 + R_3 + \dots$$

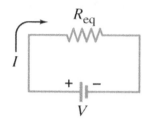

In a series circuit, the current through each resistor is the same ($I_{\text{series}} = I_1 = I_2 = I_3$); however, the voltage drops across each resistor. The voltage drop among resistors in series is split according to the resistance—a greater resistance equals a greater voltage drop ($V = IR$).

This can also be expanded for more than one resistor, by splitting it into components:

$$V = V_1 + V_2 + V_3 = IR_1 + IR_2 + IR_3$$

Resistors in parallel

Parallel resistors are arranged such that all resistors experience the same voltage drop across them but have different currents according to their resistances.

In a parallel circuit, there is more than one available path for the current.

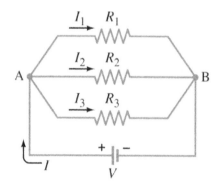

Parallel circuit offers more than one route for the current to flow

The equivalent resistance of resistors in parallel is:

$$\frac{1}{R_{equivalent}} = \frac{1}{R_1} + \frac{1}{R_2} + \frac{1}{R_3} + \dots$$

As stated earlier, for parallel resistors, the voltage across each resistor is the same ($V_{\text{parallel}} = V_1 = V_2 = V_3$); however, the current across each resistor is not.

For parallel resistors, the total current is the sum of currents across each resistor:

$$\frac{V}{R_{\text{eq}}} = \frac{V}{R_1} + \frac{V}{R_2} + \frac{V}{R_3}$$

$$I = \frac{V}{R_{\text{eq}}}$$

Most typical circuits (e.g., household circuits) are combinations of series and parallel circuits. Generally, electrical outlets in the same room are in series, but the electrical outlets in separate rooms are in parallel. This is the reason why a blown fuse may cut the power to an entire room, but not the entire house.

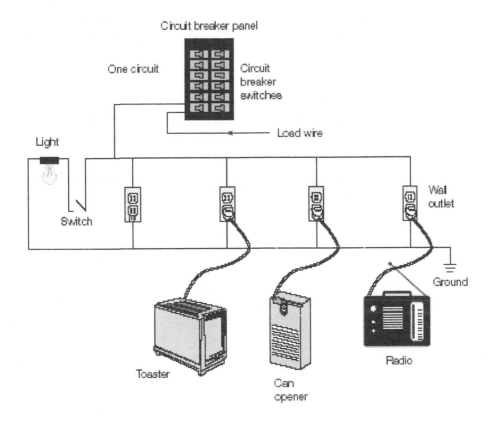

Power

The *power* (P) in a circuit is the rate at which energy converts from electrical energy into some other form, such as heat or mechanical energy.

The SI unit for power is the watt (W), which is equal to joules per second (J/s).

For a component in a DC circuit, the power is given by the equation:

$$P = IV$$

where P is the power (W), I is the current (A or ampere), and V is the voltage (V).

Using Ohm's Law, power in an electrical circuit is expressed as:

$$P = I^2R$$

Chapter Summary

Electric Potential

- Electric potential is potential energy per unit charge: $V_a = \frac{PE_a}{q}$

- A source of an electromotive force (*EMF*) transforms energy from some other form of electrical energy.

- A battery is a source of constant potential difference.

- An electric potential of a point charge:

$$V = k\frac{Q}{r} \quad \text{[single point charge V = 0 at r = ∞]} \quad = \frac{1}{4\pi\,\epsilon_0}\frac{Q}{r}$$

- Kirchhoff's rules:

  The sum of the currents entering a junction equals the sum of the currents leaving it.

  The total potential difference around a closed loop is zero.

Circuits

- Electric current is the rate of flow of electric charge.

- Conventional current is in the direction that positive charge would flow.

- A direct current is constant.

- An alternating current varies sinusoidally:

$$I = \frac{V}{R} = \frac{V_0}{R}\sin\omega t = I_0 \sin\omega t$$

- Power in an electric circuit: $P = IV$

- An RC circuit has a characteristic time constant: $\tau = RC$

Resistance

- Resistance is the ratio of voltage to current: $V = IR$

- Ohmic materials have constant resistance, independent of voltage.

- Resistance is determined by shape and material: $R = \rho \dfrac{\ell}{A}$ (ρ is the resistivity)

- A battery is a source of EMF in parallel with internal resistance.

- Resistors in series: $R_{eq} = R_1 + R_2 + R_3$

- Resistors in parallel: $\dfrac{1}{R_{eq}} = \dfrac{1}{R_1} + \dfrac{1}{R_2} + \dfrac{1}{R_3}$

Practice Questions

1. A 3 Ω resistor is connected in parallel with a 6 Ω resistor; both resistors are connected in series with a 4 Ω resistor, and all three resistors are connected to an 18 V battery as shown. If a 3 Ω resistor burnt out and exhibits infinite resistance, which of the following is true?

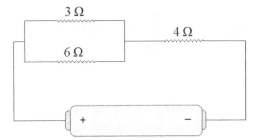

   A. The power dissipated in the circuit increases
   B. The current provided by the battery remains the same
   C. The current in the 6 Ω resistor decreases
   D. The current in the 6 Ω resistor increases

2. When a current flows through a metal wire, the moving charges are:

   I. protons   II. neutrons   III. electrons

   A. I only   **B.** II only   **C.** III only   **D.** I and II only

3. For the graph shown, what physical quantity does the slope of the graph represent?

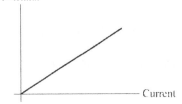

   A. 1 / Voltage
   B. Resistance
   C. Power
   D. Charge

4. What is the voltage across a 15 Ω resistor that has 5 A current passing through it?

   A. 3 V   **B.** 5 V   **C.** 15 V   **D.** 75 V

5. Consider two copper wires of equal cross-sectional area. One wire has 3 times the length of the other. How do the resistivities of these two wires compare?

   A. The longer wire has 9 times the resistivity of the shorter wire
   B. The longer wire has 27 times the resistivity of the shorter wire
   C. The longer wire has 1/3 the resistivity of the shorter wire
   D. Both wires have the same resistivity

6. When three resistors are added in series to a resistor in a circuit, the original resistor's voltage [   ] and its current [   ].

   A. decreases ... increases   **C.** decrease ... decreases
   B. increases ... increases   **D.** decreases ... remains the same

---

7. What is the quantity that is calculated with units of $kg \cdot m^2/s \cdot C^2$?

    A. Resistance   **B.** Capacitance   **C.** Potential   **D.** Resistivity

8. The addition of resistors in series to a resistor in an existing circuit, while voltage remains constant, would result in [   ] in the original resistor.

    A. an increase in current   **C.** an increase in resistance
    B. a decrease in resistance   **D.** a decrease in current

9. In an experiment, a battery is connected to a variable resistor R, where resistance can be adjusted by turning a knob. The potential difference across the resistor and the current through it are recorded for different settings of the resistor knob. The battery is an ideal potential source in series with an internal resistor. The emf of the potential source is 9 V, and the internal resistance is 0.1 Ω. What is the current if the variable resistor is set at 0.5 Ω?

    A. 15 A   **B.** 0.9 A   **C.** 4.5 A   **D.** 45 A

10. Electric current can only flow:

    A. in a region of negligible resistance   **C.** in a perfect conductor
    B. through a potential difference   **D.** in the absence of resistance

11. Which change to a circuit element will always result in an increase in the current?

    A. Increased voltage and decreased resistance
    B. Decreased voltage and increased resistance
    C. Increased voltage and increased resistance
    D. Only a decrease in resistance, the voltage has no effect on current

12. Four 6 V batteries (in a linear sequence of A → B → C → D) are connected in series to power lights A and B. The resistance of light A is 50 Ω and the resistance of light B is 25 Ω. What is the potential difference at a point between battery C and battery D? (Assume that the potential at the start of the sequence is zero)

    A. 4 volts   **B.** 12 volts   **C.** 18 volts   **D.** 26 volts

Solutions

1. D is correct.

The equivalent resistance of the 3 Ω and 6 Ω resistors is:

$1 / R_{eq} = 1 / (3 \ \Omega) + 1 / (6 \ \Omega)$

$R_{eq} = 2 \ \Omega$

The voltage across the equivalent resistor (i.e., the 6 Ω resistor) is given by the voltage divider relationship:

$V_6 = 18 \ V \ (2 \ \Omega) / (2 \ \Omega \ + 4 \ \Omega) = 6 \ V$

The current through the 6 Ω resistor is:

$I_6 = V_6 / 6 \ \Omega = 1 \ A$

After the 3 Ω resistor burns out, the voltage across the 6 Ω resistor is found using the voltage divider relationship:

$V_6 = 18 \ V \ (6 \ \Omega) / (6 \ \Omega \ + \ 4 \ \Omega) = 10.8 \ V$

Now the current through the 6 Ω resistor is:

$I_6 = V_6 / 6 \ \Omega = 1.8 \ A$

The current has increased.

2. C is correct.

In a solid, the locations of the nuclei are fixed; only the electrons move.

3. B is correct.

$V = IR$

$R = V / I$

4. D is correct.

Voltage = current × resistance

$V = IR$

$V = (5 \ A) \cdot (15 \ \Omega)$

$V = 75 \ V$

5. D is correct.

Because the material of both wires is the same (copper), the resistivity of both wires is equal.

6. C is correct.

The total resistance of a network of series resistors increases as more resistors are added to the network.

An increase in the total resistance results in a decrease in the total current through the network.

A decrease in current results in a decrease in the voltage across the original resistor:

$V = IR$

7. A is correct.

Resistance = Ohms

$\Omega = V / A$

$\Omega = [(kg \cdot m^2/s^2) / C] / [C/s]$

$\Omega = kg \cdot m^2/C^2/s$

8. D is correct.

The total resistance of a network of series resistors increases as more resistors are added.

$V = IR$

An increase in the total resistance results in a decrease in the total current through the network.

9. A is correct.

This is a circuit with two resistors in series.

Combine the two resistors into one resistor:

$R_T = R + R_{int}$

$R_T = 0.5\ \Omega + 0.1\ \Omega$

$R_T = 0.6\ \Omega$

Ohm's Law:

$V = IR$

$I = V / R$

$I = 9 \text{ V} / 0.6 \ \Omega$

$I = 15 \text{ A}$

10. B is correct.

"In a perfect conductor" and "in the absence of resistance" have the same meanings, and current can flow in conductors of varying resistances.

A semi-perfect conductor has resistance.

11. A is correct.

Ohm's Law:

$V = IR$

Increasing V and decreasing R increases I.

12. C is correct.

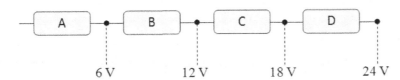

Batteries in series add voltage like resistors in series add resistance.

The resistances of the lights they power are not needed to solve the problem.

CHAPTER 7

Periodic and Harmonic Motion

- **Amplitude, Period, Frequency**

- **Simple Harmonic Motion, Displacement as a Sinusoidal Function of Time**

- **Hooke's Law ($F = -kx$)**

- **Energy of a Mass-Spring System**

- **Motion of a Pendulum**

- **Transverse and Longitudinal Waves**

- **Phase, Interference and Wave Addition**

- **Reflection and Transmission**

- **Refraction and Diffraction**

- **Amplitude and Intensity**

Amplitude, Period and Frequency

Periodic motion (i.e., sinusoidal motion) is a motion that repeats. If an object moves back and forth over the same path at a constant speed, each cycle takes the same amount of time; the resulting motion is periodic. In the periodic motion, this back-and-forth activity is *oscillation* or *vibration*.

Many systems can display oscillatory or vibratory motion; there are several types of periodic motion as well. Periodic motion can be damped (e.g., friction is present) or undamped, driven (an outside force is acting upon the system), or free.

Regardless of the motion, any oscillatory system has several inherent characteristics that define its periodic motion. These characteristics are the amplitude, frequency, and period.

In general, most questions refer to several types of oscillatory systems, but only one motion: undamped and free periodic motion (simple harmonic motion).

Amplitude (*A*): In periodic motion, the *amplitude* expresses the displacement of the system about its equilibrium (center or resting) position. Amplitude may have different units depending on the system.

Frequency (*f*): *Frequency* is the rate of oscillation, or the number of cycles per second, where a cycle is one complete vibration (when the displacement is zero). The value for frequency is usually measured in Hertz (Hz) and can be calculated by:

$$f = \frac{\# \ of \ cycles}{time}$$

In some situations, the frequency is expressed as angular frequency (ω). This value is related to frequency; however, angular frequency is measured in radians per second (rad/s).

The equation for angular frequency ω is:

$$\omega = 2\pi f$$

Period (*T*): The *period* is the time required to complete one cycle or one oscillation. The period is often measured in seconds and can be calculated by:

$$T = \frac{time}{\# \, of \, cycles}$$

The period is sometimes measured in degrees or radians.

One rotation around a circle requires 360° or 2π radians.

The value of 360° or 2π radians represents one complete cycle of an oscillating system.

From the above equation, the period (*T*) and frequency (*f*) are inversely related.

The relationship between the period and frequency is expressed as:

$$T = \frac{1}{f}$$

Simple Harmonic Motion, Displacement as a Sinusoidal Function of Time

An object or system exhibiting *simple harmonic motion* is a particular case of a periodic motion that is undamped and free. There is no force of friction present and no external, time-dependent force acting upon it. The system requires a restoring force (not a driving force), which must be proportional to the displacement (amplitude). This proportionality allows the system to oscillate about its equilibrium position while retaining the same amplitude.

Simple harmonic motion can be depicted as a sine or cosine graph, as below:

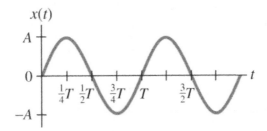

The system oscillates about its equilibrium position with the same amplitude and a fixed period (and thus constant frequency). Another important distinction is that, regardless of the magnitude of the amplitude, the period and frequency do not change. In simple harmonic motion, frequency and period are independent of amplitude. Any object's simple harmonic motion may be determined using the equation:

$$x = A \sin (\omega t)$$

$$x = A \sin (2\pi f t)$$

where x is displacement, A is amplitude, t is time, ω is the angular frequency, and f is frequency.

Sometimes the equation is written as:

$$x = A \cos (\omega t)$$

$$x = A \cos (2\pi f t)$$

Sine or cosine may be used interchangeably if the translation of these graphs is accounted for. A cosine graph has a y-intercept of A (maximum amplitude), whereas a sine graph has a y-intercept of 0 (equilibrium). These are translations, but the translations must be accounted for in the equation. Otherwise, the solution will be incorrect.

Hooke's Law

One classic example of simple harmonic motion is the oscillatory motion of a mass-spring system. When a mass is attached to a spring, the only forces acting upon it are tension and weight of the mass. In such systems, there is no driving force, and it is assumed to be completely undamped.

An important characteristic of a mass-spring system is the *spring constant*. Robert Hooke (1635-1703) discovered that, given a certain spring, there is a constant that can be found when different masses are attached, and the equilibrium position is measured. This constant is an inherent constant of all springs and relates displacement of the spring (change in length) to the restoring force the spring exerts. This relationship is Hooke's Law and is expressed as:

$$F = -k\Delta x$$

where k is the spring constant measured in (N/m), Δx is the displacement, and F is the restoring force (N).

The minus sign in Hooke's Law is by convention, and the restoring force is in the opposite direction to the displacement (because force and displacement are vectors).

In the diagram shown below:

A spring is attached to a wall, and the other side is attached to a mass (m).

For an ideal system (i.e., no friction present), when the mass is displaced, and the spring is stretched, the direction of the restoring force is opposite to the displacement and acts to the left (middle image).

Conversely, if the spring were compressed the same distance, then the restoring force would be of equal magnitude but in the opposite direction (bottom image).

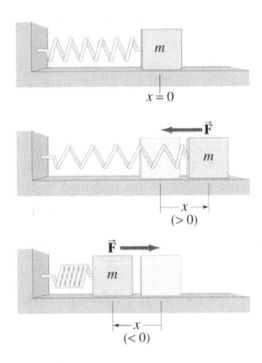

If the spring is hung vertically (shown below), the only change is in the equilibrium position, which is now at a point where the restoring spring force is equal and opposite the weight of the mass.

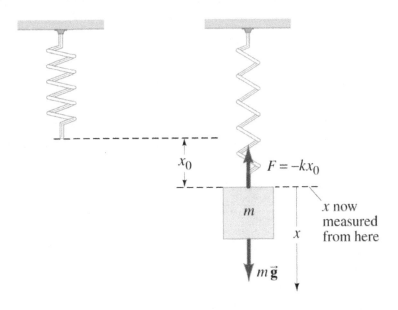

Hooke's Law ($F = -k\Delta x$) can be used to find the acceleration of the mass attached to the spring.

Regardless if the mass-spring system is horizontally- or vertically-positioned, forces always follow Newton's Second Law ($F = ma$), therefore (assuming no friction):

$$| \, ma \, | = | \, k\Delta x \, |$$

$$| \, a \, | = \left| \frac{k\Delta x}{m} \right|$$

More importantly, Hooke's Law demonstrates that mass-spring systems are examples of simple harmonic motion. When disturbed from the equilibrium position, a restoring force acts to bring the spring back towards equilibrium.

The restoring force (F) is proportional to the stretched or compressed distance, which makes the system a simple harmonic.

The amplitude (A) of this oscillation is the maximum displacement (Δx):

$$A = \Delta x$$

For example, if a mass-spring system is oriented vertically, and the mass is displaced a certain distance, the resulting motion follows a simple harmonic oscillator.

A simple harmonic oscillator is seen if a pen is attached to a mass and a roll of paper is moved across the surface of the pen during the motion of the mass:

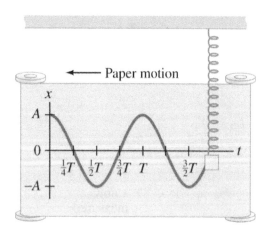

$$x = A \cos (\omega t)$$

$$F = -Ka$$

In the simple harmonic motion of a mass-spring system, the angular frequency (ω) and frequency (f) of the system can be calculated by:

$$\omega = \sqrt{\frac{k}{m}}$$

$$f = \frac{\sqrt{k/m}}{2\pi}$$

or

$$f = 2\pi\sqrt{\frac{m}{k}}$$

The period (T) can be calculated as:

$$T = \frac{2\pi}{\sqrt{k/m}}$$

or

$$T = 2\pi\sqrt{\frac{m}{k}}$$

The frequency (f) and the period (T) of a mass-spring system are only based on the mass and spring constant.

It is important to note that a vertically-angled mass-spring system has the same frequency and period, regardless of the value for gravitational acceleration.

The frequency (f) and period (T) do not change, even if the system were on the moon, in space or on Earth.

Energy of a Mass-Spring System

An oscillating mass accelerates, decelerates, changes direction, and repeats. An oscillating mass contains motion energy and stationary energy (its velocity is zero at the peaks and troughs of its movement).

The equations for the *PE* and *KE* of a mass on a spring:

$$Potential\ energy = PE = \frac{1}{2}kx^2$$

$$Kinetic\ energy = KE = \frac{1}{2}mv^2$$

When the mass is in motion and passes through the equilibrium position, the displacement is zero, as is the potential energy. However, the kinetic energy will be at its maximum because the mass is at its maximum velocity. This occurs at the point where the net force is zero.

At the maximum displacement, the value of *x* equals the amplitude (*A*). The potential energy is at its maximum, and the kinetic energy is zero (because the velocity is zero as the object changes its direction of motion). This occurs at the moment of maximum force, which is also the point of maximum acceleration of an oscillating particle.

At any point along its motion, the potential energy plus the kinetic energy of the particle will always be the same value. This value of total energy (potential energy plus kinetic energy) is constant. The sum is the same as the total energy present in the system:

$$Total\ Energy = E$$

$$E = PE + KE$$

$$E = \frac{1}{2}kx^2 + \frac{1}{2}mv^2$$

When potential energy is at its maximum (at the amplitude), kinetic energy is zero. All the energy in the system must be equal to only the potential energy.

The same relationship applies when kinetic energy is at its maximum:

$$PE_{max} = KE_{max} = E = Total\ Energy$$

The equations for maximum potential and kinetic energy are summed by:

$$PE_{max} = \frac{1}{2}kA^2 \qquad KE_{max} = \frac{1}{2}mv^2 \text{ at x} = 0$$

In the following diagram, a spring has been compressed, but it is not currently in motion. All the energy is stored in potential energy (PE):

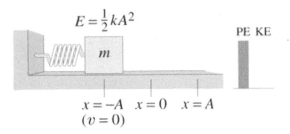

$$E = \tfrac{1}{2}kA^2$$

In the following diagram, if the mass (m) is allowed to move, the spring expands towards its equilibrium position. Once it has reached its equilibrium position, all its potential energy (PE) is transformed into kinetic energy (KE):

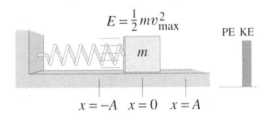

$$E = \tfrac{1}{2}mv_{\text{max}}^2$$

In the following diagram, the mass (m) reaches the maximum stretched amplitude. Kinetic energy (KE) is converted back to potential energy (PE):

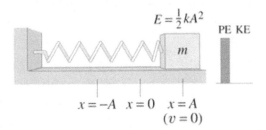

$$E = \tfrac{1}{2}kA^2$$

The mass (m) then moves back toward equilibrium but does not yet reach the equilibrium position. Therefore, most of the energy is kinetic (KE), but some energy is stored as potential energy (PE).

In the following diagram, as the mass (m) gets closer to the equilibrium position, the amount of potential energy decreases, and the amount of kinetic energy increases:

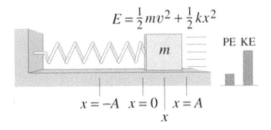

$$E = \tfrac{1}{2}mv^2 + \tfrac{1}{2}kx^2$$

The velocity of the mass (m) can also be calculated at various points during its motion.

By setting the maximum potential energy (PE) and kinetic energy (KE) equal, the maximum velocity of mass (m) is calculated as:

$$v_{max} = \sqrt{\frac{k}{m}} \times A$$

Velocity can be solved as a function of position:

$$v = \pm v_{max} \sqrt{1 - \frac{x^2}{A^2}}$$

Motion of a Pendulum

Thus far, the examples have been oscillating masses attached to springs. In this chapter, the simple harmonic motion of a pendulum is discussed. A pendulum undergoing simple harmonic motion (i.e., simple pendulum) consists of a mass at the end of an assumed massless cord or rod.

To be in simple harmonic motion, the restoring force on the pendulum must be proportional to the negative of the displacement. For example, see the diagram below:

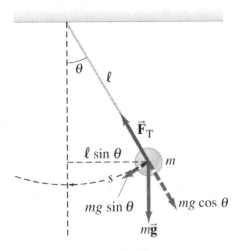

The diagram above shows that the angle θ measures the displacement of the pendulum.

The restoring force is:

$$F = -mg \sin \theta$$

$$|a| = |g \sin \theta|$$

For small displacement angles, $\sin \theta \approx \theta$.

Thus, the restoring force becomes:

$$F = -mg\theta$$

$$|a| = |g\theta|$$

Unlike mass-spring systems, the frequency (f) of a simple pendulum is dependent upon the acceleration due to gravity (g).

The frequency of a simple pendulum is also dependent upon the length of the cord (or rod) attached to the mass:

$$\omega = \sqrt{\frac{g}{l}}$$

$$f = \frac{\sqrt{\frac{g}{l}}}{2\pi}$$

where g is the acceleration of gravity (9.8 m/s²), and l is the length of the cord (or rod).

The period (T) of a simple pendulum's oscillation is:

$$T = 2\pi\sqrt{\frac{l}{g}}$$

Like mass-spring systems, simple pendulums conserve energy. The total energy of the pendulum oscillation is the sum of potential energy and kinetic energy:

$$E = PE + KE$$

Unlike the mass-spring system, PE is dependent upon gravity:

$$PE = mgh$$

where h is the height above the equilibrium position.

PE is at its maximum when the height (or x) is equal to the amplitude.

$$PE_{max} = mgl(1 - cos\ \theta)$$

Maximum KE is the same for a simple pendulum as it is for mass-spring systems:

$$KE_{max} = \frac{1}{2}mv^2$$

Wave Characteristics

Waves are periodic disturbances that transport energy through a medium but do not transport matter. Many examples of waves exist, including the light one sees, the sound one hears, and ocean waves breaking on the beach. While these examples may seem different, they share characteristics intrinsic to all waves.

Like periodic motion, the motion of a wave is defined by:

- Amplitude, A

- Frequency f and period T

- Wavelength, λ

- Wave velocity

Amplitude, frequency, and period were discussed earlier; their definition has not changed, only the context of what they describe. Wavelength (λ) and wave velocity are new terms but are understood.

Observe the diagram of a simple sine wave shown below:

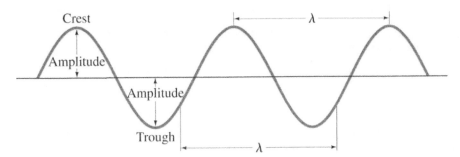

Like before, the amplitude is a representation of energy. The magnitude of the energy is not dependent upon frequency or period. The *wavelength* (λ) is the distance of one cycle of the wave and is measured in meters (m). The *wave velocity* (v) is the speed and direction of the wave. These two characteristics are related to the frequency and period by the equations:

$$f = \frac{v}{\lambda}$$

$$T = \frac{1}{f} = \frac{\lambda}{v}$$

where v is the wave velocity (units of m/s), and λ is the wavelength (units of m).

Transverse and Longitudinal Waves

Three main types of wave motion are transverse, longitudinal, and surface waves. These types can be described by the characteristics above but differ in the motion of particles within the wave. The wave is not transporting the particles. Instead, as the wave passes through a particle in a medium, the particle undergoes a specific periodic motion.

Transverse waves and longitudinal waves are shown below. For example, imagine a hand moving a slinky (figures below).

A *transverse wave* (top diagram below) oscillates particles with motion perpendicular to the wave direction.

A *longitudinal wave* (bottom diagram below) oscillates particles with motion parallel to the wave direction.

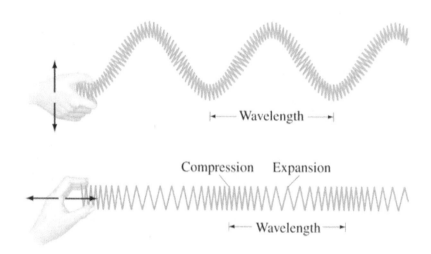

Another way to think about these types of waves is to ask, "What is oscillating, and in what direction?" Imagine there is a mark on one of the crests in the first diagram above.

For the top image above, the imaginary mark moves up and down, while energy travels through the medium from left to right.

The wave displacement is *perpendicular* to the direction of the wave motion; the imaginary mark is experiencing a transverse wave.

Imagine the mark on top of a crest in the bottom diagram above. As the hand pushes the slinky through the medium from left to right and back, the imaginary mark travels left-to-right and vice versa along with the propagated wave.

There is no vertical motion along the wave. The wave displacement is *parallel* to the direction of motion; the imaginary mark experiences a longitudinal wave. The particles in this medium move closer and then farther apart. This *compression and expansion* only occur in longitudinal waves.

Transverse waves have *crests and troughs*.

Longitudinal waves have *compressions and expansions*.

Surface waves have particles that oscillate in a circular motion, rather than vertically or horizontally. Surface waves only occur at the interface of two different mediums, where the wave is traveling in only one of the mediums.

An example of surface waves is the waves seen on the ocean. The diagram below shows a wave propagating through the ocean with a velocity v.

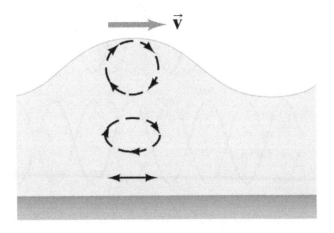

Surface waves that oscillate in a circular motion

For surface waves, the interface of the two mediums (e.g., air and water) causes the particles to move in a circular pattern (diagram above). Deeper in the ocean, the particles are further from the interface, and the motion resembles that of an ellipse.

At greater depths, the particle motion is only horizontal, and the wave behaves as a longitudinal wave. For surface waves, the further (i.e., deeper) from the interface of the two mediums, the more longitudinal the wave becomes.

Phase, Interference and Wave Addition

Phases occur when two waves interact. A phase difference between two waves means that the crests (or troughs) do not occur at the same points in space.

The diagrams below have three waves: one in-phase and two out-of-phase:

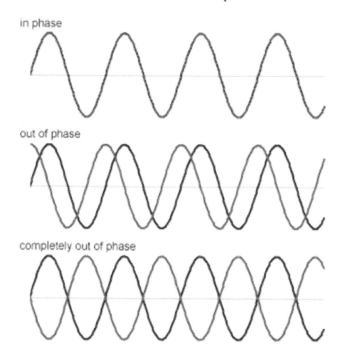

in phase

out of phase

completely out of phase

The phase of two or more waves, with respect to each, is important because it gives rise to interference effects. Interacting waves combine to create a combination wave, the amplitude of which can be determined depending on the interaction between the two-component waves.

The resulting amplitude of the interference depends upon the phase of the waves: *constructive interference* (waves are in-phase) and *destructive interference* (waves are out-of-phase).

In the diagram on the left below, two transverse waves of equal magnitude travel across a rope until they meet. At the moment that the two waves overlap, they are entirely out-of-phase and destructively interfere to produce no wave.

In the diagram on the right below, two waves of equal magnitude overlap and are completely in-phase. This produces constructive interference and results in a wave with double the magnitude of the two incoming waves.

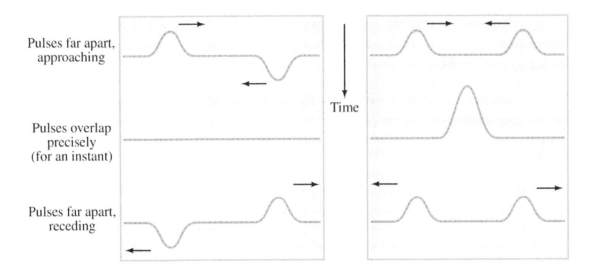

In-phase occurs when the waves are 0 or 2π radians (0 or 360°) apart in their oscillations. The peaks and troughs of one wave are perfectly aligned with the peaks and troughs of another. When two waves are in-phase and interfere, they combine. The amplitude of the resulting wave is the sum of the amplitudes of the interfering waves.

For constructive interference.

$$A_1 + A_2 = A_{net}$$

Out-of-phase occurs when the waves are not are 0 or 2π radians (0 or 360°) apart in their oscillations. All out-of-phase waves produce destructive interference. The resulting amplitude of the combined waves is less than the sum of the interfering waves.

$$0 < A_{net} < A_1 + A_2$$

Completely out-of-phase occurs when the waves are π radians (180°) apart in their oscillations. The crests of one wave are aligned with the troughs of the other wave. When two waves are completely out-of-phase, the amplitude of the resulting wave is the absolute value of the difference between the two separate amplitudes.

If the waves have the same amplitude, then the interfering waves completely destructively interfere, and no wave exists (amplitude = 0).

$$A_{net} = |A_1 - A_2|$$

The figures below show all three examples of wave interference discussed above.

Diagram (a) below demonstrates two in-phase waves and exhibits constructive interference. The resulting amplitude is the sum of the two individual amplitudes.

221

Diagram (b) demonstrates two waves that are entirely out-of-phase and exhibit destructive interference. In this example, the two individual amplitudes are equal, and the result is that no wave is produced.

Diagram (c) illustrates two waves that are not completely out-of-phase. The resulting waves destructively interfere to produce a wave with an amplitude less than that of the wave with a greater amplitude.

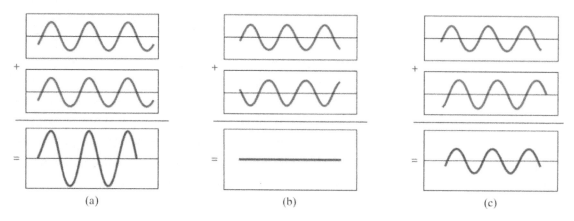

(a)   (b)   (c)

Figure a illustrates constructive interference, figure b illustrates entirely out-of-phase waves, and figure c illustrates waves that are not completely out-of-phase.

Reflection and Transmission

Reflection

Reflection occurs when waves bounce off the surface of an object or medium. All waves exhibit reflection. Examples of reflection are the reflection of light off a mirror to see an image, echoes produced by the reflection of sound waves, and the glare from sunlight reflecting off the water.

These reflections occur when a wave encounters an obstacle or an interface between two different mediums; the wave is forced to change direction.

Reflections of waves depend upon the object or medium the wave reflects off.

Imagine a wave traveling down a string, as in the figure below.

In the diagram on the left, if the wave hits an immobile object, it is reflected, but its reflection is inverted.

In the diagram on the right, the end of the string is connected to a point, so it is free to move. The wave on the string is reflected in the opposite direction, but its reflection is upright instead of inverted.

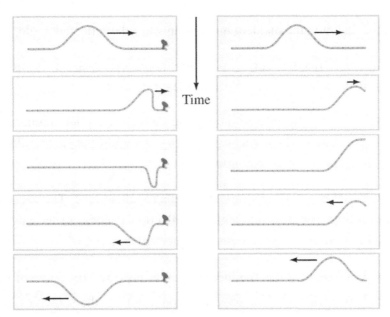

Law of Reflection

The Law of Reflection governs the reflection of light off surfaces and interfaces of two different mediums. The Law of Reflection states that *the angle of incidence of the incoming light ray is equal to the angle of reflection of the outgoing light ray, concerning the normal line of the reflecting surface.*

$$\theta_{incident} = \theta_{reflected}$$

Billiards is an example, in which the balls are waves and the edges of the table surface from which they reflect. A billiards player understands the reflection angle of the ball off an edge equals the incoming angle of the ball, concerning the normal of the surface.

The diagram below represents an incident light ray on a reflecting surface:

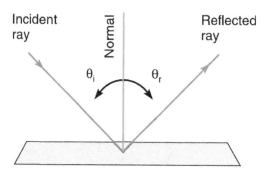

From the diagram, the incident angle is equal to the reflected angle.

The Law of Reflection only applies to smooth surfaces, which are assumed to be ideal reflectors. Plane mirrors are modeled as ideal reflectors.

If the surface is rough and not smooth, the angle of reflection of one wave is not equal to the angle of reflection of the other wave, even if they left the same point with the same angle. Rough surfaces scatter incoming waves.

The figure below is an ideal reflector and a rough surface. The ideal reflector obeys the Law of Reflection, and thus the angle of reflection is equal to the angle of incidence, allowing an observer to see the source of the light (e.g., a mirror).

The rough surface scatters the incoming light rays, and the angle of reflection is not equal to the angle of incidence. The observer would not see the source of light but instead see only the surface of the rough-surfaced reflector.

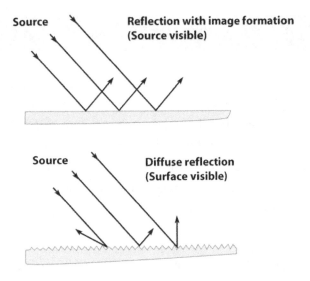

Transmission

Transmission occurs when a wave encounters a different medium. Unlike reflection, the transmission is the phenomenon where some or all the wave energy is transmitted through a different medium. Transmission is usually not total. An incoming wave is usually partially reflected from an interface of two different mediums, while the remaining portion is transmitted through the new medium.

Transmission and reflection of water is an example. When light travels through the atmosphere and encounters the surface of a lake, some of the light is reflected, but some of the light is transmitted through the water. Glare on lakes indicates reflection. However, when a person jumps into the water, it becomes see-through, indicating transmission of light.

From the figure below, consider two strings of different densities that are attached. For a wave traveling down the lower-density section, it both reflects off and transmit some of its energy to the higher-density section.

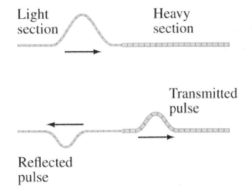

Refraction and Diffraction

Refraction

When a wave encounters a boundary between two different mediums or enters a medium where the wave speed is different, the wave is refracted. Specifically, when waves are transmitted from one medium to another, the different physical properties cause the light to bend and therefore change direction within the new medium. This is *refraction* and is commonly observed in light waves. Refraction is possible with any wave that encounters such a boundary.

For light, the speed that the wave travels is the *light propagation speed*. This speed depends upon the medium through which the light propagates. In a vacuum, light travels at a constant 3×10^8 m/s. In different mediums, such as glass or water, the light propagating speed is less than the speed in a vacuum. Which direction the light bends during refraction depends on the light speed for the different mediums.

Snell's Law expresses the direction the light bends when traveling through mediums with different wave propagation speeds. Snell's Law relates the speed and angle of the incoming wave to that of the refracted wave:

$$n_1 \sin (\theta_1) = n_2 \sin (\theta_2)$$

where n is the index of refraction, and θ is the angle of the wave concerning the normal of the medium interface.

The index of refraction is the relation of the light propagation speed in a medium to that of the speed of light propagation in a vacuum.

n is always greater than 1 because light cannot travel faster than in a vacuum.

$$n = \frac{c}{v}$$

where n is the index of refraction, c is the speed of light in a vacuum, v is the wave propagation speed for that medium.

Indices of refraction (*n*) for some common materials. *c* is the speed of light in a vacuum.

Substance	Index of refraction	Light speed
Air	Approx. 1	~c
Water	1.333	0.75c
Glass	1.5	0.67c
Diamond	2.4	0.42c

The figures below depict the refraction of light from water to air and vice versa.

When a wave moves to a denser medium (i.e., higher refractive index), it bends *toward the normal.*

When a wave moves to a less dense medium (i.e., smaller refractive index), it bends *away from the normal.*

When light refracts from water to air (left diagram), it bends *away* from the normal.

When light refracts from air to water (right diagram), it bends *toward* the normal.

Given the angle of incidence, the angle of refraction is computed by Snell's Law.

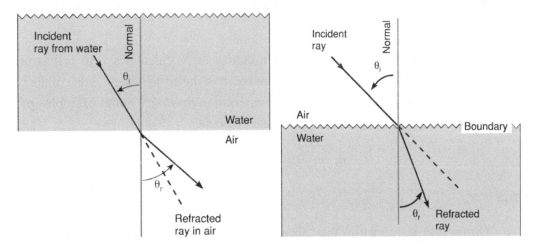

Consider the refraction of white light through a prism. The prism is an exciting example of refraction because it separates the mixture of colors in sunlight (white light) into a rainbow. The observation of a rainbow through a prism is only possible because the index of refraction (*n*) varies with speed (and therefore with wavelength).

Different wavelengths refract at different angles. This difference in refraction produces an assortment of colored light (e.g., a rainbow), where the refraction occurs in suspended water droplets instead of through a prism.

Violet light has the shortest wavelength for visible light and is refracted the most. This refraction gives the sky a blue color.

Red light has the longest wavelength for visible light and is refracted the least. When the angle of refraction is greater, red sunsets are observed in the sky.

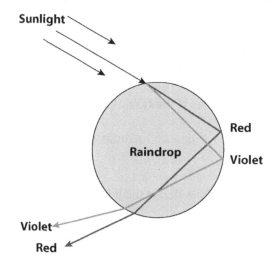

An essential aspect of refraction is the *critical angle*. The critical angle is the greatest angle a wave can make with the boundary between two mediums and not be refracted into the second medium. At the critical angle, a wave is refracted parallel to the surface of the interface boundary.

Angles greater than the critical angle causes the incident wave to reflect off the boundary completely. Thus, at angles greater or equal to the critical angle, none of the waves passes through the boundary; there is "*total internal reflection.*" Some examples of total internal reflection are fiber optics and gemstone brilliance.

$$n_1 \, sin \, (\theta_{critical}) = n_2 \, sin \, (90°)$$

Diffraction

Diffraction is refraction that occurs when a wave encounters an obstacle in the medium within which it is traveling. A wave then spreads out (dissipates), to move around the obstacle, or through an opening (an *aperture*) in the obstacle, producing a "*shadow region.*"

The figures demonstrate diffraction around an obstacle and through an aperture:

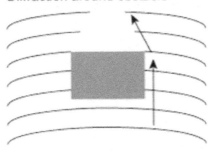

Diffraction around obstacle

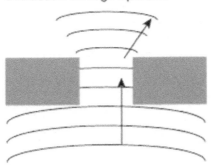

Diffraction through aperture

Some types of waves diffract more efficiently than others. For example, consider a sound wave compared to a light wave.

Music (sound waves) can be heard from around the corner of a building, but the speaker (light waves as the visual image) that it is emitting cannot be seen around the corner. Conversely, shining light through a hole does not produce a dot of light, but a diffused circle of light. The amount of diffraction depends on how the wavelength and the size of the obstacle (or aperture) compare.

If the opening is larger than the wavelength, diffraction is minimal, and for the most part, the wave continues as before.

If the opening is much smaller than the wavelength, the diffraction is noticeable, and the wave bends into a circular orientation.

If the wave encounters an obstacle, its reaction is the opposite. For example, the figures below depict different waves diffracting off different objects.

If the obstacle is much smaller than the wavelength, the wave barely diffracts, as in diagram for water waves passing blades of grass (top left).

If the object is comparable to or larger than the wavelength, diffraction is more significant. This is seen in the diagrams for a stick in the water (top right), short-wavelength waves passing a large log (bottom left), or long-wavelength waves passing the same log (bottom right).

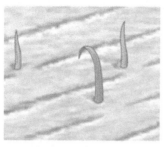

Water waves passing
blades of grass

Stick in water

Short-wavelength
waves passing log

Long-wavelength
waves passing log

Amplitude and Intensity

Like the oscillation that starts the wave, the energy transported by a wave is proportional to the square of the amplitude.

Recall that the amplitude is the maximum height of a crest or the maximum displacement from the equilibrium position.

Amplitude correlates with the energy of the wave.

A greater amplitude means the wave has higher energy.

A lesser amplitude means the wave has lower energy.

Intensity is the energy per area per time, which translates to power (Watts) per area (m^2).

$$I = \frac{P}{A}$$

Thus, amplitude and intensity are correlated similarly to amplitude and energy.

A higher amplitude (and therefore greater energy) leads to a higher intensity.

Chapter Summary

Periodic Motion Summary

- Periodic motion is a motion that repeats

- Amplitude relates the displacement and potential energy

- Frequency gives cycles per second

- The period is the time to complete one cycle

- At the equilibrium position, $PE = 0$, KE = maximum

- At the maximum displacement (amplitude) $x = A$, PE = maximum, $KE = 0$

- At any point, $PE + KE$ = maximum PE = maximum KE = constant

- From the velocity at the equilibrium position, the amplitude is calculated by setting the maximum KE = maximum PE

- From the amplitude, the velocity at the equilibrium position is calculated by setting the maximum PE = maximum KE

Wave Characteristics Summary

- The speed of a wave depends on the medium through which it travels.

  Wave speed is determined by $v = f\lambda$, where f is the frequency (f = # cycles/time), and λ is the wavelength.

  $f = 1/T$, the speed $v = \lambda/T$.

- Changing the period, frequency, or wavelength of a wave affects the other two quantities. This change does not affect the speed of the wave if it remains in the same medium.

- Superimposition is when waves interact constructively or destructively (e.g., interference creates larger or smaller amplitudes).

- Waves reflect and transmit when traveling through different mediums.

- Waves transmitted through two different mediums with different indices of refraction (n) bend. Snell's Law: $n_1 \sin(\theta_1) = n_2 \sin(\theta_2)$.

- Angles equal to or greater than the critical angle exhibit total internal reflection: $n_1 \sin (\theta_{critical}) = n_2 \sin (90°)$.

- Diffraction occurs for all waves around objects or through apertures.

- Standing waves on a string fixed at both ends form with wavelengths of

$$\lambda_n = 2L/n$$

Standing waves on a string fixed at both ends form with frequencies of

$$f_n = nv/2L$$

where L is the length of the string, v is the speed of the wave, and n is a whole positive number.

Practice Questions

1. Considering a vibrating mass on a spring, what effect on the system's mechanical energy is caused by doubling of the amplitude only?

A. Increases by a factor of two   **C.** Increases by a factor of three

B. Increases by a factor of four   **D.** Produces no change

2. Find the wavelength of a train whistle that is heard by a fixed observer as the train moves toward him with a velocity of 50 m/s. The wind blows at 5 m/s from the observer to the train. The whistle has a natural frequency of 500 Hz. (Use v of sound = 340 m/s)

A. 0.75 m   **B.** 0.43 m   **C.** 0.58 m   **D.** 7.5 m

3. The efficient transfer of energy taking place at a natural frequency occurs in a phenomenon called:

A. reverberation   **B.** the Doppler effect   **C.** beats   **D.** resonance

4. A simple pendulum and a mass oscillating on an ideal spring both have period T in an elevator at rest. If the elevator now accelerates downward uniformly at 2 m/s², what is true about the periods of these two systems?

A. The period of the pendulum increases, but the period of the spring remains the same

B. The period of the pendulum increases and the period of the spring decreases

C. The period of the pendulum decreases, but the period of the spring remains the same

D. The periods of the pendulum and of the spring both increase

5. All of the following is true of a pendulum that has swung to the top of its arc and has not yet reversed its direction, EXCEPT:

A. The PE of the pendulum is at a maximum

B. The displacement of the pendulum from its equilibrium position is at a maximum

C. The KE of the pendulum equals zero

D. The acceleration of the pendulum equals zero

6. The explanation for refraction must involve a change in:

    I. frequency   II. speed   III. wavelength

A. I only   **B.** II only   **C.** III only   **D.** I and II only

7. Consider the wave shown in the figure. The amplitude is:

A. 1 m   **C.** 4 m

B. 2 m   **D.** 8 m

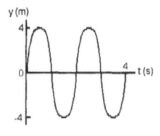

8. Increasing the mass *m* of a mass-and-spring system causes what kind of change on the resonant frequency *f* of the system?

   A. The *f* decreases
   B. There is no change in the *f*
   C. The *f* decreases only if the ratio k / m is < 1
   D. The *f* increases

9. A simple pendulum that has a bob of mass *M* has a period T. What is the effect on the period if *M* is doubled while all other factors remain unchanged?

   A. T/2   **B.** $T/\sqrt{2}$ **C.** 2T   **D.** T

10. A skipper on a boat notices wave crests passing the anchor chain every 5 s. The skipper estimates that the distance between crests is 15 m. What is the speed of the water waves?

   A. 3 m/s   **B.** 5 m/s   **C.** 12 m/s   **D.** 9 m/s

11. For an object undergoing simple harmonic motion, the:

   A. maximum potential energy is larger than the maximum kinetic energy
   B. acceleration is greatest when the displacement is greatest
   C. displacement is greatest when the speed is greatest
   D. acceleration is greatest when the speed is greatest

12. As the frequency of a wave increases, which of the following must decrease?

   A. The speed of the wave   **C.** The amplitude of the wave
   B. The velocity of the wave   **D.** The period of the wave

13. What is the period for a weight on the end of a spring that bobs up and down one complete cycle every 2 s?

   A. 0.5 s   **B.** 1 s   **C.** 2 s   **D.** 3 s

14. After rain, one sometimes sees brightly colored oil slicks on the road. These are due to:

   A. selective absorption of different λ by oil   **C.** polarization effects
   B. diffraction effects   **D.** interference effects

15. If two traveling waves with amplitudes of 3 cm and 8 cm interfere, which of the following best describes the possible amplitudes of the resultant wave?

   A. Between 5 and 11 cm   **C.** Between 3 and 5 cm
   B. Between 3 and 8 cm   **D.** Between 8 and 11 cm

Solutions

1. B is correct.

$$PE = \frac{1}{2}kx^2$$

Doubling the amplitude x increases PE by a factor of 4.

2. C is correct.

Because wind is blowing in the reference frame of both the train and the observer, it does not need to be taken into account.

$$f_{observed} = [v_{sound} / (v_{sound} - v_{source})] \times f_{source}$$

$$f_{observed} = [340 \text{ m/s} / (340 \text{ m/s} - 50 \text{ m/s})] \cdot 500 \text{ Hz}$$

$$f_{observed} = 586 \text{ Hz}$$

$$\lambda = v / f$$

$$\lambda = (340 \text{ m/s}) / 586 \text{ Hz}$$

$$\lambda = 0.58 \text{ m}$$

3. D is correct.

Resonance is the phenomenon where one system transfers its energy to another at that system's resonant frequency (natural frequency). It is a forced vibration that produces the highest amplitude response for a given force amplitude.

4. A is correct.

Period of a pendulum:

$$T_P = 2\pi\sqrt{(L / g)}$$

Period of a spring:

$$T_S = 2\pi\sqrt{(m / k)}$$

The period of a spring does not depend on gravity and is unaffected.

5. D is correct.

At the top of its arc, the pendulum comes to rest momentarily; the *KE* and the velocity equal zero.

Since its height above the bottom of its arc is at a maximum at this point, its (angular) displacement from the vertical equilibrium position is at a maximum also.

The pendulum constantly experiences the forces of gravity and tension and is therefore continuously accelerating.

6. B is correct.

Refraction is the bending of a wave when it enters a medium where its speed is different. Refraction occurs in sound waves and light waves.

7. C is correct.

The amplitude of a wave is the magnitude of its oscillation from its equilibrium point.

8. A is correct.

$$f = (1/2\pi) \times \sqrt{(k/m)}$$

An increase in m causes a decrease in f.

9. D is correct.

$$T = 2\pi[\sqrt{(L / g)}]$$

No effect on the period because T is independent of mass.

10. A is correct.

speed = wavelength × frequency

period = 1 / frequency

$v = \lambda f$

$v = \lambda / T$

$v = 15 \text{ m} / 5 \text{ s}$

$v = 3 \text{ m/s}$

11. B is correct.

When the displacement is greatest, the force on the object is greatest. When force is maximized, then acceleration is maximum.

12. D is correct.

$$\lambda = vf$$

$$f = v / \lambda$$

$$f = 1 / T$$

The period is the reciprocal of the frequency.

If f increases, then T decreases.

13. C is correct.

The definition of the period is the time required to complete one cycle.

Period = time / # cycles

$T = 2$ s / 1 cycle

$T = 2$ s

14. D is correct.

When it rains the brightly colored oil slicks on the road are due to thin film interference effects.

This is when light reflects from the upper and lower boundaries of the oil layer and form a new wave due to interference effects. These new waves are perceived as different colors.

15. A is correct.

Constructive interference: the maximal magnitude of the amplitude of the resultant wave is the sum of the individual amplitudes:

3 cm + 8 cm = 11 cm

Destructive interference: the minimal magnitude of the amplitude of the resultant wave is the difference between the individual amplitudes:

8 cm – 3 cm = 5 cm

The magnitude of the amplitude of the resultant wave is between 5 and 11 cm.

CHAPTER 8

Sound

- **Production of Sound**

- **Relative Speed of Sound in Solids, Liquids, and Gases**

- **Intensity of Sound**

- **Attenuation: Damping**

- **Doppler Effect**

- **Pitch**

- **Ultrasound**

- **Resonance in Pipes and Strings**

- **Beats**

- **Shock Waves**

Production of Sound

Sound is a wave that is experienced in everyday life. Everything that is being heard is the result of the sound wave. This includes the noise of traffic, the wind through trees, and a jet flying by overhead. However, many sounds are not audible.

Like other waves, the sound is produced by vibrations in a medium.

Specifically, the sound is a mechanical longitudinal wave that travels through a medium as vibrations.

Vibrations produce pressure waves, which oscillate parallel to the direction of propagation.

If the vibrations have a frequency too low to hear, they are *infrasound*.

Comparatively, if the frequency is too high to hear, they are *ultrasound*.

Musical instruments produce sounds through vibrations in various ways— strings, membranes, metal or wood shapes, or air columns. Vibrations may be started by plucking, striking, bowing, or blowing. They are transmitted to the air and then to the perceivers' ears.

For example, a drum produces sound by vibrating a thin membrane when struck. The vibrating membrane creates a longitudinal wave through the air to a person's ears, which results in the perception of sound.

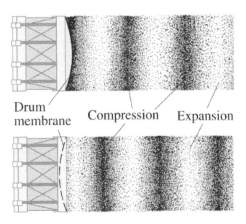

Longitudinal waves produced by the beating of a drum

The strings on a guitar can be effectively shortened by fingering, which raises the fundamental pitch.

The pitch of a string at a given length can be altered by using a different density string.

The strings on stringed instruments produce a fundamental tone whose wavelength is twice the length of the string. There are also various harmonics present.

A piano uses both methods (string length and string density) to cover its more than seven-octave range—the lower notes are produced by strings that are much longer and much thicker than the strings that produce the higher notes.

Wind instruments create sound through standing waves in a tube, and they have a vibrating column of air when played.

During a storm, lightning is seen before thunder is heard, even though they occur at the same time because the speed of light (300,000,000 m/s or 3.0×10^8 m/s) is much faster than the speed of sound (300 m/s or 3.0×10^2 m/s).

Relative Speed of Sound in Solids, Liquids, and Gases

Like all waves, sound waves do not transport matter. Even though a sound wave travels, the medium through which the sound wave propagates does not travel. The particles within the medium vibrate around their initial position (horizontally because the wave is longitudinal) and return to their initial position after the wave has propagated. It is important to remember that waves carry energy, not matter.

Two values affect the speed of sound: the *elasticity* and *density* of the medium.

Sound travels through a medium by transferring energy from one particle to the other. A rigid medium, or one with little elasticity, will have strong attractions between its molecules. Therefore, the molecules can vibrate at a much higher speed and transfer energy faster than a more elastic material.

The speed of sound is faster through solids than through liquids, and faster through liquids than through gases. Sound cannot travel in a vacuum; sound requires a medium, and in a vacuum, there are no particles to vibrate and transmit the wave.

As previously stated, the speed of sound depends upon the density and elasticity of the medium. The equation gives the speed of sound is:

$$v = \sqrt{\frac{\beta}{\rho}}$$

Where β is the bulk modulus, which indicates how the medium responds to compression (how elastic or inelastic it is), and ρ is the density of the medium.

Generally, a substance with a large density is made of larger molecules.

Larger molecules mean more mass, thus requiring more kinetic energy to vibrate them. Since waves are made of kinetic energy, they travel slower through a medium with larger molecules and a higher mass and faster through a medium with smaller molecules and a lower mass.

If the medium is a gas, the temperature can also change the speed of sound. Say two equally sized jars contain the same gas but with different densities. Since there is so much space between particles in a gas, the ideal gas laws play a much larger role than individual particle characteristics, such as mass.

A higher density at the same volume means an increase in temperature.

An increase in temperature means the addition of heat energy, or kinetic energy, to the system.

More kinetic energy means the gas molecules bounce around faster than at cooler temperatures, and transfer energy at a quicker rate.

Sound waves travel faster through the warmer medium.

$$v = \sqrt{\frac{\gamma RT}{M}}$$

where γ is the adiabatic constant of the gas, R is the ideal gas constant (8.314 J/mol K), T is the temperature in Kelvin (K), and M is the molecular mass of the gas (kg/mol).

Some examples of speed comparison through different media:

- Sound will travel faster through wood than it will through the air. Wood is inelastic, whereas air is exceptionally compressible.

- Sound travels faster through American Redwood, which has a density of 28 lb/ft^3, than through African Teak, which has a density of about 45 lb/ft^3.

    Their elasticities are similar, which is why density matters.

- Even though gases are less dense than solids, sound travels slower in a gas (e.g., helium) because it is too compressible.

- Sound travels much faster over a hot desert than it does over a cold tundra; the temperature is higher. Therefore, the speed of sound is higher is the hot desert.

At room temperature and normal atmospheric pressure, the speed of sound is approximately 343 m/s.

Below is a table of sound speed through various mediums, at constant temperature and pressure, unless otherwise noted:

Speed of Sound in Various Materials (20 °C and 1 atm)

Material	Speed (m/s)
Air	343
Air (0 °C)	331
Helium	1,005
Hydrogen	1,300
Water	1,440
Seawater	1,560
Concrete	≈3,000
Hardwood	≈4,000
Glass	≈4,500
Iron and steel	≈5,000
Aluminum	≈5,100

Intensity of Sound

The *intensity* of a wave is equal to the energy transported per unit time across a unit area. The human ear detects sounds with intensity between 10^{-12} W/m^2 and 1 W/m^2.

However, perceived loudness is not proportional to the intensity; the two are related, though, as in the table below.

The Intensity of Sample Sounds

Source of the Sound	Sound Level (dB)	Intensity (W/m^2)
Jet plane at 30m	140	100
Threshold of pain	120	1
Siren at 30m	100	1×10^{-2}
Heavy street traffic	80	1×10^{-4}
Noisy restaurant	70	1×10^{-5}
Talk, at 50cm	65	3×10^{-6}
Quiet radio	40	1×10^{-8}
Whisper	30	1×10^{-9}
Rustle of leaves	10	1×10^{-11}
Threshold of hearing	0	1×10^{-12}

The loudness of a sound is much more closely related to the logarithm of the intensity. Sound level is measured in decibels (dB) and is defined as:

$$\beta = 10 log \left(\frac{I}{I_0}\right)$$

where β is the sound level in decibels (dB), and I is the intensity in power per area, or energy per unit time per unit area, given in Watts per meters squared (W/m^2).

I_0 is the threshold of hearing at 10^{-12} W/m^2.

The intensity follows an inverse square law of $I \propto 1 / r^2$, where r is the distance between the source and detector (observer).

In conjunction with the above equation, as the distance increases, the decibels decrease.

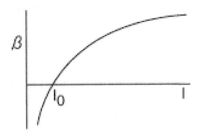

Sound vs. intensity graph where horizontal line signifies audible sounds

Intensity	Decibels
I_0	0
$10\ I_0$	10
$100\ I_0$	20
$1,000\ I_0$	30

An increase in sound level of 3 dB, which is a doubling in intensity, is a small change in loudness. In a large area (substantial value of r), this change in intensity is insignificant.

However, in a smaller space (smaller value of r), any change in intensity will be extremely noticeable.

The decibel system is based on human perception.

The decibel value for sound with an intensity of I_0 is zero. Below this intensity, the sound is not audible.

As intensity increases, the perception of loudness increases, but to a much lesser degree.

Attenuation: Damping

Sound attenuation is the gradual loss of intensity as sound travels through a medium, and is the greatest for soft, elastic, viscous, or less dense material.

Vibration causes the sound, and the characteristics of this vibration determine how the sound wave acts as it travels through the medium. A wave can oscillate in free harmonic motion, in which the amplitude remains unchanged throughout the vibration.

A wave can also exhibit damped harmonic motion, in which a frictional or dragging force inhibits the vibrations oscillation.

If the damping is small, it can be treated as an "envelope" that modifies the undamped oscillation:

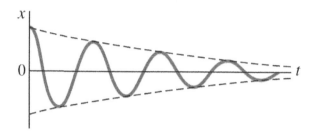

However, if the damping is significant, it no longer resembles a general oscillation (Simple Harmonic Motion, or SHM) wave:

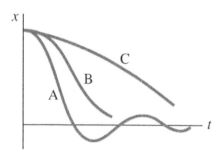

There are a few representative shapes on a graph distance vs. time graph when there is a large damping force acting on the system.

Underdamping (labeled as line A in the graph above) is when there are a few small oscillations before the oscillator comes to rest.

Critical damping (labeled B in the graph above) is the fastest way to get to equilibrium.

Over-damping (labeled C in the graph above) occurs when the system is slowed so much that it takes a long time to get to equilibrium.

There are systems where damping is unwanted, such as clocks and watches.

Moreover, there are systems in which dampening is desirable, and often need to be as close to critical damping as possible.

A system for which dampening is desirable includes earthquake protection for buildings and automobile shock absorbers (pictured below).

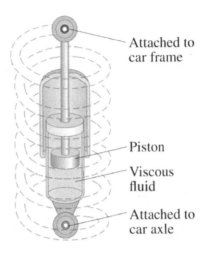

Automobile shocks dampen the vibrations from the bumps on the road surface

Doppler Effect

The Doppler shift describes the relationship between frequency detected and frequency emitted by a source when a source and detector are in relative motion.

$$f_d = f_e[(v_s \pm v_d) / (v_s \mp v_e)]$$

where f_d is the frequency detected by the observer, f_e is the frequency emitted by the source v_d is the velocity of the detector, v_e is the velocity of the source, and v_s is the speed of the wave.

When the source and a detector are moving with respect to each other, the f of the detected wave is shifted from the f of the emitted wave (Doppler shift).

The f_d increases when the source and detector are approaching.

The f_d decreases when the source and detector are receding.

When calculating the Doppler shift between a source and detector, the individual velocities are with respect to each other. If the source and detector are moving away at equal speeds, this is equivalent to the source moving at double its speed away from a stationary detector. This allows one of the velocities to be set to zero in the calculation.

The Doppler Effect states that *the frequency of the sounds varies if there is relative motion between the source of the sound and the observer of the sound.*

If the relative motion between the sound source and observer is towards, the frequency is perceived as higher.

If the relative motion between the sound source and observer is away, the frequency is perceived as lower. Therefore, oncoming sirens seem to sound louder than when they have already passed.

The equation expresses this:

$$f' = \frac{v \pm v_o}{v \mp v_s} \times f$$

where f' is the perceived frequency, f is the wave frequency, v_o is the velocity of the observer or detector, v_s is the velocity of the source, and v is a reference value equal to the velocity of sound through the given medium.

First, decide whether to add or subtract the velocities from the speed of sound through the medium. Think about the problem logically.

If the observer is walking away from the source, the wavelength becomes longer, and the perceived pitch decreases. The velocity of the observer must be subtracted in the numerator.

If the source is getting closer to the observer, the wavelengths are getting shorter, and the perceived frequency increases. The denominator must get smaller, and the velocity of the source must be subtracted in the denominator.

Use care when analyzing the movement of the source and remember how fractions react as their denominator is either increased or decreased.

Situations where the observed frequency is higher than the actual:

- Source moving toward stationary observer: $f' = \dfrac{v}{v - v_s} \times f$

- Observer moving toward stationary source: $f' = \dfrac{v + v_o}{v} \times f$

- Source and observer both moving toward each other: $f' = \dfrac{v + v_o}{v - v_s} \times f$

Situations where the observed frequency is lower than the actual:

- Source moving away from the stationary observer: $f' = \dfrac{v}{v + v_s} \times f$

- Observer moving away from the stationary source: $f' = \dfrac{v - v_o}{v} \times f$

- Source and observer both moving away from each other: $f' = \dfrac{v - v_o}{v + v_s} \times f$

Situations where the observed frequency could be higher or lower than the actual:

- Source is moving toward the observer; the observer is moving away from the source:

$$f' = \frac{v - v_o}{v - v_s} \times f$$

- Source is moving away from the observer; the observer is moving toward the source:

$$f' = \frac{v + v_o}{v + v_s} \times f$$

When the source and observer are moving at the same speed, and in the same direction, there is no frequency shift. Their relative motion is zero. This instance shows that reference frames are important.

When the source of waves and a detector are moving with respect to each other, the frequency of the detected wave shifts from the frequency of the emitted wave (*Doppler shift*).

The detected frequency increases when the source and detector are approaching.

The detected frequency decreases when the source and detector are receding.

The f_{det} is the detected frequency, v_s is the speed of the wave in the medium, v_{det} is the speed of the detector, v_{em} is the speed of the emitter, and f_{em} is the emitted frequency.

Choose the sign in the numerator to reflect the direction the detector is moving (positive if approaching, negative if receding).

Choose the sign in the denominator to reflect the direction the source is moving (negative if approaching, positive if receding).

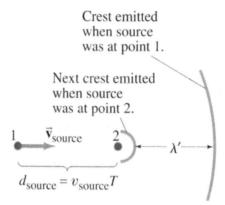

The change in the wavelength is given by:

$$\lambda' = d - d_{source}$$
$$\lambda' = \lambda - v_{source}$$
$$\lambda' = \lambda - v_{source} \times \frac{\lambda}{v_{snd}}$$
$$\lambda' = \lambda(1 - \frac{v_{source}}{v_{snd}})$$

If the observer is moving concerning the source, the wavelength remains the same, but the wave speed is different for the observer:

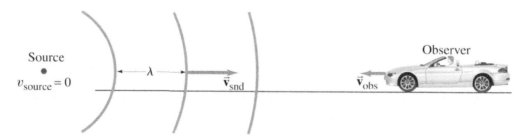

Pitch

Pitch is the human perception of the frequency of sound.

High pitch results from high vibrations and shorter wavelengths; a higher frequency.

Low pitch results from low vibrations and longer wavelength; a lower frequency.

Humans hear sound waves with frequencies between 20-20,000 Hz. The upper limit of this range decreases with age.

Waves with frequencies above 20,000 Hz are *ultrasonic*.

Waves with frequencies below 20 Hz are *infrasonic*.

Ultrasound

The sound has three fundamental properties: reflection, refraction, and diffraction.

Ultrasound imaging uses the reflective property of sound. A source emits a sound wave with an ultrasonic frequency, which reflects off a surface (e.g., internal organ) and travels back into the detector to form an image.

Ultrasound is sound with frequencies of 20,000 Hz or higher.

Ultrasound is used for medical imaging.

Repeated traces are made as the transducer is moved, and a complete picture is built.

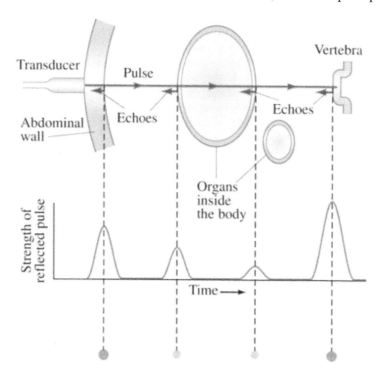

Sonar is used to locate objects underwater by measuring the time it takes a sound pulse to reflect to the receiver.

Sonar techniques are used to learn about the internal structure of the Earth.

Sonar usually uses ultrasound waves, as the shorter wavelengths are less likely to be diffracted by obstacles.

Resonance in Pipes and Strings

In standing wave patterns, there are points along the medium that appear to be still.

These still points are *nodes* and are described as points of no displacement.

There are other points along the medium that undergo the maximum displacement during each vibrational cycle. These maximum displacement points are *antinodes,* and they are opposite of nodes.

A standing wave pattern consists of an alternating pattern of nodes and antinodes.

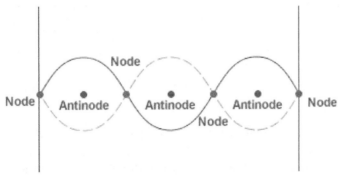

If a tube is open at both ends, like most wind instruments, and a wave of sound passes through it, the characteristics of the wave can be analyzed if the amount of nodes or antinodes the wave has can be determined.

In a tube, an open-end always has a displacement antinode, and a closed-end in the tube always has a displacement node. The pressure in the air varies in the same way air displacement does but shifted.

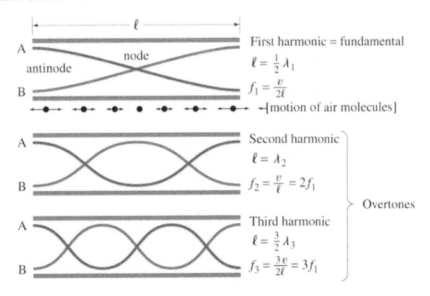

Tube open at both ends illustrating the displacement of air

Everywhere there is a *displacement antinode*; there is a *pressure node*. Everywhere there is a *displacement node*; there is a *pressure antinode*.

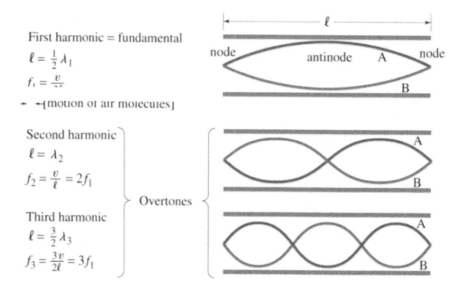

First harmonic = fundamental

$\ell = \frac{1}{2}\lambda_1$

$f_1 = \frac{v}{\lambda_1}$

[motion of air molecules]

Second harmonic

$\ell = \lambda_2$

$f_2 = \frac{v}{\ell} = 2f_1$

Third harmonic

$\ell = \frac{3}{2}\lambda_3$

$f_3 = \frac{3v}{2\ell} = 3f_1$

Overtones

Tube open at both ends illustrating the pressure variation of air

A tube closed at one end, like some organ pipes, has a displacement node and a pressure antinode at the closed end. The number of each node and antinode contained within the pipe depends on the harmonic level (e.g., first harmonic, second harmonic, etc.).

The *fundamental frequency*, also the fundamental, is the first harmonic ($n = 1$).

The next frequency is the second harmonic ($n = 2$).

This continues to the nth harmonic.

Higher harmonics in pipes, either open or closed, have shorter wavelengths and higher frequencies, but the same wave speed.

For the nth harmonic on a string, an n number of half wavelengths fit precisely along the length of the string.

The frequency of a wave can be obtained by:

$$f = \frac{v}{\lambda}$$

If a pipe is open at both ends, or if a string is unfixed at both ends, its length is:

$$L = \frac{n}{2} \times \lambda$$

If a pipe has one closed-end, or if a string has one fixed end, its length is:

$$L = \frac{2n - 1}{4\lambda}$$

For an open-ended tube, resonance occurs when:

$$f_n = n \times \frac{v}{2L}$$ where n can be any integer

Resonance occurs when an outside force acts at a frequency close to the standard frequency of some component of the system. This depends on whether the tube is closed on one end or open at both ends.

For a tube with one closed end, resonance occurs when:

$$f_n = n \frac{v}{4L}$$ and $\lambda = \frac{4L}{n}$ where n must be an *odd* integer

An instrument does not play just one sound. They are known for their overtones, which combine with other instruments' overtones to create music, as opposed to merely noise. A trumpet sounds different from a flute, and the reason is overtones—which ones are present and how strong they are.

The plots below show the frequency spectra for a clarinet, a piano, and a violin. The differences in overtone strength are apparent.

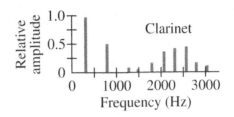
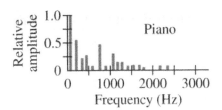

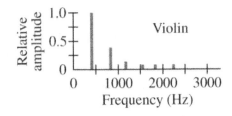

Beats

Sound waves interfere in the same way that other waves do, causing *beats*.

Beats are the slow "envelope" around two waves that are relatively close in frequency, as the two speakers exhibit below.

The region of overlapping sound waves is what produces a beat.

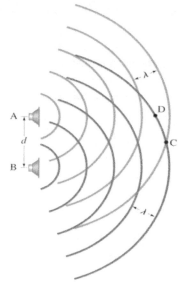

The two frequencies are graphed on a linear axis (top graph below). Although they start in the same place, one frequency is higher than the other.

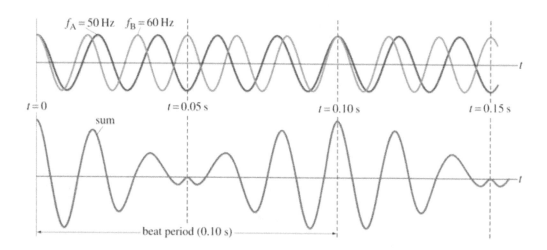

The combination, or interference, of these two results in the wave shown above in the lower graph. This is an out-of-phase interference, meaning the amplitude of this combined wave is equal to the addition of the two individual amplitudes of the two waves shown in the top graph shown above.

A *beat period* is the length of time it takes for the beat to start all over again.

The wave in the lower graph does not oscillate with a constant amplitude as the graph above; it repeats if the component waves stay constant.

The beat frequency equation is:

$$f_{beat} = |f_1 - f_2|$$

where f_1 and f_2 are the frequencies of the interfering waves.

If two notes are played at the same time that are close in pitch but not the same, a pulse or "wobble" is heard. This is the beat, and its frequency is f_{beat}.

Musicians are tuning their instruments by listening for this beat. They try to eliminate it, thereby matching the frequency of their instrument with the frequency of the reference pitch.

Shock Waves

If a source is moving faster than the speed of the waves that it is producing in a given medium, then a *shock wave* is formed. The diagram shows an object with a velocity of zero (top left), a velocity less than the speed of sound (top right), a velocity equal to the speed of sound (bottom left), and velocity higher than the speed of sound (bottom right). This is the only situation in which a shock wave occurs. The object in the bottom left creates a shock wave front, but the waves do not pile up as in the bottom right.

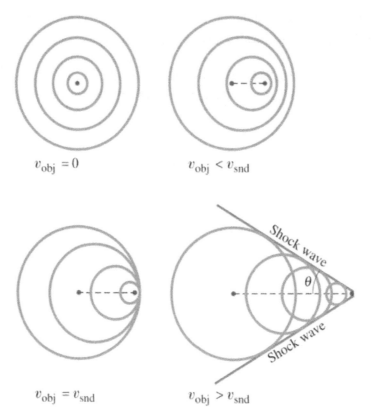

$$v_{obj} = 0 \qquad\qquad v_{obj} < v_{snd}$$

$$v_{obj} = v_{snd} \qquad\qquad v_{obj} > v_{snd}$$

Shock waves are analogous to the bow waves produced by a boat going faster than the wave speed of the water. An airplane exceeding the speed of sound in air produces two sonic booms, one from the nose and one from the tail of the plane.

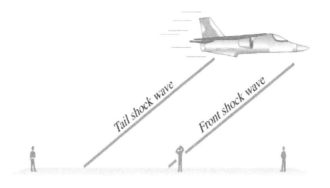

Chapter Summary

- Sound is a mechanical longitudinal wave that travels through a medium as vibrations. The vibrations produce pressure waves, which oscillate parallel to the direction of propagation. Two essential values affect the speed of sound: the elasticity and the density of the medium.

$$v = \sqrt{\frac{\beta}{\rho}}$$

  where β is the bulk modulus, which indicates how the medium responds to compression (how elastic or inelastic it is), and ρ is the density of the medium.

- *Intensity* of a wave is equal to the energy transported per unit time per unit area.

- The loudness of a sound is much more closely related to the logarithm of the intensity. Sound level is measured in decibels (dB) and is defined as:

$$\beta = 10 log\left(\frac{I}{I_0}\right)$$

  where β is the sound level in decibels (dB), and I is the intensity in power per area, or energy per unit time per unit area, given in Watts per meters squared (W/m^2).

- The Doppler shift describes the relationship between the frequency detected and the frequency emitted by the source when the source and detector are in relative motion.

$$f_d = f_c[(v_s \pm v_d) / (v_s \mp v_c)]$$

  where f_d is the frequency detected by the observer, f_c is the frequency emitted by the source v_d is the velocity of the detector, v_c is the velocity of the source, and v_s is the speed of the wave.

- In standing wave patterns, there are points along the medium that appear still. These no displacement points are *nodes*. Other points along the medium undergo a maximum displacement during each vibrational cycle. The maximum displacement points are *antinodes*.

- The frequency of a wave can be obtained by:

$$f = \frac{v}{\lambda}$$

- For a pipe that is open at both ends or a string that is unfixed at both ends, the length can be found by:

$$L = \frac{n}{2} \times \lambda$$

- If a pipe has one closed-end, or if a string has one fixed end, its length can be found by:

$$L = \frac{2n - 1}{4\lambda}$$

- For an open-ended tube, resonance occurs when:

$$f_n = n \times \frac{v}{2L} \qquad \text{where n can be any integer}$$

- Sound waves interfere in the same way that other waves do, causing a phenomenon of *beats*. The beat frequency is given by the equation:

$$f_{beat} = |f_1 - f_2|$$

where f_1 and f_2 are the frequencies of the interfering waves.

- If a source is moving faster than the speed of the waves that it is producing in a given medium, then a *shock wave* is formed.

Practice Questions

1. Two tuning forks have frequencies of 460 Hz and 524 Hz. What is the beat frequency if both are sounding simultaneously and resonating?

    A. 52 Hz   **B.** 64 Hz   **C.** 396 Hz   **D.** 524 Hz

2. Which of the of the following is true of the properties of a light wave as it moves from a medium of the lower refractive index to a medium of the higher refractive index?

    A. Speed decreases   **C.** Frequency decreases

    B. Speed increases   **D.** Frequency increases

3. Resonance can be looked at as forced vibration with the:

    A. matching of constructive and destructive interference

    B. matching of wave amplitudes

    C. maximum amount of energy input

    D. least amount of energy input

4. The Doppler effect occurs when a source of sound moves:

        I. toward the observer

        II. away from the observer

        III. with the observer

    A. I only   **B.** II only   **C.** I and III only   **D.** I and II only

5. Which of the following increases when a sound becomes louder?

    A. Amplitude   **B.** Period   **C.** Frequency   **D.** Wavelength

6. Sound intensity is defined as the:

    A. sound power per unit volume   **C.** sound energy passing through a unit of area

    B. sound power per unit time   **D.** sound energy passing an area per unit time

7. A violin with string length 36 cm and string density 3.8 g/cm resonates with the first overtone of an organ pipe with one end closed. The pipe length is 3 m. What is the tension in the string so that the sound wave resonates at its fundamental frequency? (Use the speed of sound $v = 340$ m/s)

    A. 1,390 N   **B.** 1,946 N   **C.** 1,414 N   **D.** 987 N

8. A speaker is producing a total of 10 W of sound, and Rahul hears the music at 20 dB. His roommate turns up the power to 100 W. What level of sound does Rahul now hear?

    A. 15 dB   **B.** 30 dB   **C.** 40 dB   **D.** 100 dB

9. Seven seconds after a flash of lightning, thunder shakes a house. Approximately how far was the lightning strike from the house? (Use the speed of sound $v = 340$ m/s)

    A. Requires more information   **C.** About one kilometer away
    B. About five kilometers away   **D.** About two kilometers away

10. The natural frequencies for a stretched string of length L and wave speed v are $nv / (2L)$, where n equals:

    A. 0, 1, 3, 5, ...   **B.** 1, 2, 3, 4, ...   **C.** 2, 4, 6, 8, ...   **D.** 0, 1, 2, 3, ...

11. What is the source of all electromagnetic waves?

    A. electric fields   **C.** heat
    B. vibrating charges   **D.** magnetic fields

12. When a radio is tuned to a certain station, the frequency of the internal electrical circuit is matched to the frequency of that radio station. In tuning the radio, what is being affected?

    A. Beats   **B.** Reverberation   **C.** Forced vibrations   **D.** Resonance

13. A standing wave is oscillating at 670 Hz on a string, as shown in the figure. What is the wave speed?

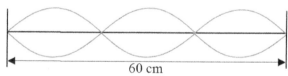

60 cm

    A. 212 m/s   **B.** 178 m/s   **C.** 268 m/s   **D.** 404 m/s

14. A 50 m/s train is moving directly toward Carlos, who is standing near the tracks. The train is emitting a whistling sound at 415 Hz. What frequency does Carlos hear? (Use speed of sound $v = 340$ m/s)

    A. 290 Hz   **B.** 476 Hz   **C.** 481 Hz   **D.** 487 Hz

15. Two tuning forks are struck simultaneously, and beats are heard every 500 ms. What is the frequency of the sound wave produced by one tuning fork, if the other produces a sound wave of 490 Hz frequency?

    A. 490 Hz   **B.** 498 Hz   **C.** 492 Hz   **D.** 506 Hz

Solutions

1. B is correct.

Beat frequency equation:

$$f_{beat} = |f_2 - f_1|$$

$$f_{beat} = |524 \text{ Hz} - 460 \text{ Hz}|$$

$$f_{beat} = 64 \text{ Hz}$$

2. A is correct.

The frequency of a wave does not change when it enters a new medium.

$$v = (1 / n)c$$

where c = speed of light in a vacuum and n = refractive index.

The speed v decreases when light enters a medium with a higher refractive index.

3. D is correct.

Resonance is the phenomenon where one system transfers its energy to another at that system's resonant frequency (natural frequency). It is forced vibrations with the least energy input.

4. D is correct.

The Doppler effect is the observed change in frequency when a sound source is in motion relative to an observer (away or towards). If the sound source moves with the observer, then there is no relative motion between the two and the Doppler effect does not occur.

5. A is correct.

When a sound becomes louder, the energy of the sound wave becomes higher.

Amplitude is directly related to the energy of the sound wave:

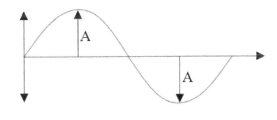

more energy = higher amplitude

less energy = lower amplitude

6. D is correct.

Intensity is the power per unit area:

$$I = W/m^2$$

Loudness is a subjective measurement of the strength of the ear's perception to sound.

7. C is correct.

An overtone is any frequency higher than the fundamental.

In a stopped pipe (i.e., open at one end and closed at the other):

Harmonic #	Tone
1	fundamental tone
3	1st overtone
5	2nd overtone
7	3rd overtone

The first overtone is the 3rd harmonic.

Find wavelength:

$$\lambda_n = (4L / n), \text{ for stopped pipe}$$

$$\text{where n} = 1, 3, 5, 7…$$

$$\lambda_3 = [(4)\cdot(3 \text{ m}) / 3)]$$

$$\lambda_3 = 4 \text{ m}$$

Find frequency:

$$f = v / \lambda$$

$$f = (340 \text{ m/s}) / (4 \text{ m})$$

$$f = 85 \text{ Hz}$$

Find velocity of a standing wave on the violin:

$$f = v / 2L$$

$$v = (2L)\cdot(f)$$

$$v = (2)\cdot(0.36 \text{ m})\cdot(85 \text{ Hz})$$

$$v = 61 \text{ m/s}$$

Convert linear density to kg/m:

$$\mu = (3.8 \text{ g/cm})\cdot(1 \text{ kg/10}^3 \text{ g})\cdot(100 \text{ cm} / 1 \text{ m})$$

$$\mu = 0.38 \text{ kg/m}$$

Find tension:

$$v = \sqrt{(T / \mu)}$$

$$T = v^2\mu$$

$$T = (61 \text{ m/s})^2 \times (0.38 \text{ kg/m})$$

$$T = 1{,}414 \text{ N}$$

8. B is correct.

I = Power / area

The intensity *I* is proportional to the power, so an increase by a factor of 10 in power leads to an increase by a factor of 10 in intensity.

$$I \text{ (dB)} = 10\log_{10} (I / I_0)$$

dB is related to the logarithm of intensity.

If the original intensity was 20 dB then:

$$20 \text{ dB} = 10\log_{10} (I_1 / I_0)$$

$$2 = \log_{10} (I_1 / I_0)$$

$$100 = I_1 / I_0$$

The new intensity is a factor of 10 higher than before:

$$I_2 = 10\, I_1$$

$$1{,}000 = I_2 / I_0$$

$$I \text{ (dB)} = 10 \log_{10} (1{,}000)$$

$$I \text{ (dB)} = 30 \text{ dB}$$

9. D is correct.

velocity = distance / time

$$v = d / t$$

$$d = vt$$

$$d = (340 \text{ m/s}){\cdot}(7 \text{ s})$$

$$d = 2{,}380 \text{ m} \approx 2 \text{ km}$$

10. B is correct.

A stretched string has all harmonics of the fundamental.

11. B is correct.

All electromagnetic waves arise from accelerating charges. When a charge is vibrating it is accelerating (change in the direction of motion is acceleration).

12. D is correct.

When tuning a radio, the tuner picks up certain frequencies by resonating at those frequencies. This filters out the other radio signals, so only that specific frequency is amplified. By changing the tuner on the radio, a particular frequency is chosen that the tuner resonates at and the signal is amplified.

13. C is correct.

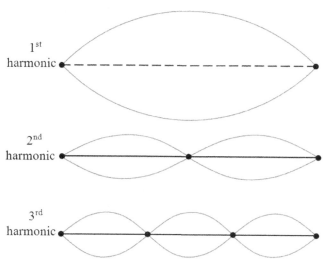

From the diagram, the wave is a 3rd harmonic standing wave.

Find wavelength:

$\lambda_1 = 2L$

$\lambda_n = 2L / n$

where n = 1, 2, 3, 4...

$\lambda_n = (2 \times 0.6 \text{ m}) / 3$

$\lambda_n = 0.4 \text{ m}$

Find speed:

$\lambda = v / f$

$v = \lambda f$

$v = (0.4 \text{ m}) \cdot (670 \text{ Hz})$

$v = 268 \text{ m/s}$

14. D is correct.

Doppler equation for an approaching sound source:

$$f_{observed} = [v_{sound} / (v_{sound} - v_{source})]f_{source}$$

$$f_{observed} = [(340 \text{ m/s}) / (340 \text{ m/s} - 50 \text{ m/s})] \cdot (415 \text{ Hz})$$

$$f_{observed} = 487 \text{ Hz}$$

The observed frequency is always higher when the source is approaching.

15. C is correct.

If beats are heard every 500 ms (i.e., ½ s), or 2 beats per second.

Since $f_{beat} = 2$ Hz, the frequencies of the two tuning forks differ by 2 Hz.

One tuning fork has an f of 490 Hz:

$$f \text{ is } (490 \text{ Hz} - 2 \text{ Hz}) = 488 \text{ Hz}$$

or

$$f \text{ is } (490 \text{ Hz} + 2 \text{ Hz}) = 492 \text{ Hz}$$

Appendix

Common AP Physics 1 Formulas and Conversions

Constants and Conversion Factors

1 unified atomic mass unit	$1 \text{ u} = 1.66 \times 10^{-27} \text{ kg}$
	$1 \text{ u} = 931 \text{ MeV}/c^2$
Proton mass	$m_p = 1.67 \times 10^{-27} \text{ kg}$
Neutron mass	$m_n = 1.67 \times 10^{-27} \text{ kg}$
Electron mass	$m_e = 9.11 \times 10^{-31} \text{ kg}$
Electron charge magnitude	$e = 1.60 \times 10^{-19} \text{ C}$
Avogadro's number	$N_0 = 6.02 \times 10^{23} \text{ mol}^{-1}$
Universal gas constant	$R = 8.31 \text{ J/(mol·K)}$
Boltzmann's constant	$k_B = 1.38 \times 10^{-23} \text{ J/K}$
Speed of light	$c = 3.00 \times 10^8 \text{ m/s}$
Planck's constant	$h = 6.63 \times 10^{-34} \text{ J·s}$
	$h = 4.14 \times 10^{-15} \text{ eV·s}$
	$hc = 1.99 \times 10^{-25} \text{ J·m}$
	$hc = 1.24 \times 10^3 \text{ eV·nm}$
Vacuum permittivity	$\varepsilon_0 = 8.85 \times 10^{-12} \text{ C}^2/\text{N·m}^2$
Coulomb's Law constant	$k = 1/4\pi\varepsilon_0 = 9.0 \times 10^9 \text{ N·m}^2/\text{C}^2$
Vacuum permeability	$\mu_0 = 4\pi \times 10^{-7} \text{ (T·m) / A}$
Magnetic constant	$k' = \mu_0/4\pi = 10^{-7} \text{ (T·m) / A}$
Universal gravitational constant	$G = 6.67 \times 10^{-11} \text{ m}^3/\text{kg·s}^2$
Acceleration due to gravity at Earth's surface	$g = 9.8 \text{ m/s}^2$
1 atmosphere pressure	$1 \text{ atm} = 1.0 \times 10^5 \text{ N/m}^2$
	$1 \text{ atm} = 1.0 \times 10^5 \text{ Pa}$
1 electron volt	$1 \text{ eV} = 1.60 \times 10^{-19} \text{ J}$
Balmer constant	$B = 3.645 \times 10^{-7} \text{ m}$
Rydberg constant	$R = 1.097 \times 10^7 \text{ m}^{-1}$
Stefan constant	$\sigma = 5.67 \times 10^{-8} \text{ W/m}^2\text{K}^4$

Units			Prefixes	
Name	**Symbol**	**Factor**	**Prefix**	**Symbol**
meter	m	10^{12}	tera	T
kilogram	kg	10^{9}	giga	G
second	s	10^{6}	mega	M
ampere	A	10^{3}	kilo	k
kelvin	K	10^{-2}	centi	c
mole	mol	10^{-3}	mili	m
hertz	Hz	10^{-6}	micro	μ
newton	N	10^{-9}	nano	n
pascal	Pa	10^{-12}	pico	p
joule	J			
watt	W			
coulomb	C			
volt	V			
ohm	Ω			
henry	H			
farad	F			
tesla	T			
degree Celsius	°C			
electronvolt	eV			

Values of Trigonometric Functions for Common Angles

θ	$\sin\theta$	$\cos\theta$	$\tan\theta$
0°	0	1	0
30°	1/2	$\sqrt{3}/2$	$\sqrt{3}/3$
37°	3/5	4/5	3/4
45°	$\sqrt{2}/2$	$\sqrt{2}/2$	1
53°	4/5	3/5	4/3
60°	$\sqrt{3}/2$	1/2	$\sqrt{3}$
90°	1	0	∞

Newtonian Mechanics

		a = acceleration
	$v = v_0 + a\Delta t$	A = amplitude
	$x = x_0 + v_0\Delta t + \frac{1}{2}a\Delta t^2$	E = energy
Translational Motion	$v^2 = v_0^2 + 2a\Delta x$	F = force
	$\vec{a} = \dfrac{\sum \vec{F}}{m} = \dfrac{\vec{F}_{net}}{m}$	f = frequency
		h = height
	$\omega = \omega_0 + \alpha t$	I = rotational inertia
	$\theta = \theta_0 + \omega_0 t + \frac{1}{2}\alpha t^2$	J = impulse
Rotational Motion	$\omega^2 = \omega_0^2 + 2\alpha\Delta\theta$	K = kinetic energy
		k = spring constant
	$\vec{\alpha} = \dfrac{\sum \vec{\tau}}{I} = \dfrac{\vec{\tau}_{net}}{I}$	ℓ = length
		m = mass
Force of Friction	$|\vec{F}_f| \leq \mu|\vec{F}_n|$	N = normal force
Centripetal Acceleration	$a_c = \dfrac{v^2}{r}$	P = power
		p = momentum
Torque	$\tau = r_\perp F = rF\sin\theta$	L = angular momentum
		r = radius of distance
Momentum	$\vec{p} = m\vec{v}$	T = period
Impulse	$\vec{J} = \Delta\vec{p} = \vec{F}\Delta t$	t = time
		U = potential energy
Kinetic Energy	$K = \frac{1}{2}mv^2$	v = velocity or speed
		W = work done on a system
Potential Energy	$\Delta U_g = mg\Delta y$	
Work	$\Delta E = W = F_\parallel d = Fd\cos\theta$	x = position
		y = height
Power	$P = \dfrac{\Delta E}{\Delta t} = \dfrac{\Delta W}{\Delta t}$	

		α = angular
Simple Harmonic Motion	$x = A\cos(\omega t) = A\cos(2\pi f t)$	acceleration
Center of Mass	$x_{cm} = \dfrac{\sum m_i x_i}{\sum m_i}$	μ = coefficient of
		friction
Angular Momentum	$L = I\omega$	θ = angle
Angular Impulse	$\Delta L = \tau \Delta t$	τ = torque
Angular Kinetic Energy	$K = \dfrac{1}{2}I\omega^2$	ω = angular speed
Work	$W = F\Delta r\,\cos\theta$	
Power	$P = Fv\,\cos\theta$	
Spring Force	$\left|\vec{F_s}\right| = k\left|\vec{x}\right|$	
Spring Potential Energy	$U_s = \dfrac{1}{2}kx^2$	
Period of Spring Oscillator	$T_s = 2\pi\sqrt{m/k}$	
Period of Simple Pendulum	$T_p = 2\pi\sqrt{\ell/g}$	
Period	$T = \dfrac{2\pi}{\omega} = \dfrac{1}{f}$	
Gravitational Body Force	$\left|\vec{F_g}\right| = G\dfrac{m_1 m_2}{r^2}$	
Gravitational Potential Energy of Two Masses	$U_G = -\dfrac{Gm_1 m_2}{r}$	

Electricity and Magnetism

Electric Field	$\vec{E} = \dfrac{\vec{F}_E}{q}$	$A = area$
		$B = magnetic\ field$
		$C = capacitance$
Electric Field Strength	$\left|\vec{E}\right| = \dfrac{1}{4\pi\varepsilon_0}\dfrac{|q|}{r^2}$	$d = distance$
		$E = electric\ field$
Electric Field Strength	$\left|\vec{E}\right| = \dfrac{|\Delta V|}{|\Delta r|}$	$\epsilon = emf$
		$F = force$
Electrostatic Force Between Charged Particles	$\left|\vec{F}_E\right| = \dfrac{1}{4\pi\varepsilon_0}\dfrac{|q_1 q_2|}{r^2}$	$I = current$
		$l = length$
Electrostatic Potential due to a Charge	$V = \dfrac{1}{4\pi\varepsilon_0}\dfrac{q}{r}$	$P = power$
		$Q = charge$
Current	$I = \dfrac{\Delta Q}{\Delta t}$	$q = point\ charge$
		$R = resistance$
Resistance	$R = \dfrac{\rho l}{A}$	$r = separation$
		$t = time$
Power	$P = I\Delta V$	$U = potential\ energy$
		$V = electric\ potential$
Current	$I = \dfrac{\Delta V}{R}$	$v = speed$
		$\kappa = dielectric\ constant$
Resistors in Series	$R_s = \sum\limits_i R_i$	$\rho = resistivity$
		$\theta = angle$
Resistors in Parallel	$\dfrac{1}{R_p} = \sum\limits_i \dfrac{1}{R_i}$	$\Phi = flux$

Sound

Standing Wave/ Open Pipe Harmonics	$\lambda = \dfrac{2L}{n}$	*f = frequency*
		L = length
Closed Pipe Harmonics	$\lambda = \dfrac{4L}{n}$	*m = mass*
		M = molecular mass
Harmonic Frequencies	$f_n = nf_1$	*n = harmonic number*
Speed of Sound in Ideal Gas	$v_{sound} = \sqrt{\dfrac{yRT}{M}}$	*R = gas constant*
		T = tension
Speed of Wave Through Wire	$v = \sqrt{\dfrac{T}{m/L}}$	*v = velocity*
		y = adiabatic constant
Doppler Effect (Approaching Stationary Observer)	$f_{observed} = \left(\dfrac{v}{v - v_{source}}\right)f_{source}$	*λ = wavelength*
Doppler Effect (Receding Stationary Observer)	$f_{observed} = \left(\dfrac{v}{v + v_{source}}\right)f_{source}$	
Doppler Effect (Observer Moving towards Source)	$f_{observed} = \left(1 + \dfrac{v_{observer}}{v}\right)f_{source}$	
Doppler Effect (Observer Moving away from Source)	$f_{observed} = \left(1 - \dfrac{v_{observer}}{v}\right)f_{source}$	

Geometry and Trigonometry

Rectangle	$A = bh$	A = area
		C = circumference
Triangle	$A = \dfrac{1}{2}bh$	V = volume
		S = surface area
Circle	$A = \pi r^2$	b = base
	$C = 2\pi r$	h = height
		l = length
Rectangular Solid	$V = lwh$	
		w = width
Cylinder	$V = \pi r^2 l$	r = radius
	$S = 2\pi rl + 2\pi r^2$	θ = angle
Sphere	$V = \dfrac{4}{3}\pi r^3$	
	$S = 4\pi r^2$	
Right Triangle	$a^2 + b^2 = c^2$	
	$\sin\theta = \dfrac{a}{c}$	
	$\cos\theta = \dfrac{b}{c}$	
	$\tan\theta = \dfrac{a}{b}$	

Physics Glossary

A

Absolute humidity (or saturation value) − the maximum amount of water vapor that could be present in 1 m³ of the air at any given temperature.

Absolute magnitude − a classification scheme which compensates for the differences in the distance to stars; calculates the brightness that stars would appear to have if they were all at a defined, standard distance of 10 parsecs.

Absolute scale − temperature scale set so that zero is the theoretical lowest temperature possible (this would occur when all random motion of molecules has ceased).

Absolute zero − the theoretical lowest temperature possible, at which molecular motion vanishes; −273.16 °C or 0 K.

Absorptance − the ratio of the total absorbed radiation to the total incident radiation.

Acceleration − the rate of change of velocity of a moving object with respect to time; the SI units are m/s²; by definition, this change in velocity can result from a change in speed, a change in direction or a combination of changes in both speed and direction.

Acceleration due to gravity − the acceleration produced in a body due to the Earth's attraction; denoted by the letter g (SI unit – m/s²); on the surface of the Earth, its average value is 9.8 m/s²; increases when going towards the poles from the equator; decreases with altitude and with depth inside the Earth; the value of g at the center of the Earth is zero.

Achromatic − capable of transmitting light without decomposing it into its constituent colors.

Acoustics − the science of the production, transmission, and effects of sound.

Acoustic shielding − a sound barrier that prevents the transmission of acoustic energy.

Adiabatic − any change in which there is no gain or loss of heat.

Adiabatic cooling − the decrease in temperature of an expanding gas that involves no additional heat flowing out of the gas; the cooling from the energy lost by expansion.

Adiabatic heating − the increase in temperature of the compressed gas that involves no additional heat flowing into the gas; the heating from the energy gained by compression.

Afocal lens − a lens of zero convergent power whose focal points are infinitely distant.

Air mass – a large, more or less uniform body of air with nearly the same temperature and moisture conditions throughout.

Albedo – the fraction of the total light incident on a reflecting surface, especially a celestial body, which is reflected back in all directions.

Allotropic forms – elements that can have several different structures with different physical properties (e.g., graphite and diamond).

Alpha (α) particle – the nucleus of a helium atom (two protons and two neutrons) emitted as radiation from a decaying heavy nucleus (α-decay).

Alternating current – an electric current that first moves in one direction, then in the opposite direction with a regular frequency.

Amorphous – term that describes solids that have neither definite form nor structure.

Amp – unit of electric current; equivalent to coulomb/second.

Ampere – the full name of the unit amp; the SI unit of electric current; one ampere is the flow of one coulomb of charge per second.

Amplitude – the maximum absolute value attained by the disturbance of a wave or by any quantity that varies periodically.

Amplitude (of an oscillation) – the maximum displacement of a body from its mean position during an oscillatory motion.

Amplitude (of waves) – the maximum displacement of particles of the medium from their mean positions during the propagation of a wave.

Angle of contact – the angle between tangents to the liquid surface and the solid surface inside the liquid; both the tangents are drawn at the point of contact.

Angle of incidence – the angle of an incident (arriving) ray or particle to a surface; measured from a line perpendicular to the surface (the normal).

Angle of reflection – the angle of a reflected ray or particle from a surface; measured from a line perpendicular to the surface (the normal).

Angle of refraction – the angle between the refracted ray and the normal.

Angle of repose – the angle of inclination of a plane with the horizontal such that a body placed on the plane is on the verge of sliding but does not.

Angstrom – a unit of length; $1 = 10^{-10}$ m.

Angular acceleration − the rate of change of angular velocity of a body moving along a circular path; denoted by a.

Angular displacement − the angle described at the center of the circle by a moving body along a circular path. It is measured in radians.

Angular momentum − also a moment of momentum; the cross-product of position vector and momentum.

Angular momentum quantum number − from quantum mechanics model of the atom, one of four descriptions of the energy state of an electron wave; describes the energy sublevels of electrons within the main energy levels of an atom.

Angular velocity − the rate of change of angular displacement per unit of time.

Annihilation − a process in which a particle and an antiparticle combine and release their rest energies in other particles.

Antineutrino − the antiparticle of neutrino; has zero mass and spin ½.

Archimedes principle − a body immersed in a fluid experiences an apparent loss of weight which is equal to the weight of the fluid displaced by the body.

Astronomical unit − the radius of the Earth's orbit is defined as one astronomical unit (A.U.).

Atom − the smallest unit of an element that can exist alone or in combination with other elements.

Atomic mass unit − relative mass unit (amu) of an isotope based on the standard of the carbon-12 (^{12}C) isotope; one atomic mass unit (1 amu) = 1/12 the mass of a ^{12}C atom = 1.66×10^{-27} Kg.

Atomic number − the number of protons in the nucleus of an atom.

Atomic weight − weighted average of the masses of stable isotopes of an element as they occur in nature; based on the abundance of each isotope of the element and the atomic mass of the isotope compared to ^{12}C.

Avogadro's number − the number of carbon-12 (^{12}C) atoms in exactly 12.00 g of C that is 6.02×10^{23} atoms or other chemical units; the number of chemical units in one mole of a substance.

Avogadro's Law − under the same conditions of temperature and pressure, equal volumes of all gases contain an equal number of molecules.

Axis − the imaginary line about which a planet or other object rotates.

B

Background radiation – ionizing radiation (e.g., alpha, beta, gamma rays) from natural sources.

Balanced forces – when a number of forces act on a body and the resultant force is zero; see *Resultant forces*.

Balmer lines – lines in the spectrum of the hydrogen atom in the visible range; produced by the transition between n 2 and n = 2, with n being the principal quantum number.

Balmer series – a set of four line spectra; narrow lines of color emitted by hydrogen atom electrons as they drop from excited states to the ground state.

Bar – a unit of pressure; equal to 10^5 Pascals.

Barometer – an instrument that measures atmospheric pressure; used in weather forecasting and determining elevation above sea level.

Baryon – subatomic particle composed of three quarks.

Beat – a phenomenon of the periodic variation in the intensity of sound due to the superposition of waves differing slightly in frequency; rhythmic increases and decreases of volume from constructive and destructive interference between two sound waves of slightly different frequencies.

Bernoulli's theorem – states that the total energy per unit volume of a non-viscous, incompressible fluid in a streamline flow will remain constant.

Beta (β) particle – high-energy electron emitted as ionizing radiation from a decaying nucleus (β-decay); also a beta ray.

Big bang theory – current model of galactic evolution in which the universe is assumed to have been created by an intense and brilliant explosion from a primeval fireball.

Binding energy – the net energy required to break a nucleus into its constituent protons and neutrons; also the energy equivalent released when a nucleus is formed.

Black body – an ideal body which would absorb all incident radiation and reflect none.

Black body radiation – electromagnetic radiation emitted by an ideal material (the black body) that perfectly absorbs and perfectly emits radiation.

Black hole – the remaining theoretical core of a supernova that is so dense that even light cannot escape.

Bohr model – the structure of the atom that attempted to correct the deficiencies of the solar system model and account for the Balmer series.

Boiling point − the temperature at which a phase change of liquid to gas takes place through boiling; the same temperature as the condensation point.

Boundary − the division between two regions of differing physical properties.

Boyle's Law − for a given mass of a gas at constant temperature, the volume of the gas is inversely proportional to the pressure.

Brewster's Law − states that the refractive index of a material is equal to the tangent of the polarizing angle for the material.

British thermal unit (Btu) − the amount of energy or heat needed to increase the temperature of one pound of water one degree Fahrenheit.

Brownian motion − the continuous random motion of solid microscopic particles when suspended in a fluid medium due to their ongoing bombardment by atoms and molecules.

Bulk's modulus of elasticity − the ratio of normal stress to the volumetric strain produced in a body.

Buoyant force – the upward force on an object immersed in a fluid.

C

Calorie − a unit of heat; 1 Calorie = 4.186 joule.

Candela − the SI unit of luminous intensity defined as the luminous intensity in a given direction of a source that emits monochromatic photons of frequency 540×10^{12} Hz and has a radiant intensity in that direction of 1/683 W/sr.

Capacitance − the ratio of charge stored per increase in potential difference.

Capacitor − electrical device used to store charge and energy in the electrical field.

Capillarity − the rise or fall of a liquid in a tube of very fine bore.

Carnot's theorem − no engine operating between two temperatures is more efficient than a reversible engine working between the same two temperatures.

Cathode rays − negatively charged particles (electrons) that are emitted from a negative terminal in an evacuated glass tube.

Celsius scale of temperature − the ice-point is taken as the lower fixed point (0 °C), and the steam-point is taken as the upper fixed point (100 °C); the interval between the ice-point and the steam-point is divided into 100 equal divisions; the unit division on this scale is 1 °C; previously the centigrade scale; the temperatures on the Celsius scale and the Fahrenheit scale are related by the relationship, C/100 = (F − 32) / 180; the temperature of a healthy person is 37 °C or 98.6 °F.

Centrifugal force − an apparent outward force on an object in circular motion; a consequence of the third law of motion.

Centripetal force − the radial force required to keep an object moving in a circular path.

Chain reaction − a self-sustaining reaction where some of the products are able to produce more reactions of the same kind (e.g., in a nuclear chain reaction, neutrons are the products that produce more nuclear reactions in a self-sustaining series).

Charles' Law − for a given mass of a gas at constant pressure, the volume is directly proportional to the temperature.

Chromatic aberration − an optical lens defect causing color fringes due to the lens bringing different colors of light to focus at different points.

Circular motion − the motion of a body along a circular path.

Closed system − the system which cannot exchange heat or matter with the surroundings.

Coefficient of areal expansion − the fractional change in surface area per degree of temperature change; see *Coefficient of thermal expansion.*

Coefficient of linear expansion − the fractional change in length per degree of temperature change; see *Coefficient of thermal expansion.*

Coefficient of thermal expansion − the fractional change in the size of an object per degree of change in temperature at a constant pressure; the SI unit is K^{-1}.

Coefficient of volumetric expansion − the fractional change in volume per degree of temperature change; see *Coefficient of thermal expansion.*

Coherent source − a source in which there is a constant phase difference between waves emitted from different parts of the source.

Compression − a part of a longitudinal wave in which the density of the particles of the medium is higher than the normal density.

Compressive stress − a force that tends to compress the surface as the Earth's plates move into each other.

Condensation (sound) − a compression of gas molecules; a pulse of increased density and pressure that moves through the air at the speed of sound.

Condensation (water vapor) – where more vapor or gas molecules are returning to the liquid state than are evaporating.

Condensation nuclei – tiny particles such as tiny dust, smoke, soot or salt crystals suspended in the air on which water condenses.

Condensation point – the temperature at which a gas or vapor changes back to liquid; see *Boiling point*.

Conduction – the transfer of heat from a region of higher temperature to a region of lower temperature by increased kinetic energy moving from molecule to molecule.

Constructive interference – the condition in which two waves arriving at the same place at the same time and in phase add amplitudes to create a new wave.

Control rods – rods inserted between fuel rods in a nuclear reactor to absorb neutrons and control the rate of the nuclear chain reaction.

Convection – transfer of heat from a region of higher temperature to a region of lower temperature by the displacement of high-energy molecules (e.g., the displacement of warmer, less dense air (higher kinetic energy) by cooler, denser air (lower kinetic energy)).

Conventional current – the opposite of electron current; considers an electric current to consist of a drift of positive charges that flow from the positive terminal to the negative terminal of a battery.

Coulomb – unit used to measure the quantity of electric charge; equivalent to the charge resulting from the transfer of 6.24 billion particles such as the electron.

Coulomb's Law – relationship between charge, distance, and magnitude of the electrical force between two bodies; the force between any two charges is directly proportional to the product of charges and inversely proportional to the square of the distance between the charges.

Covalent bond – a chemical bond formed by the sharing of a pair of electrons.

Covalent compound – chemical compound held together by a covalent bond or bonds.

Crest – the point of maximum positive displacement on a transverse wave.

Critical angle – the limit to the angle of incidence when all light rays are reflected internally.

Critical mass – the mass of fissionable material needed to sustain a chain reaction.

Curvilinear motion – the motion of a body along a curved path.

Cycle – a complete vibration.

Cyclotron – a device used to accelerate the charged particles.

D

De-acceleration – negative acceleration when the velocity of a body decreases with time.

Decibel – unit of the sound level; if P1 & P2 are two amounts of power, the first is said to be n decibels greater, where $n = 10 \log 10 \, (P1/P2)$.

Decibel scale – a nonlinear scale of loudness based on the ratio of the intensity level of a sound to the intensity at the threshold of hearing.

Density – the mass of a substance per unit volume.

Destructive interference – the condition in which two waves arriving at the same point at the same time out of phase add amplitudes that cancel to create zero total disturbance; see *Constructive interference*.

Dewpoint temperature – the temperature at which condensation begins.

Dew – condensation of water vapor into droplets of liquid on surfaces.

Diffraction – the bending of light around the edge of an opaque object.

Diffuse reflection – light rays reflected in many random directions, as opposed to the parallel rays reflected from a perfectly smooth surface such as a mirror.

Diopter – unit of measure of the refractive power of a lens.

Direct current – an electrical current which always flows in one direction.

Direct proportion – when two variables increase or decrease together in the same ratio (at the same rate).

Dispersion – the splitting of white light into its component colors of the spectrum.

Displacement – a vector quantity for the change in the position of an object as it moves in a particular direction; also the shortest distance between the initial position and the final position of a moving body.

Distance – a scalar quantity for the length of the path traveled by a body irrespective of the direction it goes in.

Doppler effect – an apparent change in the frequency of sound or light due to the relative motion between the source of the sound or light and the observer.

E

Echo − a reflected sound that can be distinguished from the original sound, usually arriving 0.1 s or more after the original sound.

Einstein mass-energy relation − $E = mc^2$; E is the energy released, m is the mass defect and c is the speed of light.

Elastic potential energy − the potential energy of a body by its configuration (i.e., shape).

Elastic strain − an adjustment to stress in which materials recover their original shape after stress is released.

Electric circuit − consists of a voltage source that maintains an electrical potential, a continuous conducting path for a current to follow and a device where work is done by the electrical potential; a switch in the circuit is used to complete or interrupt the conducting path.

Electric current − the flow of electric charge; the electric force field produced by an electrical charge.

Electric field line − an imaginary curve tangent to which at any given point gives the direction of the electric field at that point.

Electric field lines − a map of an electric field representing the direction of the force that a test charge would experience; the direction of an electric field shown by lines of force.

Electric generator − a mechanical device that uses wire loops rotating in a magnetic field to produce electromagnetic induction to generate electricity.

Electric potential energy − potential energy due to the position of a charge near other charges.

Electrical conductors − materials that have electrons that are free to move throughout the material (e.g., metals); allows electric current to flow through the material.

Electrical energy − a form of energy from electromagnetic interactions.

Electric force − a fundamental force that results from the interaction of electrical charges; it is the most powerful force in the universe.

Electrical insulators − electrical nonconductors, or materials that obstruct the flow of electric current.

Electrical nonconductors − materials that have electrons that do not move easily within the material (e.g., rubber); also electrical insulators.

Electrical resistance − the property of opposing or reducing electric current.

Electrolyte − water solution of ionic substances that will conduct an electric current.

Electromagnet – a magnet formed by a solenoid that can be turned on and off by turning the current on and off.

Electromagnetic force – one of four fundamental forces; the force of attraction or repulsion between two charged particles.

Electromagnetic induction – the process in which current is induced in a coil whenever there is a change in the magnetic flux linked with the coil.

Electromagnetic waves – the waves which are due to oscillating electrical and magnetic fields and do not need any material medium for their propagation; can travel through a material medium (e.g., light waves and radio waves); travel in a vacuum with a speed of 3×10^8 m/s.

Electron – subatomic particle that has the smallest negative charge possible; usually found in an orbital of an atom but is gained or lost when atoms become ions.

Electron configuration – the arrangement of electrons in orbits and sub-orbits about the nucleus of an atom.

Electron current – the opposite of conventional current; considers electric current to consist of a drift of negative charges that flows from the negative terminal to the positive terminal of a battery.

Electron pair – a pair of electrons with different spin quantum numbers that may occupy an orbital.

Electron volt – the energy gained by an electron moving across a potential difference of one volt; equal to 1.60×10^{-19} Joules.

Electronegativity – the comparative ability of atoms of an element to attract bonding electrons.

Electrostatic charge – an accumulated electric charge on an object from a surplus of electrons or a deficiency of electrons.

Element – a pure chemical substance that cannot be broken down into anything simpler by chemical or physical means; there are over 100 known elements, the fundamental materials of which all matter is made.

Endothermic process – the process in which heat is absorbed.

Energy – the capacity of a body to do work; a scalar quantity; the SI unit is the Joule; there are five forms: mechanical, chemical, radiant, electrical and nuclear.

Escape velocity – the minimum velocity with which an object must be thrown upward to overcome the gravitational pull and escape into space; the escape velocity depends on the mass and radius of the planet/star, but not on the mass of the body being thrown upward.

Evaporation − process of more molecules leaving a liquid for the gaseous state than returning from the gas to the liquid; can occur at any given temperature from the surface of a liquid; takes place only from the surface of the liquid; causes cooling; faster if the surface of the liquid is large, the temperature is higher, and the surrounding atmosphere does not contain a large amount of vapor of the liquid.

Exothermic process − the process in which heat is evolved.

F

Fahrenheit scale of temperature − the ice-point (lower fixed point) is taken as 32 °F, and the steam-point (upper fixed point) is taken as 212 °F; the interval between these two points is divided into 180 equal divisions; the unit division on the Fahrenheit scale is 1 °F; the temperatures on the Celsius scale and the Fahrenheit scale are related by the relationship, $C/100 = (F − 32) / 180$; the temperature of a healthy person is 37 °C or 98.6 °F.

Farad − the SI unit of capacitance; the capacitance of a capacitor that, if charged to 1 C, has a potential difference of 1 V.

Faraday − the electric charge required to liberate a gram equivalent of a substance; 1 Faraday = 96,485 coulomb/mole.

Fermat's principle − an electromagnetic wave takes a path that involves the least time when propagating between two points.

First Law of Motion − every object remains at rest or in a state of uniform straight-line motion unless acted on by an unbalanced force.

Fluid − matter that has the ability to flow or be poured; the individual molecules of a fluid are able to move, rolling over or by one another.

Focus − the point to which rays that are initially parallel to the axis of a lens or mirror converge or from which they appear to diverge.

Force − a push or pull which tends to change the state of rest or of uniform motion, the direction of motion or the shape and size of a body; a vector quantity; the SI unit is a Newton, denoted by N; one N is the force which when acting on a body of mass 1 kg produces an acceleration of 1 m/s^2.

Force of gravitation − the force with which two objects attract by their masses; acts even if the two objects are not connected; an action-at-a-distance force.

Fracture strain − an adjustment to stress in which materials crack or break as a result of the stress.

Fraunhofer lines − the dark lines in the spectrum of the sun or a star.

Freefall − the motion of a body falling to Earth with no other force except the force of gravity acting on it; all free-falling bodies are weightless.

Freezing point − the temperature at which a phase change of liquid to solid takes place; the same temperature as the melting point for a given substance.

Frequency − the number of oscillations completed in 1 second by an oscillating body.

Frequency (of oscillations) − the number of oscillations made by an oscillating body per second.

Frequency (of waves) − the number of waves produced per second.

Friction − the force that resists the motion of one surface relative to another with which it is in contact; caused by the humps and crests of surfaces, even those on a microscopic scale; the area of contact is small, and the consequent high pressure leads to local pressure welding of the surface; in motion the welds are broken and remade continually.

Fuel rod − long zirconium alloy tubes containing fissionable material for use in a nuclear reactor.

Fundamental charge – the smallest common charge known; the magnitude of the charge of an electron and a proton, which is 1.60×10^{-19} coulomb.

Fundamental frequency − the lowest frequency (longest wavelength) at which a system vibrates freely and can set up standing waves in an air column or on a string.

Fundamental properties − a property that cannot be defined in simpler terms other than to describe how it is measured; the fundamental properties are length, mass, time and charge.

G

g − symbol representing the acceleration of an object in free fall due to the force of gravity; its magnitude is 9.80 m/s^2.

Gamma (γ) ray − a high energy photon of short wavelength electromagnetic radiation emitted by decaying nuclei (γ-decay).

Gases – a phase of matter composed of molecules that are relatively far apart moving freely in constant, random motion and have weak cohesive forces acting between them, resulting in the characteristic indefinite shape and indefinite volume of a gas.

Graham's Law of Diffusion – the rate of diffusion of a gas is inversely proportional to the square root of its density.

Gram-atomic weight – the mass in grams of one mole of an element that is numerically equal to its atomic weight.

Gram-formula weight – the mass in grams of one mole of a compound that is numerically equal to its formula weight.

Gram-molecular weight – the gram-formula weight of a molecular compound.

Gravitational constant G – appears in the equation for Newton's Law of Gravitation; numerically, it is equal to the force of gravitation, which acts between two bodies with a mass of 1 kg each separated by a distance of 1 m; the value of G is 6.67×10^{-11} Nm²/kg².

Gravitational potential at a point – the amount of work done against the gravitational forces to move a particle of unit mass from infinity to that point.

Gravitational potential energy – the potential energy possessed by a body by its height from the ground; equals *mgh*.

Gravity – the gravitational attraction at the surface of a planet or other celestial body.

Greenhouse effect – the process of increasing the temperature of the lower parts of the atmosphere through redirecting energy back toward the surface; the absorption and re-emission of infrared radiation by carbon dioxide, water vapor, and a few other gases in the atmosphere.

Ground state – the energy state of an atom with its electrons at the lowest energy state possible for that atom.

H

Half-life − the time required for one-half of the unstable nuclei in a radioactive substance to decay into a new element.

Heat − a form of energy that makes a body hot or cold; measured by the temperature-effect, it produces in any material body; the SI unit is the Joule (J).

Heisenberg uncertainty principle − states that there is a fundamental limit to the precision with which certain pairs of physical properties of a particle (i.e., complementary variables) can be known simultaneously (e.g., one cannot measure both the exact momentum and the exact position of a subatomic particle at the same time − the more one is certain of one, the less certain one can be of the other).

Hertz − unit of frequency (Hz); equivalent to one cycle per second.

Hooke's Law − within elastic limit, stress is directly proportional to strain.

Horsepower − unit of power; 1 hp = 746 Watts.

Humidity − the ratio of water vapor in a sample of air to the volume of the sample.

Huygens' principle − each point on a light wavefront can be regarded as a source of secondary waves, the envelope of these secondary waves determining the position of the wavefront at a later time.

Hypothesis − a tentative explanation of a phenomenon that is compatible with the data and provides a framework for understanding and describing that phenomenon.

I

Ice-point − the melting point of ice under 1 atm pressure; equal to 0 °C or 32 °F.

Ideal gas equation − $PV = nRT$.

Impulse − equal to the product of the force acting on a body and the time for which it acts; if the force is variable, the impulse is the integral of Fd_t from t_0 to t_1; the impulse of a force acting for a given time interval is equal to change in momentum produced over that interval; $J = m(v - u)$, assuming that the mass m remains constant while the velocity changes from v to u; the SI units are kg m/s.

Impulsive force − the force which acts on a body for a short time but produces a large change in the momentum of the body.

Incandescent − matter emitting visible light as a result of high temperature (e.g., a light bulb, a flame from any burning source, the Sun).

Incident ray − line representing the direction of motion of incoming light approaching a boundary.

Index of refraction − the ratio of the speed of light in a vacuum to the speed of light in a material.

Inertia − the property of matter that causes it to resist any change in its state of rest or of uniform motion; there are three kinds of inertia: the inertia of rest, the inertia of motion and the inertia of direction; the mass of a body is a measure of its inertia.

Infrasonic − sound waves at a frequency below the range of human hearing (less than 20 Hz).

Insulators − materials that are poor conductors of heat or electricity (e.g., wood or glass); materials with air pockets slow down the movement of heat because the air molecules are far apart.

Intensity − a measure of the energy carried by a wave.

Interference − the redistribution of energy due to the superposition of waves with a phase difference from coherent sources, resulting in alternate light and dark bands.

Intermolecular forces − forces of interaction between molecules.

Internal energy − the sum of the kinetic energy and potential energy of all molecules of an object.

Inverse proportion − the relationship in which the value of one variable increases while the value of a second variable decreases at the same rate (in the same ratio).

Ionization − process of forming ions from molecules.

Ionized − an atom or a particle that has a net charge because it has gained or lost electrons.

Isobaric process − in which pressure remains constant.

Isochoric process − in which volume remains constant.

Isostasy − a balance or equilibrium between adjacent blocks of Earth's crust.

Isothermal process − in which temperature remains constant.

Isotope − atoms of the same element with the same atomic number (i.e., number of protons) but with a different mass number (i.e., number of neutrons).

J

Joule − the unit used to measure work and energy; can also be used to measure heat; 1 J = 1N·m.

Joule's Law of Heating – states that the heat produced when a current (I) flows through a resistor (R) for a given time (t) is given by $Q = I^2Rt$.

K

Kelvin scale of temperature − the ice-point (the lower fixed point) is taken as 273.15 K, and the steam-point (the upper fixed point) is taken as 373.15 K; the interval between these two points is divided into 100 equal parts; each division is equal to 1 K.

Kelvin's statement of Second Law of Thermodynamics − it is impossible that, at the end of a cycle of changes, heat has been extracted from a reservoir and an equal amount of work has been produced without producing some other effect.

Kepler's Laws of Planetary Motion − the three laws describing the motion of the planets.

Kepler's First Law – in planetary motion, each planet moves in an elliptical orbit, with the Sun located at one focus.

Kepler's Second Law – a radius vector between the Sun and a planet moves over equal areas of the ellipse during equal time intervals.

Kepler's Third Law – the square of the period of an orbit is directly proportional to the cube of the radius of the major axis of the orbit.

Kilocalorie − the amount of energy required to raise the temperature of 1 kg of water by 1 °C; 1 Kcal = 1,000 calorie.

Kilogram − the fundamental unit of mass in the metric system of measurement.

Kinetic energy − energy possessed by a body due to its motion; $KE = \frac{1}{2}mv^2$, where m is mass and v is velocity.

L

Laser – a device that produces a coherent stream of light through stimulated emission of radiation.

Latent heat – energy released or absorbed by a body during a constant-temperature phase change.

Latent heat of vaporization – the heat absorbed when one gram of a substance changes from the liquid phase to the gaseous phase; also, the heat released when one gram of gas changes from the gaseous phase to the liquid phase.

Latent heat of fusion – the quantity of heat required to convert one-unit mass of a substance from a solid state to a liquid state at its melting point without any change in its temperature; the SI unit is J kg^{-1}.

Latent heat of sublimation – the quantity of heat required to convert one unit of mass of a substance from a solid state to a gaseous state without any change in its temperature.

Law of Conservation of Energy – states that energy can neither be created nor destroyed, but can be transformed from one form to another.

Law of Conservation of Mass – states that mass (including single atoms) can neither be created nor destroyed in a chemical reaction.

Law of Conservation of Matter – states that matter can neither be created nor destroyed in a chemical reaction.

Law of Conservation of Momentum – states that the total momentum of a group of interacting objects remains constant in the absence of external forces.

Lenz's Law – states that the induced current always flows in such a direction that it opposes the cause producing it.

Light-year – the distance that light travels in a vacuum in one year (365.25 days); approximately 9.46×10^{15} m.

Line spectrum – an emission (of light, sound or other radiation) spectrum consisting of separate isolated lines (discrete frequencies or energies); can be used to identify the elements in a matter of unknown composition.

Lines of force – lines drawn to make an electric field strength map, with each line originating on a positive charge and ending on a negative charge; each line represents a path on which a charge would experience a constant force; having the lines closer indicates a stronger electric field.

Liquids – a phase of matter composed of molecules that have interactions stronger than those found in gas but not strong enough to keep the molecules near the equilibrium positions of a solid, resulting in the characteristic definite volume but the indefinite shape of a liquid.

Liter − a metric system unit of volume; usually used for liquids.

Longitudinal strain − the ratio of change in the length of a body to its initial length.

Longitudinal waves − the wave in which the particles of the medium oscillate along the direction of propagation of a wave (e.g., sound waves).

Loudness − a subjective interpretation of a sound that is related to the energy of the vibrating source, related to the condition of the transmitting medium and the distance involved.

Luminosity − the total amount of energy radiated into space each second from the surface of a star.

Luminous − an object or objects that produce visible light (e.g., the Sun, stars, light bulbs, burning materials).

Lyman series − a group of lines in the ultraviolet region in the spectrum of hydrogen.

M

Magnetic domain − tiny physical regions in permanent magnets, approximately 0.01 to 1 mm, that have magnetically aligned atoms, giving the domain an overall polarity.

Magnetic field − the region around a magnet where its magnetic force is experienced by other magnetic objects; a model used to describe how magnetic forces on moving charges act at a distance.

Magnetic poles − the ends, or sides, of a magnet about which the force of magnetic attraction seems to be concentrated.

Magnetic quantum number − from quantum mechanics model of the atom, one of four descriptions of the energy state of an electron wave; describes the energy of an electron orbital as the orbital is oriented in space by an external magnetic field, a kind of energy sub-sublevel.

Magnetic reversal − the changing of polarity of the Earth's magnetic field as the north magnetic pole and the south magnetic pole exchange positions.

Magnetic wave − the spread of magnetization from a small portion of a substance where an abrupt change in the magnetic field has taken place.

Magnification − the ratio of the size of the image to the size of the object.

Magnitude − the size of a measurement of a vector; scalar quantities that consist of a number and unit only.

Malus Law – states that the intensity of the light transmitted from the analyzer varies directly as the square of the cosine of the angle between the plane of transmission of the analyzer and the polarizer.

Maser – microwave amplification by stimulated emission of radiation.

Mass – the quantity of matter contained in a body; the SI unit is the kg; remains the same everywhere; a measure of inertia, which means resistance to a change of motion.

Mass defect – the difference between the sum of the masses of the individual nucleons forming a nucleus and the mass of that nucleus.

Mass number – the sum of the number of protons and neutrons in a nucleus; used to identify isotopes (e.g., ^{238}Uranium).

Matter – anything that occupies space and has mass.

Mean life – the average time during which a system, such as an atom or a nucleus, exists in a specified form.

Mechanical energy – the sum of the potential energy and the kinetic energy of a body; energy associated with the position of a body.

Mechanical wave – those waves that need a material medium for their propagation (e.g., sound waves and water waves); also elastic waves.

Megahertz – unit of frequency; equal to 106 Hertz.

Melting point – the temperature at which a phase change of solid to liquid takes place.

Metal – matter is having the physical properties of conductivity, malleability, ductility, and luster.

Meter – the fundamental metric unit of length.

MeV – unit of energy; equal to 1.6×10^{-13} joules.

Millibar – a measure of atmospheric pressure equivalent to 1,000 dynes per cm^2.

Miscible fluids – fluids that can mix in any proportion.

Mixture – matter made of unlike parts that have a variable composition and can be separated into their component parts by physical means.

Model – a mental or physical representation of something that cannot be observed directly; usually used as an aid to understanding.

Modulus of elasticity – the ratio of stress to the strain produced in a body.

Modulus of rigidity – the ratio of tangential stress to the shear strain produced in a body.

Mole − the amount of a substance that contains Avogadro's number of atoms, ions, molecules or any other chemical unit; 6.02×10^{23} atoms, ions or other chemical units.

Momentum − a measure of the quantity of motion in a body; the product of the mass and the velocity of a body; SI units are kg·m /s.

Monochromatic light − consisting of a single wavelength.

N

Natural frequency − the frequency of oscillation of an elastic object in the absence of external forces; depends on the size, composition, and shape of the object.

Negative electric charge − one of the two types of electric charge; repels other negative charges and attracts positive charges.

Negative ion − atom or particle that has a surplus or imbalance of electrons and a negative charge.

Net force − the resulting force after all vector forces have been added; if a net force is zero, all the vector forces have canceled, and there is not an unbalanced force.

Newton (N) − a unit of force defined as $kg·m/s^2$; 1 Newton is needed to accelerate a 1 kg mass by 1 m/s^2.

Newton's First Law of Motion – a body continues in a state of rest or of uniform motion in a straight line unless it is acted upon by an external (unbalanced) force.

Newton's Law of Gravitation − the gravitational force of attraction acting between any two particles is directly proportional to the product of their masses and inversely proportional to the square of the distance between them; the force of attraction acts along the line joining the two particles; real bodies having spherical symmetry act as point masses with their mass assumed to be concentrated at their center of mass.

Newton's Second Law of Motion − the rate of change of momentum is equal to the force applied; the force acting on a body is directly proportional to the product of its mass and acceleration produced by force in the body.

Newton's Third Law of Motion − states that to every action there is an equal and opposite reaction; the action and the reaction act on two different bodies simultaneously.

Noise − sounds made up of groups of waves of random frequency and intensity.

Non-uniform acceleration – when the velocity of a body increases by unequal amounts in equal intervals of time.

Non-uniform speed – when a body travels unequal distances in equal intervals of time.

Non-uniform velocity – when a body covers unequal distances in equal intervals of time in a particular direction, or when it covers equal distances in equal intervals but changes its direction.

Normal – a line perpendicular to the surface of a boundary.

Nuclear energy – the form of energy from reactions involving the nucleus.

Nuclear fission – the splitting of a heavy nucleus into more stable, lighter nuclei with an accompanying release of energy.

Nuclear force – one of four fundamental forces; a strong force of attraction that operates over short distances between subatomic particles; overcomes the electric repulsion of protons in a nucleus and binds the nucleus together.

Nuclear fusion – nuclear reaction of low mass nuclei fusing together to form a more stable and more massive nucleus with an accompanying release of energy.

Nuclear reactor – a steel vessel in which a controlled chain reaction of fissionable materials releases energy.

Nucleons – a collective name for protons and neutrons in the nucleus of an atom.

Nucleus – the central, positively charged, dense portion of an atom; contains protons and neutrons.

O

Ohm – unit of resistance; 1 ohm = 1volt/ampere.

Ohm's Law – states that the current flowing through a conductor is directly proportional to the potential difference across the ends of the conductor.

Open system – a system across whose boundaries both matter and energy can pass.

Optical fiber – a long, thin thread of fused silica; used to transmit light; based on total internal reflection.

Orbital – the region of space around the nucleus of an atom where an electron is likely to be found.

Origin − the only point on a graph where the *x* and the *y* variables both have a value of zero at the same time.

Oscillatory motion − the to and fro motion (periodic in nature) of a body about its mean position; also vibratory motion.

P

Pascal − a unit of pressure, equal to the pressure resulting from a force of 1 Newton acting uniformly over an area of 1 m^2.

Pascal's Law – states that the pressure exerted on a liquid is transmitted equally in all directions.

Paschen series − a group of lines in the infrared region in the spectrum of hydrogen.

Pauli exclusion principle − no two electrons in an atom can have the same four quantum numbers; a maximum of two electrons can occupy a given orbital.

Peltier effect − the evolution or absorption of heat at the junction of two dissimilar metals carrying current.

Period (of a wave) − the time taken by a wave to travel through a distance equal to its wavelength; denoted by T; time period of a wave = 1/frequency of the wave.

Period (of an oscillation) − the time taken to complete one oscillation; does not depend upon the mass of the bob and amplitude of oscillation; directly proportional to the square root of the length and inversely proportional to the square root of the acceleration due to gravity.

Periodic wave − a wave in which the particles of the medium oscillate continuously about their mean positions regularly at fixed intervals of time.

Periodic motion − a motion which repeats itself at regular intervals of time.

Permeability − the ability to transmit fluids through openings, small passageways or gaps.

Phase − when the particles in a wave are in the same state of vibration (i.e., in the same position and in the same direction of motion).

Phase change − the action of a substance changing from one state of matter to another; always absorbs or releases internal potential energy that is not associated with a temperature change.

Photons − quanta of energy in the light wave; the particle associated with light.

Photoelectric effect – the emission of electrons in some materials when the light of a suitable frequency falls on them.

Physical change – a change of the state of a substance but not in the identity of the substance.

Planck's constant – proportionality constant in the ratio of the energy of vibrating molecules to their frequency of vibration; a value of 6.63×10^{-34} J·s.

Plasma – a phase of matter; a very hot highly ionized gas consisting of electrons and atoms that have been stripped of their electrons because of high kinetic energies.

Plasticity – the property of a solid whereby it undergoes a permanent change in shape or size when subjected to a stress.

Plastic strain – an adjustment to stress in which materials become molded or bent out of shape under stress and do not return to their original shape after the stress is released.

Polarized Light – light whose constituent transverse waves are all vibrating in the same plane.

Polaroid – a film that transmits only polarized light.

Polaroid or polarizer – a device that produces polarized light.

Positive electric charge – one of the two types of electric charge; repels other positive charges and attracts negative charges.

Positive ion – atom or particle that has a net positive charge due to an electron or electrons being torn away.

Positron – an elementary particle having the same mass as that of an electron but equal and positive charge.

Potential Energy – energy possessed by a body by its position or configuration; see the *Gravitational potential energy* and *Elastic potential energy*.

Power – scalar quantity for the rate of doing work; the SI unit is Watt; 1 W = 1 J/s.

Pressure – a measure of force per unit area (e.g., kilograms per square meter (kg/m^2).

Primary coil – part of a transformer; a coil of wire connected to a source of alternating current.

Primary colors – three colors (red, yellow and blue) which can be combined in various proportions to produce any other color.

Principal quantum number – from quantum mechanics model of the atom, one of four descriptions of the energy state of an electron wave; describes the main energy level of an electron in terms of its most probable distance from the nucleus.

Principle of calorimetry – states that if two bodies of different temperature are in thermal contact, and no heat is allowed to go out or enter into the system, then heat lost by the body with higher temperature is equal to the heat gained by the body of lower temperature (i.e., heat lost = heat gained).

Progressive wave – a wave which transfers energy from one part of a medium to another.

Projectile – an object thrown into space either horizontally or at an acute angle and under the action of gravity; the path followed by a projectile is its trajectory; the horizontal distance traveled by a projectile is its range; the time taken from the moment it is thrown until the moment it hits the ground is its time of flight.

Proof – a measure of ethanol concentration of an alcoholic beverage; double the concentration by volume (e.g., 50% by volume is 100 proof).

Properties – qualities or attributes that, taken together, are usually unique to an object (e.g., color, texture, and size).

Proportionality constant – a constant applied to a proportionality statement that transforms the statement into an equation.

Pulse – a wave of short duration confined to a small portion of the medium at any given time; also a wave pulse.

Q

Quanta – fixed amounts; usually referring to fixed amounts of energy absorbed or emitted by matter.

Quantum limit – the shortest wavelength; present in a continuous x-ray spectrum.

Quantum mechanics – model of the atom based on the wave nature of subatomic particles and the mechanics of electron waves; also wave mechanics.

Quantum numbers – numbers that describe the energy states of an electron; in the Bohr model of the atom, the orbit quantum numbers could be any whole number (e.g., 1, 2, 3, etc.); in the quantum mechanics model of the atom, four quantum numbers are used to describe the energy state of an electron wave (n, m, l, and s).

Quark – one of the hypothetical basic particles; has a charge with the magnitude of one-third or two-thirds of the charge on an electron.

R

Rad – a measure of radiation received by a material (radiation-absorbed dose).

Radiant energy – the form of energy that can travel through space (e.g., visible light and other parts of the electromagnetic spectrum).

Radiation – the emission and propagation of waves transmitting energy through space or through some medium.

Radioactive decay – the natural, spontaneous disintegration or decomposition of a nucleus.

Radioactive decay constant – a specific constant for a particular isotope that is the ratio of the rate of nuclear disintegration per unit of time to the total number of radioactive nuclei.

Radioactive decay series – series of decay reactions that begins with one radioactive nucleus that decays to a second nucleus that decays to a third nucleus and so on, until a stable nucleus is reached.

Radioactive decay law – the rate of disintegration of a radioactive substance is directly proportional to the number of undecayed nuclei.

Radioactivity – spontaneous emission of particles or energy from an atomic nucleus as it disintegrates.

Rarefaction – a part of a longitudinal wave in which the density of the particles of the medium is less than the normal density.

Real image – an image generated by a lens or mirror that can be projected onto a screen.

Rectilinear motion – the motion of a body in a straight line.

Reflected ray – a line representing the direction of motion of light reflected from a boundary.

Refraction – the bending of a light wave, a sound wave or another wave from its straight-line path as it travels from one medium to another.

Refractive index – the ratio of the speed of light in a vacuum to that in the medium.

Relative density – (i.e., *specific gravity*) is the ratio of the density (mass of a unit volume) of a substance to the density of given reference material. *Specific gravity* usually means relative density with respect to water. The term *relative density* is more common in modern scientific usage.

Relative humidity – the percentage of the amount of water vapor present in a certain volume of the air to the amount of water vapor needed to saturate it.

Resolving power – a quantitative measure of the ability of an optical instrument to produce separable images of different points of an object.

Resonance – when the frequency of an external force matches the natural frequency of the body.

Restoring force – the force which tends to bring an oscillating body back to its mean position whenever it is displaced from the mean position.

Resultant force – a single force, which acts on a body to produce the same effect on it as done by all other forces collectively; see *Balanced forces*.

Reverberation – apparent increase in the volume of sound caused by reflections from the boundary surfaces, usually arriving within 0.1 seconds after the original sound.

Rigid body – an idealized extended body whose size and shape is fixed and remains unaltered when forces are applied.

S

Saturated air – air in which an equilibrium exists between evaporation and condensation; the relative humidity will be 100 percent.

Saturated solution – the apparent limit to dissolving a given solid in a specified amount of water at a given temperature; a state of equilibrium that exists between dissolving solute and solute coming out of solution.

Scalar quantity – a physical quantity described completely by its magnitude.

Scientific law – a relationship between quantities; usually described by an equation in the physical sciences; describes a wider range of phenomena and is more important than a scientific principle.

Scientific principle – a relationship between quantities concerned with a specific or narrow range of observations and behavior.

Second – the standard unit of time in both the metric and English systems of measurement.

Second Law of Motion – the acceleration of an object is directly proportional to the net force acting on that object and inversely proportional to the mass of the object.

Secondary coil – part of a transformer; a coil of wire in which the voltage of the original alternating current in the primary coil can be stepped up or down by way of electromagnetic induction.

Second's pendulum – a simple pendulum whose time period on the surface of the Earth is 2 seconds.

Semiconductors – elements whose electrical conductivity is intermediate between that of a conductor and an insulator.

Shear strain − the ratio of the relative displacements of one plane to its distance from the fixed plane.

Shear stress − the restoring force developed per unit area when deforming force acts tangentially to the surface of a body, producing a change in the shape of the body without any change in volume.

Siemens − the derived SI unit of electrical conductance; equal to the conductance of an element that has a resistance of 1 ohm; also written as ohm^{-1}.

Simple harmonic motion − the vibratory motion that occurs when the restoring force is proportional to the displacement from the mean position and is directed opposite to the displacement.

Simple pendulum − a heavy point mass (actually a small metallic ball), suspended by a light inextensible string from the frictionless rigid support; a simple machine based on the effect of gravity.

Snell's Law – states that the ratio of sin i to sin r is a constant and is equal to the refractive index of the second medium with respect to the first.

Solenoid − a cylindrical coil of wire that becomes electromagnetic when a current is run through it.

Solids − a phase of matter with molecules that remain close to fixed equilibrium positions due to strong interactions between the molecules, resulting in the characteristic definite shape and definite volume of a solid.

Sonic boom − sound waves that pile up into a shock wave when a source is traveling at or faster than the speed of sound.

Specific gravity – see *Relative density*.

Specific heat − the amount of heat energy required to increase the temperature of 1 g of a substance by 1 °C; each substance has its specific heat value.

Speed – a scalar quantity for the distance traveled by a body per unit of time; if a body covers the distance in time, then its speed is given by distance/time; SI units are m/s.

Spin quantum number − from quantum mechanics model of the atom, one of four descriptions of the energy state of an electron wave; describes the spin orientation of an electron relative to an external magnetic field.

Standing waves – the condition where two waves of equal frequency traveling in opposite directions meet and form stationary regions of maximum displacement due to constructive interference and stationary regions of zero displacement due to destructive interference.

State of motion − when a body changes its position with respect to a fixed point in its surroundings; the states of rest and motion are relative to the frame of reference.

State of rest – when a body does not change its position with respect to a fixed point in its surrounding; the states of rest and motion are relative to the frame of reference.

Steam-point – the temperature of steam over pure boiling water under 1 atm pressure; taken as the upper fixed point (100 °C or 212 °F) for temperature scales.

Stefan-Boltzmann Law – the amount of energy radiated per second per unit area of a perfectly black body, is directly proportional to the fourth power of the absolute temperature of the surface of the body.

Superconductors – some materials in which, under certain conditions, the electrical resistance approaches zero.

Super-cooled – water in the liquid phase when the temperature is below the freezing point.

Supersaturated – containing more than the normal saturation amount of a solute at a given temperature.

Surface tension – the property of a liquid due to which its surface behaves like a stretched membrane.

T

Temperature – a numerical measure of the hotness or coldness of a body; according to the molecular model, it is a measure of the average kinetic energy of the molecules of the body; heat flows from a body at higher temperature to a body at a lower temperature.

Tensional stress – the opposite of compressional stress; occurs when one part of a plate moves away from another part that does not move.

Tesla – the SI unit of magnetic flux density; the magnetic flux density of a magnetic flux of 1 Wb through an area of 1 m^2.

Thermal Capacity – the quantity of heat required to raise the temperature of the whole body by one degree (1 K or 1 °C).

Thermal equilibrium – when two bodies in contact are at the same temperature, and there is no flow of heat between them; also, the common temperature of the bodies in thermal equilibrium.

Thermal expansion – the increase in the size of an object when heated.

Thermometer – a device used for the numerical measurement of temperature; the mercury thermometer is commonly used.

Third Law of Motion − whenever two objects interact, the force exerted on one object is equal in size and opposite in direction to the force exerted on the other object; forces always occur in matched pairs that are equal and opposite.

Total internal reflection − condition where all light is reflected back from a boundary between materials; occurs when light travels from a denser to a rarer medium, and the angle of incidence is greater than the critical angle.

Transformation of energy − the conversion of one form of energy into another (e.g., when a body falls, its potential energy is converted to kinetic energy).

Transverse wave − a wave in which the particles of the medium oscillate in a direction perpendicular of the direction of propagation of the wave (e.g., water waves, light waves, radio waves).

Trough − the point of maximum negative displacement on a transverse wave.

U

Ultrasonic − sound waves too high in frequency (above 20,000 Hz) to be heard by the human ear.

Unbalanced forces − when a number of forces act on a body and the resultant force is not zero.

Uniform acceleration − when the velocity of a body increases by equal amounts in equal intervals of time.

Uniform circular motion − the motion of an object in a circular path with uniform speed; accelerated motion.

Uniform speed − when a body travels equal distances in equal intervals of time.

Uniform velocity − when a body travels along a straight line in a particular direction and covers equal distances in equal intervals of time.

Universal Law of Gravitation − every object in the universe is attracted to every other object with force directly proportional to the product of their masses and inversely proportional to the square of the distance between the centers of the two masses.

Unpolarized light − light consisting of transverse waves vibrating in all possible random directions.

V

Van der Waals force − general term for weak attractive intermolecular forces.

Vapor − the gaseous state of a substance that is normally in a liquid state.

Vector quantity − a quantity which needs both magnitude and direction to describe it.

Velocity − distance traveled by a body in a particular direction per unit time; the displacement of the body per unit time; a vector quantity; the SI units are m/s.

Vibration − a back and forth motion that repeats itself.

Virtual image − an image formed when the reflected or refracted light rays appear to meet; this image cannot be projected on a screen.

Volt − unit of potential difference equivalent to joules/coulomb.

Voltage drop – the difference in electric potential across a resistor or other part of a circuit that consumes power.

W

Watt − SI unit for power; equivalent to joule/s.

Wave − a disturbance or oscillation that moves through a medium.

Wavelength − the distance between the two nearest points on a wave which are in the same phase; the distance between two adjacent crests or two adjacent troughs.

Wave (mechanical) − a periodic disturbance produced in a material medium due to the vibratory motion of the particles of the medium.

Wave mechanics − alternate name for quantum mechanics derived from the wavelike properties of subatomic particles.

Wave motion − the movement of a disturbance from one part of a medium to another involving the transfer of energy but not the transfer of matter.

Wave period − the time required for two successive crests or other successive parts of the wave to pass a given point.

Wave velocity − the distance traveled by a wave in one second; it depends on the nature of the medium through which it passes.

Weight − the force with which a body is attracted towards the center of the Earth; the SI unit is N; the gravitational units are kg·wt and g·wt; the weight of a body is given by *mg*.

Weightlessness − the state when the apparent weight of a body becomes zero; all objects while falling freely under the action of gravity are seemingly weightless.

Wien's Displacement Law – states that for a black body, the product of the wavelength corresponding to its maximum radiance and its absolute temperature is constant.

Work − work is done when a force acting on a body displaces it; Work = Force × Displacement in the direction of the force; work is a scalar quantity; the SI unit is Joule.

Y

Young's Modulus of Elasticity − the ratio of normal stress to the longitudinal strain produced in a body.

Z

Zeeman effect − the splitting of the spectral lines in a spectrum when the source is exposed to a magnetic field.

Zeroth Law of Thermodynamics – states that if body A is in thermal equilibrium with body B, and B is also in thermal equilibrium with C, then A is necessarily in thermal equilibrium with C.

Your purchase helps support global environmental causes

Sterling Test Prep is committed to protecting our planet by supporting environmental organizations for conservation, ecological research, and preservation of vital natural resources. A portion of our profits is donated to help these organizations continue their critical missions.

  The Ocean Conservancy advocates for a healthy ocean with sustainable solutions based on science and cleanup efforts.

RAINFOREST TRUST The Rainforest Trust saves critical lands for conservation through land purchases and protected area designations in over 16 countries.

 Pacific Whale Foundation saves whales from extinction and protects our oceans through science and advocacy.

We want to hear from you

Your feedback is important to us because we strive to provide the highest quality prep materials. Email us any comments or suggestions.

info@sterling–prep.com

Customer Satisfaction Guarantee

Contact us to resolve any issues to your satisfaction.

*We reply to all emails – **check your spam folder***

Thank you for choosing our products to achieve your educational goals!

Advanced Placement (AP) prep books

Biology Practice Questions

Biology Review

Physics 1 Practice Questions

Physics 1 Review

Physics 2 Practice Questions

Physics 2 Review

Environmental Science

Psychology

U.S. History

World History

European History

U.S. Government and Politics

Comparative Government and Politics

Human Geography

Visit our Amazon store

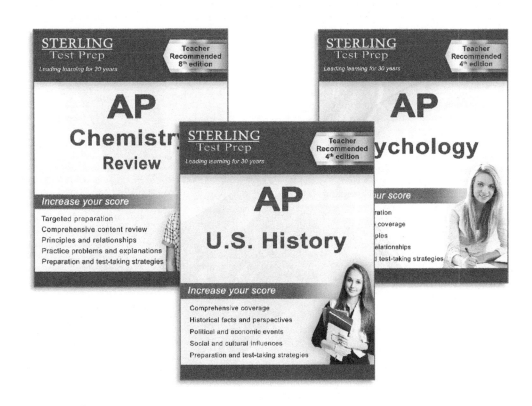

AP Chemistry, Biology and Physics online practice tests

Our advanced online testing platform allows you to take AP practice questions on your computer to generate a Diagnostic Report for each test.

By using our online AP tests and Diagnostic Reports, you will:

Assess your knowledge of subjects and topics to identify your areas of strength and weakness

Learn important scientific topics and concepts for comprehensive test preparation

Improve your test-taking skills

To access AP questions online
at special pricing for book owners, visit:

http://ap.sterling-prep.com/bookowner.htm

Made in the USA
Las Vegas, NV
27 April 2024

89232446R00175